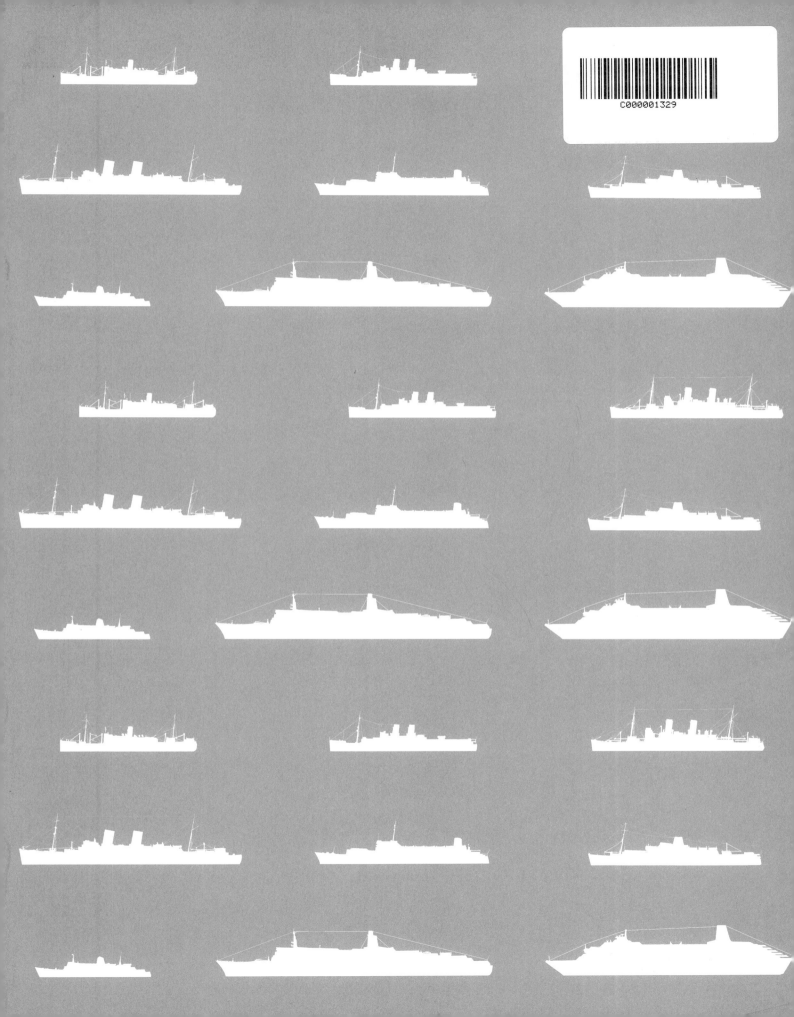

Favourite British Liners

©2011 Carmania Press and Anthony Cooke, London.
P.O. Box 56435
London, SE3 0SZ

e-mail: carmania@btconnect.com

www.carmaniapress.co.uk

ISBN 978-0-9563355-2-4

Design and lay-out: Maurizio Eliseo.

Editorial secretary: Antonella Pollara.

Produced by Thalia SaS, Trieste (Italy).

Printed by Tisak Zambelli, Rijeka, Croatia.

ANTHONY COOKE

FAVOURITE
BRITISH LINERS

CARMANIA PRESS LONDON

Acknowledgements

I must thank the many people who have helped to make this book possible. Above all, I am grateful to Maurizio Eliseo of Thalia SaS in Trieste for encouraging me to persevere and for designing and laying out a very beautiful book. Co-operating with him in our various projects has always been a joy; his colleague Antonella Pollara has also been a great help.

Then, I must express my gratitude to the late Arthur W. Crook for allowing me to use his text for the chapter on how ships such as the first *Oriana* were built in the 'Sixties and for being very tolerant of my alterations, intended to make it more accessible to the layman. With his long experience of shipbuilding in various countries, he added an extra touch of authority to the book.

My thanks also go to Martin Grant, who has read large parts of my text and has been a strict editor, imposing grammatical and historical discipline on a sometimes wayward author. And thanks are due to Stephen J. Card for his splendid painting of the *Southern Cross* on the dustjacket.

I am also grateful to the friends who have made illustrations available, particularly John Clarkson of Ships in Focus and William Mayes of Overview Press who have been very generous with their photographs despite the fact that they are rival publishers of maritime books – we have a very friendly rivalry. Also, Ambrose Greenway, Clive Harvey, Peter Knego, Bruce Peter and Paolo Piccione – a quintet of distinguished authors - have, as usual, opened their collections to me and have added many wonderful illustrations to the book.

Others, including well-known authors, have very willingly assisted with images or information: in alphabetical order they are Kenneth Barton, Stefan and Petra Behn, Andrew Bell, John Bokor-Ingram, Jonathan Boonzaier, Sheila Bourne, Ahmet Cakir, Stephen Card, Luis Miguel Correia, Colin Deller, C. J. Douglas, Jennifer Dunn, the late Laurence Dunn, Brian Gardner, the late R. Bruce Grice, Kevin Griffin, Ann Haynes, Andres Hernandez, David Hutchings, Allan Jordan, Hugh Lalor, Chris Mason, Jim Nurse, Thomas N. Olesen, Kai Ortel, Barbara Peden, James Pottinger, Nils Schwerdtner, Theodore W. Scull, Ian Shiffman of Table Bay Underway, Roy Turner and Charles Zuckerman.

Index

Introduction

This book is pure self-indulgence. The ships covered here are some of my own Favourite British Liners. They include obvious choices – *Aquitania*, *Oriana*, *Canberra* and *QE2*, for instance. Although they had their faults, these were great ships and, above all, they had character. Loyal passengers and crew members grew to love them.

But the book also contains others which are less well-known but whose histories I find fascinating. The *Aba*, for instance, was a significant player in the early development of the diesel-driven ship, dating back to the times when the crusading magazine "The Motor Ship" found it necessary to publish maps of the World shewing the very limited number of ports where it was possible for these vessels to refuel. If *Aba* represented the cutting edge of a new technology when she was built, *Rajula* was already old-fashioned when she left the shipyard. She was a rather small, very ordinary ship which spent her entire peace-time life on an unglamorous but busy route Out East. Who would have guessed then that she would attract such loyalty from her crews and from her Indian passengers? Or, presumably, such gratitude from her owners for whom she proved to be a hugely profitable investment.

Inevitably there are omissions. Some readers may be disappointed that I have chosen to include, for instance, *Britannic* and *Reina del Mar* but not the mighty *Queen Mary*. I love the *Queen Mary* and my stays on board her at

In this atmospheric photograph taken in March, 1954, the second *Mauretania* lies at Pier 90 in Manhattan. The tug boat crews are on strike and the *Empress of Scotland* (in the background) is attempting to dock without their aid; later the *Mauretania* will leave under similar circumstances. In the meantime police keep watch in case of trouble. *(Maurizio Eliseo collection)*

Long Beach have been among the most thrilling episodes in my ship-collecting career but so much has already been written about her. What more is there to say? Why not give her magnificent but often overlooked fleet-mate, the second *Mauretania*, a moment in the spotlight instead?

Some themes emerge from this book. Until the coming of the jet airliners, British passenger shipping covered the World. Our liners, often also carrying large cargoes of manufactured goods on their outward voyages and of food on the return leg, sailed not just on the famous route to New York but to Canada, South America, East Africa, West Africa, South Africa, Australia and New Zealand, India and the Far East. Much of this trade was a legacy of Empire. There was, however, increasing competition, especially from Germany, whose shipping industry was resurgent after the First World War, and from Italy, not to mention France, the Netherlands and, on the North Atlantic, the United States.

The 1920s, which it is tempting to think of as 'The Roaring 'Twenties', a decade of headlong indulgence, were also a time of great hardship for shipping, shipbuilding and the heavy industries generally. Shipyards with empty berths and workers without jobs were grateful for the orders placed, in an act of faith, by British shipowners in the hope that liners such as *Arandora Star* and *Isipingo* could be employed profitably.

Those hard times had their victims. The collapse of the mighty empire which Lord Kylsant had built on what we now see to have been unstable foundations shook the whole British shipping establishment who had to rally round to salvage some famous lines from the wreckage. The careers of such ships as *Asturias* and *Britannic* were changed forever but at least they survived while many others did not.

It becomes clear that there was an innate conservatism among the designers of many British ships. It was not until the 'Sixties, for instance, that *Oriana* became the first British liner to be given a bulbous bow. The Germans, the Italians and the Americans had incorporated them in their hull designs thirty years earlier. A few British companies, though, were adventurous. Canadian Pacific found that the high-pressure water-tube boilers on ships such as the *Duchess of Bedford* and the *Empress of Japan* were very economical in operation.

Until the 'Sixties, British shipowners also tended to be conservative in the design of the interiors of their liners, partly because of the perceived tastes of many of their passengers. Nevertheless, there was a shift in the late 'Twenties when a few ships such as the *Duchess of Bedford* were built with less ornate, lighter public rooms – partly, it has to be said, because they were less expensive to maintain. Then in the 'Sixties there was a sudden explosion of trendy creativity in

ships such as *Oriana*, *Canberra* and the *QE2*. But even then, vessels such as *Transvaal Castle* were still being built which harked back to a certain extent to the conservatism of a previous age. It seems to me that it was at that time that interior furnishing took a backward step – not necessarily because of the new styles but because of the materials which were being used and a decline in the quality of the workmanship which went into British ships. A visit to Peter Knego's house in California, which he has filled with furniture and fittings rescued from old liners, makes it clear that, even in the hard-pressed late 'Forties and early 'Fifties, the interiors of British-built ships had 'reeked of quality'.

Other themes which emerge include the way in which after the Second World War it became ever more difficult to run ships carrying both passengers and cargo – hence the emergence of the passenger-only *Southern Cross* which, being a one-class ship, also recognised that the number of first class passengers travelling from continent to continent by sea was declining. Finally, the growth in the market for cruises is illustrated by the final ship in this book, the second *Oriana* which, although built in Germany, might be said to be the one of the last of the truly British deep sea passenger vessels.

Eighteen ships are included here, forming, I hope, an interesting cross-section of the British passenger fleet during the Twentieth Century. There is one additional chapter, not written by me but by the late Arthur W. Crook. It came into *Favourite British Liners* almost by accident. As a Lloyd's Surveyor, Arthur had been involved in the building in Italy of the outstanding Panamanian-flagged *Oceanic*, for years one of the most popular ships in the cruise market out of New York. Before that, while working in the Naval Architect's department at the Vickers-Armstrongs yard at Barrow-in-Furness, he had been involved in the design of the first *Oriana*. Some time ago, for a projected book about the *Oceanic*, he wrote an account of how large passenger ships were built in those days. It seemed to me that, at a time when we in Britain have turned our backs on engineering, it might be of interest for readers to learn about just how much was involved in constructing such sophisticated ships and about the incredible resources and skills which used to be required. So, in slightly modified form to make it more relevant to *Oriana*, that text has been included as a chapter in this book.

I hope you will enjoy reading *Favourite British Liners* as much as I have enjoyed researching and writing it.

Anthony Cooke
London, 2011

Aquitania

Completed 1914.

45,647 gross tons.

Length overall: 901 ft. 6ins.

Breadth: 97 ft. 0ins.

Draught: 34 ft. 0ins.

Quadruple screw.

Direct-drive turbines.

Service speed: 23 knots.

Scrapped: 1950.

The *Aquitania* at Naples in the mid-'Thirties. *(Maurizio Eliseo collection)*

The Cunard Steam Ship Company introduced their *Lusitania* and *Mauretania* in 1907, the two biggest ocean liners yet built and also the quickest. Indeed, from 1909 until 1929 *Mauretania* held the Blue Riband for the fastest westbound crossing of the North Atlantic. She was a dearly loved ship, not only in Britain but also among some Americans (including the future President Franklin Delano Roosevelt). Many years later, the eminent German maritime historian Arnold Kludas described her unequivocally as 'the most famous express steamer of all time'. But it was still necessary for Cunard to use four ships to maintain their weekly express service from Liverpool to New York and the two new speedsters had to run in conjunction with the archaic old *Campania* (a record-breaker in her day but much smaller, less luxurious and a full five knots slower) and either the *Caronia* or the *Carmania* (modern but even slower). It was a singularly ill-matched service. Cunard needed another new liner which would be compatible with *Lusitania* and *Mauretania* and would be quick enough to enable them to run the weekly service with just three vessels. She must also be able to match the size and luxury of the new steamers soon to be introduced by the White Star and Hamburg America companies.

When they ordered the *Lusitania* and *Mauretania*, Cunard had not only received a loan from the British government to help finance the building costs but it was agreed that the operation of the two ships should be subsidised. In return, they – and subsequent Cunard expresses – were to be designed so as to be suitable for naval service in the event of a national emergency. The new ship, to be called *Aquitania*, was therefore built with gun mountings but she was not subsidised. The company decided that she must be even bigger than the earlier pair, must be able to carry more passengers and must be more economical to operate. While she would be fast enough for the express service, she would not have that expensive extra knot or so which would have been necessary had Cunard wanted a third record-breaker. On the 8th December, 1910, it was announced that the contract for the new ship had been awarded to the John Brown yard at Clydebank, who had built the *Lusitania*. This caused disappointment on Tyneside, where Swan, Hunter & Wigham Richardson, builders of the *Mauretania*, had also been in contention but had quoted a higher price. The new liner was to be 111 feet longer than the *Mauretania* and fractionally larger than the White Star Line's recently launched *Olympic*. She was, in fact, to be so big that John Brown not only had to spend heavily on enlarging one of their slipways but they also paid the Clyde Navigation Trustees £10,000 to help towards the cost of the necessary widening and deepening of the river. In Liverpool, the new Gladstone Graving Dock was built specifically to be able to accommodate ships of the *Aquitania*'s size and in New York the port authorities now needed to lengthen the Cunard pier.

The keel of the new giant was laid on the 5th June, 1911. Nearly two years later, on the 21st April, 1913, she was launched by the Countess of Derby. According to Bruce Peter's grandfather, the late Ernest Glen, the new ship's hull was painted pale grey at the request of 'cinematograph photographers' who were to record the occasion – black would apparently not have shewn up sufficiently well against the background. The correspondent of *The Shipping Gazette & Lloyd's List* wrote an almost lyrical account of the occasion, describing how the launch was watched by 'an immense concourse' and how the foremast was already suspended from a crane, ready for installation on the new ship once she was afloat. Those were great days at Clydebank – the John Brown yard had been simultaneously building the largest liner in Britain, the largest battle cruiser and the largest battleship. But there could be no avoiding the fact

Final preparations at Liverpool for the *Aquitania*'s maiden voyage on the 30th May, 1914. Note the thousands of rivets on the hull, the telescopic gangway, the steamer trunks and the hats. Several of the early photographs in this chapter were taken by a representative of the German shipbuilders Blohm & Voss who sailed anonymously on the first crossing. *(Maurizio Eliseo collection)*

that in Germany an even larger liner, the *Imperator*, was about to enter service and that a still bigger one, the *Vaterland*, had been launched two weeks previously.

By the 10th May, 1914, the *Aquitania* was ready to run her trials – although fitting out was far from complete and, indeed, up to 800 workmen toiled away until almost the last minute before she sailed on her maiden voyage on the 30th. So large was she that before she left the shipyard there had been anxiety over whether the tide would be high enough for her to be towed down the Clyde. In fact, there was an awkward moment as she was manoeuvred round a bend at Dalmuir and the tow had to be briefly suspended. She aroused so much interest that it was said that Sunday services at several churches were delayed to enable members of the congregations to see the great liner pass. On her speed trials on the 12th, she proved able to sustain 24 knots, comfortably above the 23 knots which Cunard had specified. Afterwards, she made her way to the Mersey, where she arrived on the 14th.

The Edwardian age was over and the old order was about to be swept aside by the most devastating war the World had ever known but, unwittingly, the Atlantic steamship companies were building vast monuments to those doomed times. There is no doubt that the *Aquitania* was one of the most magnificent of them all.

As was customary, all sorts of statistics were produced to boggle the minds of an astonished public. Her generators, for instance, produced sufficient electricity to supply a town of 110,000 inhabitants. She had the most powerful Marconi wireless equipment yet fitted to a merchant ship. Her 21 double-ended boilers were heated by no less than 168 coal-fired furnaces. (Nothing was said about the 'black gang', the men who, under the most appalling conditions, performed the brutal work of stoking those furnaces.) Her turbines contained over a million tiny blades.

After the huge success of the *Lusitania* and *Mauretania*, it went without saying that the *Aquitania* would be powered by steam turbines. She was, in fact, given four forward turbines, one high-pressure, one intermediate pressure and two low-pressure, all built in the engine works at the John Brown yard and based on the designs of the pioneering Sir Charles Parsons. They produced 56,000 shp and were directly coupled to the four propellers. (As the *Aquitania* was being towed down the Clyde, she passed the hull of another Cunard group liner, the *Transylvania*, still on the 'ways' at Scotts' yard at Greenock. That much smaller liner was to be driven by turbines which would transmit their power through a system of gearing. In theory they would be much more efficient but, perhaps surprisingly, engineering technology had not yet reached the stage where it was possible to cut the teeth of the huge gearwheels with suffi-

The Chief Engineer presides over the control platform in the *Aquitania*'s engine room. The large dials indicate that she is steaming at Full Speed Ahead. *(Maurizio Eliseo collection)*

cient precision and some of the early geared turbine ships tended to be troublesome.)

Designed by Cunard's own naval architect, Laurence Peskett, *Aquitania* was a nine-decker. In an attempt to mitigate the more unpleasant aspects of sea travel, she was fitted with Frahm's anti-rolling tanks. With the *Titanic* catastrophe fresh in their minds, the public and the authorities were much concerned with safety at sea and *Aquitania* was described as 'a ship within a ship' (i.e.: for much of her length, her hull had a double skin up to the waterline). It was emphasised that two of her lifeboats were fitted with Marconi wireless equipment and with paraffin engines which would enable them to tow other boats. It was ironic, therefore, that *Aquitania*'s maiden departure should be sadly overshadowed by the news just received of the sinking of the Canadian Pacific liner *Empress of Ireland* following a collision in fog. Over 1,000 lives had been lost.

But the newspapers and their readers were still very interest-

ed by *Aquitania*'s amazing first class interiors. She was sometimes known as 'The Ship Beautiful'. That was no doubt a tag thought up by somebody in a smoke-filled room in the Cunard offices rather than a description customarily used by her passengers, but there is no doubt that she was one of the most handsome liners ever built, and one of the most palatial – in her first and second class areas, that is. Arthur Davis, who had partnered the great Charles Mewès in the design of some very grand hotels and gentlemen's clubs and also of the public rooms on some notable ocean liners, had scoured history for styles which would impress the *Aquitania*'s wealthiest passengers and might even give them the illusion of being safely on dry land rather than enduring the discomfort and perils of an ocean voyage. Modern purists tend to scoff at the eclecticism of the interiors of the liners of that time but there can be no denying that, in this case at least, the result was wonderfully handsome and hugely impressive.

The restaurant, with a two deck-high central section, was in

Louis XVI style. For those who wished to dine even more exclusively, there was the grill room furnished in the Jacobean manner. Then there were two lounges. In one, a splendid copy of the Palladian style, the ceiling was adorned by an original eighteenth century allegorical painting which had been carefully transferred from a stately home. The other lounge, almost equally magnificent, had an oak floor which could be used for dancing and an apse containing a stage. The huge smoking room (for gentlemen only, of course) was furnished in oak in the Restoration style. In that room at least, Mr. Davis had acknowledged that he was working on a ship – inspiration had come from a very naval room at The Greenwich Hospital and the treatment of the windows was said to suggest the admiral's walk on an old wooden warship. There were two 'garden lounges' with ivy-covered trellises; and there was a 'long gallery', in truth an enclosed promenade running 150-feet along one side of the vessel. Leading

off it were a barber's shop and a room where typists were at the disposal of business-minded passengers. Open-air swimming pools and lidos had not yet become features of ocean liners, but on the *Aquitania* and a few of the other grandest ships a pool was situated indoors, deep in the hull. In her case, this space was decorated in what was claimed to be the Egyptian manner and was adjoined by a gymnasium with all the latest devices to enable the more energetic gentlemen passengers to counter the effects of the sumptuous meals which were constantly being placed before them.

By the standards of the time, her first class cabins were the height of comfort and amenity. There were eight beautifully furnished, fully-equipped suites, named after artists such as Gainsborough, Reynolds and Rembrandt. Some of the other first class cabins, too, had their own en suite facilities and the rest were provided with wash-basins supplying hot and cold water. The one- and two-berth cab-

The palatial first class restaurant designed by Arthur Davis. Unusually on a ship of that period the dining chairs were not fixed to the deck. *(Maurizio Eliseo collection)*

Potted palms were a fashionable feature of the interior décor of the time. On the whole, the *Aquitania* had a rather lighter style than many ships of the period. *(Maurizio Eliseo collection)*

ins were furnished with beds but the three-berth rooms still had the traditional bunks. A curiosity was that a few of the inside cabins were referred to as inside/outside staterooms since a little natural light was provided by a narrow glazed slit which looked out over the floor of the enclosed promenade deck above – no doubt a delight for foot-fetishists. In all, *Aquitania* could accommodate up to 618 first class passengers.

Second class, situated aft and with a capacity of up to 614 passengers, was much superior to that on most liners of the day. Although not as extravagantly decorated as those in first class, the second class public rooms were almost equally stylish. They consisted of a dining room, a lounge, a drawing room, a smoking room and an attractive verandah café overlooking the stern. Second class passengers even had their own elevators and their own gymnasium. Their cabins, which included some single-berth rooms, all had cold running water. Finally, in the expectation that the boom in emigration to America would continue, the ship could accommodate up to

1,998 third class passengers. Even they enjoyed better conditions than on most ships. They slept in two-, four- and six-berth cabins. Like other big Atlantic liners of the period, the *Aquitania* carried relatively little cargo. Her holds were mainly intended for passengers' luggage, although two hatches in the bow section did give access to a small amount of cargo space.

The two masts and four tall funnels were somewhat more raked than was usual and this, together with her long, slender hull and her particularly beautiful counter stern, gave her a profile which hinted at speed and was wonderfully elegant. Those funnels were, of course, painted in the traditional Cunard colours – orange-red with black tops and each bearing three equidistant black bands. Advertisements boasted that the *Aquitania* was 'Britain's Largest Liner' and that Cunard's express line was the 'Fastest Service in the World'.

On the day before the new ship's maiden voyage, the music hall stars Vesta Tilley, George Robey and Albert Whelan gave a performance on board. Then, in the afternoon of the 30th

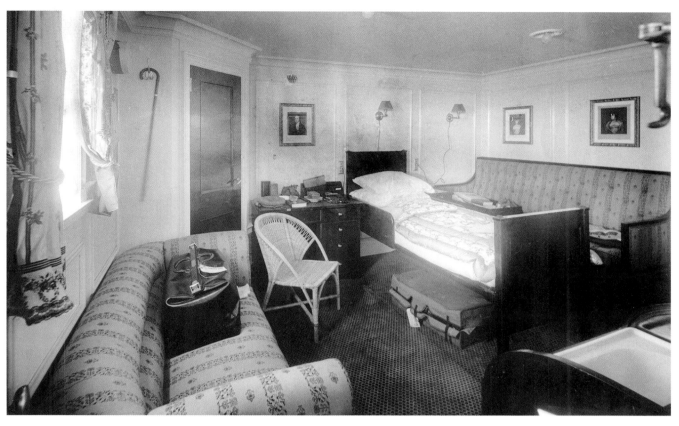

A spacious first class stateroom set up for single occupation; the bed is fitted with side restraints to keep the sleeper in situ in rough weather and there is ample stowage space for luggage underneath. *(Maurizio Eliseo collection)*

It may not have been "the biggest floating crap game in the World" but these men in the second class smoking room look like characters out of a Damon Runyon story; on many ships passengers were warned about card sharps. *(Maurizio Eliseo collection)*

May, 1914 the *Aquitania* made her first departure from the landing stage at Liverpool, arriving at New York on the 5th June, having averaged 23.1 knots. However, in August, after only three round voyages, and with Europe now plunging into war, she was taken over by the Admiralty for service as an armed merchant cruiser. Unfortunately, during her second patrol in the Western Approaches she collided with the Leyland Line's *Canadian* off the coast of Anglesey and had to return to the Mersey for repairs. In any case, the authorities had already decided that large liners such as the *Aquitania* did not, after all, make ideal warships and they returned her to Cunard. Perhaps as a result of the collision, she was now given a new wheelhouse, one deck above the bridge, from which the view would be less impeded.

She lay at Liverpool until May, 1915. By then, the disastrous Dardanelles campaign was underway and large contingents of troops had to be shipped to Gallipoli. Together with the *Mauretania*, she was taken up as a troopship and on the 18th May, she left on the first of a number of voyages to Mudros on the island of Lemnos, from where her troops could be ferried to Turkish soil. But casualties were mounting and in August she was converted into a hospital ship. She now wore the traditional hospital ship uniform – buff funnels and a white hull with a broad green band along each side, interrupted by large red crosses. Most of her luxurious furnishings and her valuable artworks had been placed in safe storage on shore but her public rooms, now crammed with beds and wounded men, were still magnificently panelled.

Aquitania's war service was, to say the least, spasmodic. By March, 1916 she was laid up again and the following month she was returned to her owners and taken to Harland & Wolff's Southampton facility to be refitted. However, in July, before the work was finished, she was reclaimed by the authorities and re-converted into a hospital ship to bring wounded men home from the Mediterranean. Then, in January, 1917, she was laid up again, this time in the Mersey.

The *Aquitania* served as a hospital ship in the First World War; here she is at Mudros together with the *Essequibo* and probably the *Lanfranc*. (Author's collection)

There she lay for nearly a year but, with America's entry into the War, she was taken up for the duty which best suited these big, fast liners – long distance ocean crossings at high speed, crammed to capacity with huge numbers of troops. In all, the *Aquitania* brought nearly 60,000 members of the American Expeditionary Force to Britain, from where they would go to meet their destiny on the battlefields of France and Flanders. On the 9th October, 1918, in an accident which foreshadowed an even more tragic one involving the *Queen Mary* in the Second World War, she collided with an escorting naval vessel, the American destroyer *U.S.S. Shaw*. The *Aquitania* cut right through the American ship, severing her bow and killing several men.

The First World War ended in November, 1918 and in January, 1919 the *Aquitania* was returned to her owners. There was still a pressing need for troopships, however, and on those immediate post-War voyages she mainly carried American and Canadian servicemen back to their own side of the Atlantic. It was not until late in 1919 that the work of restoring her to her pre-War glory could be commenced, initially in the Mersey and then at the Armstrong Whitworth yard on the Tyne, where the 7 month-long task of adapting her to burn oil fuel was carried out. As a result, the number of men needed to tend her furnaces and boilers was reduced from 350 to 50.

On the 17th July, 1920, she returned to commercial service with what was to be her last sailing from Liverpool. Cunard had decided to follow the pre-War example of their White Star rivals and base their New York express service at Southampton – more conveniently situated for London passengers and making it possible to tap the French market by calling at Cherbourg. When the spoils of war were divided up, Cunard were allotted the Hamburg America superliner *Imperator* to compensate them for the loss of the *Lusitania*. She became their *Berengaria* and maintained the three-ship weekly service together with the *Aquitania* and the *Mauretania*.

In the 'Twenties, as often after a terrible war, discontent was rife among the workforce and on one voyage in May, 1921, the *Aquitania* was only able to sail because 350 clerks from the Cunard offices in Southampton and Liverpool acted as replacements for stewards who were on strike. Another problem facing Cunard and the other Atlantic lines was that in 1921 and 1924 laws came into force in America imposing very strict quotas which reduced the number of migrants allowed to settle there by nearly two-thirds. The days when, on westbound voyages, the stark third class quarters could be filled with hopefuls seeking a new life were over. Many companies sought to replace the lost passengers with the new 'tourist class' – often school teachers and others who had long holidays and who could be tempted by the prospect of relatively cheap travel in comfort if not in luxury. Accordingly, in a 1926 refit the *Aquitania*'s accommodation was rearranged to become 610 in first class, 950 in second and 640 in tourist class quarters which were a great improvement over the former third class.

The ship was given a number of other refits over the years. In 1922, for instance, more first class cabins had been given private facilities, shared with just one neighbouring cabin. In 1933, further internal rebuilding in first class produced some more de luxe staterooms with private bathrooms. In addition, cinema equipment was installed. This must have represented a welcome innovation. In those days before the advent of the Cruise Director, entertainment would, apart from dancing to the music of the ship's orchestra, be largely organised by a committee self-appointed from among the passengers. There would perhaps be 'horse-racing', deck games and the dreaded passengers' concerts. Only very occasionally were professional entertainers engaged. However, in an advertisement for *Aquitania*'s cruise out of New York over the Independence Day weekend in 1933, Cunard announced that Hildegarde would perform for the first class passengers. She was a noted and very stylish cabaret artiste who played the piano (wearing long white gloves!) and sang popular songs of the day.

The *Aquitania* was used less for cruising than some of the other liners of the time, but nevertheless she did make some notable pleasure voyages. In 1932, there were two long cruises from New York to the Mediterranean and two shorter New York – Bermuda round trips. She returned to the Mediterranean twice in 1934 and twice in 1935. Then, in 1936 and 1937, she made her most ambitious cruises, from New York to the Caribbean and Rio de Janeiro. Finally, in 1938 there was a Christmas cruise to the Caribbean.

Over the years, she and her captains suffered a number of misfortunes. In July, 1928, in the days when the masters of the great Atlantic liners were well-known public figures, Sir James Charles collapsed in his cabin at Cherbourg as he was nearing the end of the final voyage of his long career. He was taken to hospital in Southampton but died within minutes of arrival. In December, 1931, Captain R. B. Irving was cut by flying glass when the bridge windows were shattered during a gale. More seriously, he was taken critically ill while in command in April, 1934. He eventually recovered sufficiently to take charge of the ship again, but many months later.

The *Aquitania* was twice aground on the approach to Southampton Water, on the 24th January, 1934 and on the 10th April, 1935. On the first occasion she got off quickly with the help of six tugs but the second time she was aground for a whole day and it took eleven tugs to

Aquitania being handled by tugs on a windy day; the twin flags of the Cunard and White Star lines flap on her mainmast. *(Author's collection)*

shift her. Fortunately, she seemed to have suffered no damage and her scheduled sailing was not delayed. On a happier note, she took part in the Coronation Review at Spithead in May, 1937.

She must have been a popular ship with the Cunard management as she was consistently more economical to operate than either the *Berengaria* or the *Mauretania* and she had a fine reputation with her passengers. But with the advent of the Great Depression in the early 'Thirties, even she had struggled to cover her costs. In any case, rival companies had introduced much more modern ships – the French Line had scored a sensational success with their *Ile de France*, which in 1927 had introduced a completely new style of décor to the North Atlantic run, and they were known to be planning an even more outstanding liner. Norddeutscher Lloyd's *Bremen* and *Europa* were also very modern – in their case externally as well as internally. And the *Bremen* had snatched the Blue Riband from the *Mauretania*. The three big Cunarders were beginning to seem distinctly passé.

In any case, the Cunard company was itself planning a pair of enormous new liners which would enable it to operate the express service with just two ships. The first of these, the *Queen Mary*, came out in 1936, having already spelled the end of the *Mauretania* which made her final departure from New York in 1934, on the same day that the new ship was launched. In that year too, Cunard's Atlantic services had, at the insistence of the British government, been merged with those of the White Star Line. The ships now flew two houseflags and the combined company became known as the Cunard-White Star Line. With the former White Star *Olympic* and *Majestic* being withdrawn, the plan was that the *Aquitania* and *Berengaria* should run alongside the *Queen Mary* until the advent of the *Queen Elizabeth* in 1940. In the event, the *Berengaria*, afflicted by electrical fires, was taken out of service in 1938 and the Second World War prolonged the *Aquitania's* career.

When War broke out early in September, 1939, thousands of Americans and others were stranded in Europe and were clamouring for westward passages across the Atlantic. The *Aquitania* was one of the many liners which abandoned their scheduled programmes and hastily set sail, filled to capacity and beyond. She returned to Southampton on the 30th September. After being laid up for a few weeks, she was taken up for service as a troopship, initially making two transatlantic voyages bringing full complements of Canadians into the Clyde. On the first of these, on the 17th December, she collided with a fellow Cunarder, the *Samaria*, but was not badly damaged.

Thereafter, she was in almost constant trooping service. In the famous Convoy US3 in May – June, 1940, she carried Australian and New Zealand troops to the Clyde in company

The date is the 27th August, 1946. The *Queen Mary* (left), still in wartime grey, is leaving for another crossing while the *Aquitania* lies at her berth in Southampton. In the foreground, workmen are repairing wartime damage. *(Maurizio Eliseo collection)*

The *Aquitania* was much loved by many who served on her, including Donald Sorrell who later became a very popular Captain of the *Queen Mary*; an enthusiastic amateur artist, he made this painting of his old ship. *(Author's collection)*

Now restored to her full Cunard livery, the veteran *Aquitania* which her owners had intended to sell for scrap in 1940, remained in service until December, 1949. *(Author's collection)*

with the *Queen Mary*, the second *Mauretania*, the *Andes* and the *Empresses of Britain* and *Canada* and, for part of the way, the *Empress of Japan*. (On the way out to Sydney, the *Aquitania* had briefly been aground at Cape Town.) Other voyages took her to India, to Suez and to Singapore (where she suffered a fire while in dry dock). Following the attack on Pearl Harbor and the entry of the United States into the War in December, 1941, she was sent to make two voyages evacuating American citizens from Honolulu to San Francisco. On another occasion she carried Italian prisoners of war from Suez to Boston (via the Cape, of course) and later she took more Italians from Suez to Sydney. Soon thereafter, she was one of the big liners assigned to ferrying American troops to Britain, usually to the Clyde. Sometimes she was carrying as many as 7,500 personnel.

After the Allied victory in Europe, the flow was reversed and she began taking troops back to America. She also returned to Sydney, this time carrying homeward-bound Australian and New Zealand servicemen. In all, she travelled 526,000 nautical miles during her World War Two service and carried over 400,000 troops and other 'passengers'. For most of the time, she sailed without escort. Her wartime achievements have been less applauded than those of the two *Queens* but she performed nobly.

Such was the need for passenger ships after the War, and such was the shortage of them, that pre-War plans to scrap her were forgotten. Old and worn though she now was, she was still a ship which aroused great affection among many who knew her. Captain Donald Sorrell, later one of the best-known and most popular masters of the *Queen Mary*, was the *Aquitania*'s Staff Captain for a time. His water-colour painting of her appears in this book. Of course, she was no longer the prestigious superliner she had once been but some of her pre-War luxury, by now very dated, was restored in first class. Elsewhere, particularly on her fully booked westbound crossings, conditions must have been far from ideal. Although at first still under government control, she again wore the Cunard livery on her funnel and eventually her hull was repainted black instead of wartime grey.

In January, 1946, after a much-needed refit at Southampton, she began shuttling between Southampton and Halifax, mainly carrying British girls who had married Canadian servicemen, together with their children. She also made two final visits to New York, before the second of which – in November, 1946 – a planned drydocking was postponed in order to enable her to carry British, American, Soviet and French delegates to a meeting of the Council of Foreign Ministers at the United Nations. Later, the Australian government announced that she was to be made available for the migrant service to their country but this plan was abandoned. Instead, her charter to the British government was ended. She

did, however, find further employment when Cunard-White Star chartered her to the Canadian government, again for migrant service and still running between Southampton and Halifax. (Kenneth Barton remarks that she is still surprisingly well-remembered there and she even appears in etched glass panels at Halifax Airport.) This service lasted until the 1st December, 1949 when she made her final arrival at Southampton. There is a story, perhaps apocryphal, that Cunard-White Star had hoped to keep her going for another year but that while surveyors from the Board of Trade were inspecting her at Southampton, water began pouring into the dining room during a rainstorm. Her frailty having been so dramatically demonstrated, her certificate was not renewed. Her sale to the British Iron & Steel Corporation for scrapping was announced soon afterwards.

There was an auction of many of her fittings early in February, 1950 but not everything was put up for sale. According to Charles Zuckerman, some of the chairs from the first class dining room went to the *Franconia*, each with a small brass commemorative plate attached. In the mid-'Fifties, they were again transferred, this time to the new *Carinthia*.

On the 18th February, in what must have been a very emotional ceremony, the Cunard and White Star houseflags were hauled down, Eight Bells were struck and the Last Post was sounded. Then on the 19th, a foggy day, the *Aquitania* bade farewell to Southampton and sailed for the Clyde where she arrived on the 21st. The Royal Navy sometimes adopts a rather offhand attitude to the merchant navy but not on this occasion. As the *Aquitania* sailed up the Clyde, a submarine signalled "R.I.P.", a frigate flashed "We are proud to have met you" and a fleet auxiliary said "Goodbye, Old Faithful". On her arrival at Faslane, scrapping of the last of the great four-funnelled flyers of the North Atlantic began almost immediately.

The old liner lies at the scrapping berth at Faslane on the 5th March, 1950. *(Author's collection)*

Aba

Completed as *Glenapp*, 1918 (7,374 gross tons).

Length overall: 465 ft. 4ins.

Breadth: 55 ft. 9ins.

Draught: 30 ft. 5ins.

Diesel. Twin screw.

Service speed: 14 knots.

Conversion to passenger ship *Aba* completed 1921.

Now 7,937 gross tons with a draught of 24 ft. 3ins.

Became *Matrona*, 1947.

Capsized, 1947. Scrapped, 1948.

The *Aba* was a considerable carrier of cargo as well as passengers and mail. *(John Clarkson collection)*

Ordered by the Russian Tsarist government, she was one of the very early funnel-less motor ships. Following the 1917 revolution, the uncompleted vessel was finished as the Glen Line's troopship *Glenapp*. *(Thomas N. Olesen collection)*

You may well ask, 'Does *Aba* really qualify to figure in a book called *Favourite British Liners?*' Well, maybe not – but she was certainly very significant and, I think, deserves more attention than she usually receives from shipping historians.

She was one of the very pioneer motor ships. In 1912, the Copenhagen shipbuilders Burmeister & Wain had delivered a vessel called *Selandia* to the Østasiatiske Kompagni (East Asiatic Company), also of Copenhagen. *Selandia* was the first sizeable deep-sea vessel to be powered by oil engines of the compression ignition type developed by Dr. Rudolf Diesel. In fact, she was the World's first large motor ship. She attracted enormous attention, not least from Kaiser Wilhelm II and from Winston Churchill, then the First Lord of the Admiralty in the British government, and her maiden voyage on the East Asiatic Company's route between Europe and Siam (the present day Thailand) was watched with fascination by the shipping community. *Selandia* was primarily a cargo ship although she did carry up to 20 first class passengers – plus their servants. Many other motor-driven cargo vessels followed but the *Aba* could

accommodate 365 passengers and, some would say, was the World's first true passenger liner to be powered in that way.

The early motor ships tended to be slow and noisy and to vibrate badly. They were, though, economical in fuel, required

One of the two 8-cylinder diesel engines which powered the ship throughout her career. *(Author's collection)*

smaller crews than the steamships and had more space for cargo or passengers. Marine engine builders over Europe were eager to construct the new motors and in Britain Harland & Wolff, Ltd set up a company jointly with Burmeister & Wain to build diesels to the Danish company's design. (Although their main facility was at Belfast, Harland & Wolff also had yards on the Clyde and it was at their Glasgow engine works that they built their earliest diesels. They bought out the Danes' interest in this venture during the First World War.) It was, however, another Glaswegian firm, Barclay, Curle & Co., Ltd., who produced the first British-built motor ship. Among the later orders they received for motor-driven vessels was one from the Imperial Russian government for a freighter to be fitted with Harland &Wolff engines. (A later article in the magazine "The Motor Ship" implied that the East Asiatic Company, who had large interests in Russia at the time, were involved in this order and, indeed, Bruce Peter's researches suggest that there was some link with the order for the passenger steamer *Czaritza* which Barclay, Curle delivered to the Danish company's Russian American Line subsidiary in 1915.) In the event, work on the new ship had to be halted when the Tsarist regime was toppled in the October Revolution of 1917. With the First World War raging, the British government's Shipping Controller stepped in and allotted the ship to the Glen Line who operated on the route to the Far East and already had experience with motor vessels. They called this latest addition to their fleet *Glenapp*. Work on her was resumed early in 1918.

Most of the early motor ships did not have funnels – they either exhausted through narrow pipes attached to one of the masts or through a short tube which was usually topped by a cowl. In *Glenapp*'s case, the smoke from the two 8-cylinder, 4-stroke engines emerged through a cowl. (Amusingly, publicity photographs of the early motor vessels were sometimes 'doctored' in order to reduce the amount of exhaust they seemed to be emitting.) Developing 4,800 bhp, *Glenapp*'s engines gave her a creditable service speed of 14 knots and, according to the magazine "The Motor Ship", made her the most powerful diesel-engined vessel yet built. Her hull, which culminated in a deep counter stern, had a cargo capacity of about 260,000 cubic feet and her cargo gear was attached to four masts, one full-sized and three stumps. She was hardly a thing of beauty at that stage in her career.

She was completed in September, 1918. The First World War still had two months to run and, although basically a cargo ship, she had been fitted out to carry troops. Each side of her long single deck of superstructure was therefore lined with five lifeboats. She was employed in carrying American troops to France.

The Glen Line was a subsidiary of Elder Dempster & Co., Ltd., whose main trade was between Britain and West Africa. Elder Dempster lost many vessels during the War but afterwards they had little difficulty in replacing the freighters since many of the 'Standard' ships which had been built in large numbers for government service in those years were now being offered to British commercial owners. Replacing the lost passenger ships was a different matter. In particular, the main passenger, mail and cargo service between Liverpool and Lagos badly needed reinforcements. In 1920, it was decided that *Glenapp* should be transferred to Elder Dempster and converted into a fully-fledged passenger liner, to be named *Aba* – a considerable gesture of confidence in the speed and reliability of her diesel engines. At the time, the Elder Dempster fleet was divided between two subsidiary companies, the African Steamship Co. and the British & African Steam Navigation Co., Ltd. which in earlier days had been rivals but had been brought together under the Elder Dempster flag. *Aba* was allotted to British & African while *Adda*, a new motorliner completed in 1922, went to the African Steamship Company. (The group was in the habit of giving its prime passenger ships West African names beginning with 'A'.)

The conversion of the *Aba* was carried out by Harland & Wolff at their Govan (Glasgow) yard and transformed her appearance. She now had two masts and acquired a considerable amount of superstructure in three separate housings as well as a substantial upright funnel painted in Elder Dempster's plain buff colour. She could accommodate up to 225 passengers in first class and, very separately further aft, 105 in second class. In addition, at the African end of the route, she could carry 35 third class (i.e.: 'native') passengers. They were housed in the lower reaches of the hull at the stern, probably too close for comfort to the rumble and vibration of the propellers.

The West African run is, of course, a hot weather route and, although air-conditioning was not yet available, first and second class passengers had the benefit of airy, open promenades along the two upper decks of their separate housings; and almost all of them slept in outside cabins with windows or portholes which could be opened. High up in the ship were the first class lounge, writing room, bar and oak-panelled smoke room. Also at this upper deck level were two large suites, each of which was notable in those days for having full private facilities. Most of the other first class cabins, described by *Lloyd's List* as 'exceptionally large' and usually containing three berths but with a few singles, were on the deck below, where there was also a barber's shop. Elsewhere in the ship there was a small hospital. The large first class dining room was situated low down on main deck but was made grander and airier by a tall well which rose through the deck above. It was apparently a very elegant room, 'panelled in white with Wedgwood plaques' and, indeed, although the ship was far from large, her first class passengers were well provided for by the standards of the time. They no doubt included many senior civil servants and representatives of the big British companies trading in West Africa. Probably,

The first class reading and writing room (left) and the first class lounge after the conversion into the *Aba*; the light décor was particularly suitable for a ship trading to the coast of West Africa. *(Author's collection)*

most of the many clerics and missionaries who also travelled on this route would be in second class. (Incidentally, Elder Dempster named two of their ships, *Mary Slessor* and *David Livingstone*, after missionaries.)

Aba ran her trials in August, 1921 but it was not until the 16th November that she left Liverpool on the first voyage of her new career. Elder Dempster happily announced that, in order to complete a round voyage, she would require up to 750 tons of oil, as against the 3,000 tons of coal which would be needed by an equivalent steamer. Furthermore, the oil was carried in her double bottom, thus leaving more room in the hull for cargo. Nevertheless, the *Aba*'s conversion into a passenger-carrier had resulted in some reduction in her cargo capacity.

In the 1920s, an Elder Dempster mail ship would leave the Landing Stage at Liverpool every fortnight, usually on a Wednesday, bound for the British colonies in West Africa. On the way, she would call at Madeira and Las Palmas. Then, she would sometimes put in at Bathurst (these days called Banjul) in Gambia before heading for Freetown in Sierra Leone, Sekondi (later replaced by the newly-built deepwater harbour at

neighbouring Takoradi) on the Gold Coast, Accra also on the Gold Coast (now, of course, Ghana) and Lagos in Nigeria. Sometimes she would continue to Port Harcourt in the Niger Delta. On the return voyage, there would probably be a call at Plymouth where passengers bound for London and the South of England would disembark. The round trip, Liverpool to Liverpool, would usually take between 35 and 39 days.

Some West African ports were shallow and difficult to approach and at Sekondi, for instance, large ships would have to stand off and cargo would be unloaded 'overside' into boats. In some cases, so would passengers, who would be lowered in huge baskets.

In August, 1922 *Aba* hit the headlines when she came to the aid of the disabled Portuguese destroyer *Guadiana* and towed her for three strenuous days before bringing her into Las Palmas. *Aba* was herself the victim of a breakdown when in January, 1929, after leaving Las Palmas, she suffered a broken crankshaft and made her way very slowly on one engine to Plymouth and then to Liverpool, escorted by a tug. Lengthy repairs were carried out at Belfast and it was not until the 4th December that

The bedroom of one of the two first class "suites". Despite having bunk beds they were notable for their full private facilities; on the right, the oak-panelled first class smoking room. *(Author's collection)*

The Elder Dempster mail boats provided a vital link between Britain and the West African colonies. The company also had a large fleet of cargo ships. *(John Clarkson collection)*

she came back into service. On her first voyage back in service, misfortune struck again when, in seriously bad weather, her steering gear was put out of action by heavy seas and she had to be towed into Cobh by the famous tug *Zwarte Zee*. She was able to resume her voyage four days later. Then in January, 1931, she was briefly aground at Lagos.

By now, it was not only *Aba* which was running into trouble. Elder Dempster was a member of the interlocking Royal Mail Steam Packet Company group, presided over by Lord Kylsant. As we shall see in the chapters on *Asturias* and *Britannic*, the collapse of this huge British shipping combine had very far-reaching consequences – not least for Elder Dempster who, by 1931, were so short of money that they were unable to take delivery of their fine new flagship *Achimota*, which was eventually taken off Harland & Wolff's hands by the Australian company Huddart Parker and became their famous *Wanganella*. In December, *Aba*, perhaps by then the least serviceable of the Elder Dempster mail ships, was laid up in the River Dart which, in the gathering gloom of the Great Depression, was becoming the resting place for an increasing number of unemployed merchant vessels.

She remained there until August, 1933 and did not actually re-enter service until the 13th June, 1934. Meanwhile, in 1933, Elder Dempster had been rescued, in part by Alfred Holt & Co. of the Blue Funnel Line, and had been re-formed as Elder Dempster Lines, Ltd. By now, *Aba* was the fleet's stopgap mail ship and was only used intermittently. Her final liner voyage from West Africa ended at Liverpool on the 18th November, 1938. Thereafter, she lay idly in the River Mersey.

Fortunately, unlike some other ships which would have proved useful during the War, she was not sold for scrap. On the 10th September, 1939, seven days after war was declared, she left the Mersey, having been requisitioned to stand by as a hospital carrier at the Scapa Flow naval base. In this capacity she made sev-

eral voyages to ports on the Scottish mainland, in particular carrying casualties from the battleships *Royal Oak* (which had been sunk in a daring raid by a German submarine which had penetrated the harbour defences) and *Iron Duke* (which had been bombed there a few days later). However, in February, 1940 *Aba* was shifted, at first to Greenock and then to Liverpool, to be made ready for more taxing duties as a fully-equipped hospital ship, designated No. 34. She now had facilities for up to 450 patients and could accommodate a medical staff of 83. She, of course, wore the regulation white-hulled hospital ship livery with large red crosses on her sides and on her funnel. At night she was fully illuminated.

Her first taste of action came in May, 1940 when she was sent to support the Allied forces who were briefly attempting to stem the German advance through northern Norway. Then in July, she set out for the Middle East but for some reason the Italian authorities refused her a safe passage through the western Mediterranean despite her hospital ship status and she had to go the long way round via Cape Town and the Suez Canal. There followed a long voyage to Bombay and Durban, after which she returned to the Mediterranean where she remained for many months, carrying troops wounded in the North African, Greek and, later, Italian campaigns to ports such as Alexandria and Haifa. She also sometimes carried prisoners of war. In May, 1941, during the battle for Crete, she was bombed several times even though she was clearly marked as a hospital ship. Although damaged, she survived. The German authorities later claimed that she had been attacked because it was believed, wrongly, that the King of Greece was on board. Occasionally, *Aba*'s Mediterranean duties were interspersed by voyages to Durban.

In November, 1943, she returned to Liverpool for three months of much-needed repairs. She then went back to the Mediterranean but this time her stay was relatively short as she was damaged during an air attack on Naples in March, 1944. Three lives were lost and she had to return to Britain for repairs at Avonmouth. After that, she made a voyage to New York repatriating American casualties and then proceeded to Halifax. Two more voyages from the U.K. to Halifax followed, one rather circuitously via Ponta Delgada in the Azores. Then, after a further short stint in the Mediterranean, H.M.H.S. *Aba* was briefly employed in shuttling patients from Cherbourg to Southampton.

After more repairs, she made perhaps the most unlikely voyage of her entire career when, in July, 1945, she carried a group of Russians, who had been held as prisoners by the Germans, from Trondheim in northern Norway to Murmansk. There was, I suppose, a certain circularity in this – she was at last visiting the country for whose government she had been laid down in 1916. Then, equally aptly, she returned to once-familiar waters, carrying West African troops back to Freetown. From there she made her way to the Belgian Congo to pick up civilians whom she repatriated to Antwerp. The War was now over but there was still work for hospital ships to do and *Aba* had a further brief spell in the Mediterranean before again visiting West Africa, the Congo and Antwerp. By April, 1946 she was employed in carrying sick prisoners of war and other patients between Southampton and Hamburg. Later, after a further round trip to the Mediterranean, she made several brief troopship voyages from Liverpool to Belfast. Finally, on arrival in the Mersey on the 7th January, 1947, she was handed back to her owners.

Aba was now nearly thirty years old and still had her original engines dating from the early, almost experimental days of motor ship development. Furthermore, her war had been a very busy and taxing one. Although Elder Dempster had lost all their other mail ships, they would soon be taking delivery of two new liners which were being built for them by Vickers-Armstrongs. The lengthy and expensive process of trying to return *Aba* to her pre-War standards was not considered worthwhile. However, in those straitened times, even old and worn passenger liners could find ready buyers among the eager shipping entrepreneurs, often

Italian or Greek, who were anxious to cash in on the booming trade in carrying refugees and other migrants from war-torn Europe to more hopeful parts of the World. In April, 1947 *Aba* was bought for £55,000 by the Bawtry Steamship Co., Ltd., controlled by members of the respected Livanos family of London-Greek shipowners. Companies managed by J. Livanos & Sons also bought three other ships for emigrant use during this period. They gave *Aba* a new name, *Matrona*, and soon work began on her conversion in Bidston Dock, Birkenhead.

Unfortunately, on the 30th October, 1947, after the ill-advised removal of large quantities of ballast, she suddenly heeled over to port while the men on board scrambled for safety. She came to rest on her side, partly submerged and with one of her propellers above water. It was not until the 13th June, 1948 that she was finally righted. It had been a difficult business. Her funnel, masts, cargo gear and lifeboats had to be removed and fourteen huge pulleys were attached to the starboard side of the hull so that the ship could be heaved upright by winches installed on the quay. One account of the event states that it took just twenty minutes for the hulk to be righted – if true, it must have been a spectacular sight. She finally left Birkenhead under tow on the 3rd October bound for Barrow-in-Furness, having been sold for scrap.

The sad end of the *Aba*, while she was being converted into the emigrant ship *Matrona* in Bidston Dock, Birkenhead, in 1947. *(John Clarkson collection)*

Asturias

Completed 1926. 22,071 gross tons.

Length overall: 655 ft. 8ins. Breadth: 78 ft. 6ins.

Draught: 40 ft. 6ins.

Twin screw. Diesel engines. Service speed: 16 knots.

Engines replaced by geared steam turbines, 1934.

Service speed now 18 knots.

Gross tonnage now: 22,048.

Length overall now: 666ft. 0ins. Torpedoed, 1943.

Rebuilt as an emigrant-carrier and troopship

(22,445 gross tons), 1945-46. Scrapped, 1957.

The *Asturias* in her original motor ship form. *(Author's collection)*

An architect's rendering of the spectacular Moorish style first class winter garden. *(Bruce Peter collection)*

Having been formed in 1839 with a Royal Charter and a contract to carry Her Majesty's mails to the West Indies, the Royal Mail Steam Packet Company was very much a member of the old British shipping aristocracy. In 1851, Royal Mail ships also began running to the ports along the east coast of South America and in later years this became the company's main service. In 1903, the appointment of Owen Philipps (later Lord Kylsant) as a director, and very soon chairman, transformed what had become a rather sluggish and conventional company. Not only did he revitalise the fleet by introducing a succession of new and larger ships built on favourable terms by his friends at Harland & Wolff but, with a dizzying series of acquisitions, he made the Royal Mail company the hub of a huge interlocking combine which included such famous lines as Elder Dempster, Union-Castle, Lamport & Holt, the Nelson Line, the Pacific Steam Navigation Co., Coast Lines and, later, Aberdeen & Commonwealth, Shaw, Savill & Albion and the prestigious White Star Line. At the height of his power, Lord Kylsant controlled 2.6 million tons of shipping.

In 1923, orders were placed for two large liners which would up-grade the main Royal Mail Steam Packet passenger, mail and cargo service from Southampton to Buenos Aires, then being run by the 15,000-ton steamers *Arlanza* (1912), *Andes* (1913) and *Almanzora* (1915) in conjunction with a couple of similar but older and smaller liners. As we have seen in a previous chapter, Harland & Wolff had a licence to build marine diesel engines to the designs of the Burmeister & Wain company of Copenhagen and Lord Kylsant was a strong proponent of this type of propulsion.

The colourful children's playroom with its toy castle. *(Bruce Peter collection)*

Diesel-powered ships were cheaper to operate and they were able to carry more freight and passengers since their engines and fuel tanks took up less room than the boilers, machinery and bunkers or tanks of the steamers. Nevertheless, the decision to power such large liners with diesels was a daring one and in September, 1923 it was announced that the construction of the two ships would proceed slowly until a decision had been taken on which specific type of diesel engines were to be used. In the end, each vessel was fitted with two 8-cylinder double-acting four-cycle motors. They were the largest marine diesels yet constructed and each ship was said to develop a total of 20,000 bhp, although a figure of 15,000 bhp was quoted later.

The two sisiters conformed to the company's custom of giving their crack liners Spanish or Portuguese names beginning with the letter 'A'. Both the *Asturias* and the *Alcantara* commemorated previous vessels – the first *Alcantara* had been lost in a gallant action during the First World War in which both she and her German opponent had been sunk. Unsurprisingly, the new liners were built by Harland & Wolff at their Queen's Island yard in Belfast. By now Lord Kylsant was also chairman of Harland & Wolff who, like so many shipbuilders at that time, had a worrying number of empty slipways and were in desperate need of work. The actual owners of the *Asturias* were an associated concern within the Royal Mail group, RMSP Meat Transports, Ltd., and much of the finance for her building came from loans made by the British and Northern Ireland governments. At the time, the Kylsant companies were making much use of such loans and it was the need to repay them during a period of depressed trade which was eventually a major factor in triggering the collapse of the group.

The *Asturias*, the first of the new pair, was launched by the Duchess of Abercorn punctually at noon on the 7th July, 1925 and was completed in early 1926. Briefly, the *Asturias* was the World's biggest and most powerful motor ship.

Liners on the South American run usually had very luxurious first class public rooms; here is the social hall on the *Asturias*. (Clive Harvey collection)

A first class single cabin (left) and the first class library which seems singularly lacking in bookshelves. Note the very necessary fans in both pictures. *(Paolo Piccione collection)*

When, on the 12th January, 1926, she left the yard to run her trials on the Clyde, there was much anxious interest in Belfast. It was very important that she should be a success. Not only were Harlands working on the sister ship but they were about to launch a first motorliner for the Union-Castle company, to be named *Carnarvon Castle*. The *Asturias*'s trials occupied five days but when she returned to her builders for final adjustments the statement issued to the press was unspecific: simply that she had proved "very satisfactory" in every way. The truth may, in fact, have been that there was disappointment with her speed and almost certainly there was dismay at the way she vibrated. Nevertheless, she sailed to Southampton in good time to prepare for her scheduled maiden voyage which began late on the evening of the 26th February. She was carrying only about 300 passengers but it was stated that she would be picking up more during her Continental calls – especially, one would guess, at Lisbon, where Royal Mail ships were in the habit of embarking emigrants bound for Brazil. The advent of the *Asturias* enabled the company to increase the frequency of the service from a sailing every fortnight to one every ten days.

The *Asturias* had an appearance which was typical of the Harland & Wolff motorships designed under the supervision of the yard's naval architect, T. C. Tobin: straight upright bow; flat-fronted superstructure; two short, raked funnels with horizontal tops; and cruiser stern. She had notably tall masts. Like most passenger ships on the routes between the Argentine and Europe, she was also a big carrier of chilled or frozen meat which she would load from the *frigorificos* (meat warehouses) on the quayside at Buenos Aires. As with many other Royal Mail liners, she had a split superstructure in order to facilitate working the additional cargo which she carried beneath part of her passenger accommodation. In her case, however, the break came towards the rear of the superstructure rather than immediately behind the bridge house. Rather than booms and derricks, Royal Mail liners were often fitted with hydraulic cranes and the *Asturias* was given twelve of these which worked cargo through six hatches.

Modernity was not, though, a feature of the décor of her passenger accommodation. She and her sister were, in fact, among the last liners to emerge before the *Ile de France* changed ship interior design for ever. As built, the *Asturias* could carry up to 410 first class passengers, plus 232 in cabin class and 768 in a stark third class mainly intended for Spanish and Portuguese migrants. She was a particularly well-equipped ship, having, for instance, a Kosher kitchen. As was to be expected on this route, her first class cabins and public rooms were elaborately furnished. Particularly notable on the *Asturias* was the so-called winter garden – although, as with so many of its kind, the term 'garden' was somewhat misleading since the sole vegetation seems to have been provided by a few palms in large pots.

ROYAL MAIL LINE
between
EUROPE & SOUTH AMERICA

FIRST CLASS

PRIMERA CLASE

Kenneth Shoesmith designed some very beautiful publicity material for the Royal Mail company. *(Paolo Piccione collection)*

The room was, however, spectacularly fitted out in Moorish style with walls clad with alternating horizontal bands of red and white marble.

The other first class public rooms ranged widely in style. The dining room, with its two-deck high central section, was furnished in the French Empire manner, complete with marble and bronze gilt columns. The social hall was Georgian in style and had a stage at one end. A further lounge, domed, was modelled on the State apartments at Houghton House in Norfolk and had peacock green panelling with gilt mouldings. The smoke room was furnished in the William and Mary style with cedar wood panelling and was inspired by rooms in Belton House, Lincolnshire and in Ham House in Surrey. Harewood House, Yorkshire had provided the exemplar for the reading and writing room with its frieze of classical figures. First class passengers also had the use of an internal swimming pool in the then customary Pompeiian style. In addition, a children's playroom contained a toy castle resembling the illustrations of the still-popular Victorian author and artist Kate Greenaway.

In 1927, the *Asturias* was joined by her sister ship *Alcantara*, which began her maiden voyage on the 4th March. Their passages from Southampton to Cherbourg, Vigo, Lisbon, Rio de Janeiro, Santos, (sometimes also Montevideo) and Buenos Aires usually took 18 or 19 days. There was no doubt that they were outstanding liners but trade was difficult. Competition was increasing, particularly from the new ships being introduced by the Blue Star Line. And political and economic conditions in the Argentine and Brazil were deteriorating. Very occasionally, one or other of the sisters would be sent on a long cruise. In January, 1927, for instance, the *Asturias* set off on a 101-day voyage to the Caribbean, South America, South Africa and East Africa, returning via Suez and the Mediterranean. Two years later, she made a 40-day cruise to several Caribbean islands and to La Guaira, Cristobal, Nassau and Bermuda. In 1929, she began calling at Madeira during her regular liner voyages, hoping to pick up some of the tourist traffic to that island.

The economic collapse in the early 'Thirties affected the South American routes as much as most. In addition, foreign companies had by now introduced even bigger and faster liners, some of which were competing for the trade from the Spanish and Portuguese ports. Then in 1931 the Hamburg-Süd Amerika Line's magnificent 21-knot steamer *Cap Arcona* began calling at Southampton.

But the Kylsant group, with its vast debts, had already

Royal Mail liners often had large third class quarters, mainly for Spanish and Portuguese passengers. In this view of the third class smoking room it is notable that ladies are present. *(Author's collection)*

In 1934 the *Asturias* was converted to steam turbine propulsion and was slightly lengthened. This increased her speed and enabled her to compete more effectively with her French, German and Italian rivals. *(Author's collection)*

reached the end of the road. It did, however, control 15 per cent of the British merchant fleet and its demise would have been a catastrophe for the country's economy. From 1930, therefore, the government and some of the great and the good of the British shipping industry were trying to salvage as much as they could from the wreckage. As part of the rescue, a new company called Royal Mail Lines, Ltd. was formed in 1932 to take over the group's routes to the east coast of South America, including those of the old Royal Mail Steam Packet Co. and the Nelson Line. It eventually became part of the Furness Withy group. Meanwhile, Lord Kylsant had been sentenced to a year's imprisonment for putting his name to misleading statements in a prospectus. The *Asturias* and the *Alcantara* continued to sail throughout the whole imbroglio. By 1934, the new Royal Mail Lines company was able to tackle the problem of the sisters' unsatisfactory performance. From the 1st May until the 24th September, the *Asturias* lay at Belfast while Harland & Wolff removed her diesel engines and substituted two sets of Parsons steam turbines, single reduction-geared and with an output of 20,000 shp. New propellers were fitted and, in order to increase her speed still further, her bow was remodelled and lengthened by 10 feet. She lost her motor-liner funnels, which were replaced by two large and imposing ones of unmistakable steamship style. (The forward one was a dummy.) Probably only the *Empress of Britain* had grander stacks. During this reconstruction, the *Asturias*'s accommodation was reduced to 330 in first class and 220 in second. Third class remained at 768. Work started on the equivalent conversion of the *Alcantara* in November.

On the 15th October, the *Asturias* returned to service with a brief introductory trip from Southampton. Five days later, she set off on her first line voyage to Buenos Aires in her new form. It took 17 days, as against the previous 18 or 19 days. On the 22nd January, 1935, she started another major cruise – this time from Southampton to Algiers, Port Said, Port Tewfik, Aden, Colombo, Penang, Singapore, Padang, Batavia, Mauritius, Port Natal (i.e.: Durban), Cape Town (where she lost an anchor), Las Palmas, Madeira and back to Southampton. Later that year, she made a few shorter cruises to Norway or the Mediterranean. However, Royal Mail already had a very successful cruise ship, the *Atlantis* (the former *Andes*), and the *Asturias* henceforth concentrated almost entirely on her now more successful South American voyages, although she did make a couple of Mediterranean cruises shortly before the outbreak of war in 1939.

She arrived back from the second of these on the 26th August and, although World War II had not yet begun,

In 1943 she was torpedoed but reconstruction began in 1945 and she eventually emerged as an emigrant ship, mainly carrying passengers to Australia. Here we see her in the Suez Canal. *(Author's collection)*

she was immediately taken up by the Royal Navy. The following day she left for Belfast for conversion into the Armed Merchant Cruiser H.M.S. *Asturias*. Partly, no doubt, to reduce the target she presented to potential enemies, her dummy forward funnel was removed. Later, her mainmast was also felled. She was given eight 6-inch guns plus some lesser armament and was assigned to northern patrol duties out of Scapa Flow. In 1940, she joined her sister patrolling the South Atlantic and remained there for about three years apart from a refit at Newport News in Virginia, during which she was equipped with more modern guns and a spotter plane which could be shot off the ship by means of a catapult.

H.M.S. *Asturias* very nearly met her end on the 25th July, 1943 while she was accompanying a floating dock being towed across the South Atlantic. She was hit by the second of two torpedoes fired by an Italian submarine, the *Ammiraglio Cagni*, but, with her engine and boiler rooms flooding, she was taken in hand by the Dutch tug *Zwarte Zee*. After a perilous 400-mile tow, she was brought into Freetown, Sierra Leone on the 1st August and beached. She lay there for many months and so damaged was she that in May, 1944 she was declared a constructive total loss. However, although she deteriorated further and was by now suffering from serious infestation, the authorities later

decided that her case was not completely hopeless. In February, 1945 the *Zwarte Zee* returned and, with another tug and a naval escort, began the long tow to Gibraltar, which was reached safely on the 27th. There the *Asturias* was placed in dry dock for repair.

On the 9th June, 1945, she was officially taken up for conversion into a 'personnel ship'. By then, she was already under tow for Belfast where Harland & Wolff were to embark on the conversion. She was beyond restoration to her pre-War state but, as in the similar case of the Cunard-White Star *Georgic*, she could be made fit for trooping and, as it turned out, for emigrant service. In any case, her luxurious pre-War fittings had been destroyed when the warehouse in which they had been stored was bombed during an air raid.

In December, 1945, she was purchased by the British government's Ministry of Transport but Royal Mail Lines were to be responsible for her management. The shipyard work had been slightly delayed by fires which had broken out on board in August and November, 1945 but by the 14th September, 1946 the *Asturias* was ready to be handed over. On the 16th, she steamed into her old home port of Southampton. It must have been an emotional occasion for many people about the docks who had never expected to see her again.

The Australian government were busily encouraging migration to their country and were putting pressure on the British authorities to supply more ships to carry the newcomers. Such was the shortage of available liners in those early post-War months, however, that it was necessary to use several troopships to help fill the gap. Thus, when the *Asturias* left Southampton on the 12th October, 1946 on her first post-War voyage, she headed for Australia. She went out via the Cape but later voyages were made via Suez in both directions and included homeward calls at Bombay to pick up British civilians leaving India during the chaotic and dangerous period leading up to Independence and Partition.

In August, 1947, the *Asturias* spent time at Southampton having her accommodation made more suitable for emigrant passengers. In order to squeeze additional outward trips into her schedule, on several of her voyages she went only as far as Fremantle rather than continuing to Melbourne and Sydney. In January, 1948, she visited Wellington. Between 1949 and 1950, she called at Batavia/Djakarta and either Rotterdam or Amsterdam during some of her homeward voyages, repatriating Dutch citizens forced to leave the newly independent state of Indonesia. By now, she was officially an emigrant ship and had accommodation for 160 first class passengers, 113 third and 1,134 in dormitories.

She did, though, begin making trooping calls at Singapore and Hong Kong in 1952; and in 1953, with the regular lines on the Australian run now able to cope with most of the flow of migrants (and with her accommodation perhaps no longer acceptable for civilian passengers), she became a full-time troopship. She mainly ran to Singapore, Hong Kong, Kure and, while the Korean War was underway, Inchon or Pusan. By 1955, with fighting taking place in Cyprus, she was also visiting Famagusta and Limassol. In October, 1956, *Asturias* also made a few shuttle voyages between Southampton and Rotterdam. The following month, she was one of the ships which took British forces to fight in the unfortunate Suez campaign, after which the closure of the Suez Canal caused her final Far Eastern voyages to be diverted via the Cape.

Her last voyage Out East ended with her return to Southampton on the 27th August, 1957. On the 12th September, she left for Faslane to be scrapped. Before that, however, she had a few brief moments of film stardom, playing the part of the *Titanic* during the shooting of some deck scenes for *A Night to Remember* (some would say the best of the all the films about the *Titanic* disaster), for which her lifeboats slung from luffing davits and her Harland & Wolff deck-housing made her very suitable.

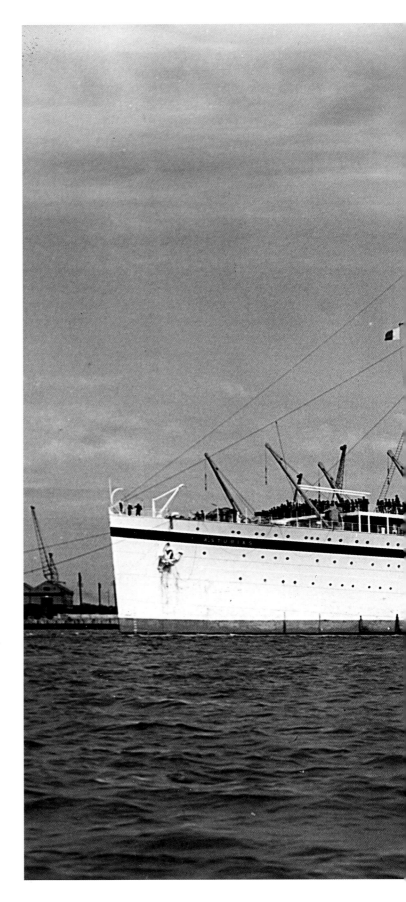

The *Asturias* ended her days as a British troopship.
(Author's collection)

Rajula

Completed 1926.

8,478 gross tons.

Length overall: 476 ft. 9ins.

Breadth: 61 ft. 9ins.   Draught: 26 ft. 2½ ins.

Twin screw.

Triple-expansion steam engines.

Service speed: 13 knots.

Became *Rangat* (8,074 gross tons), 1973.

Scrapped, 1974.

The venerable *Rajula* late in her career. *(Ambrose Greenway collection)*

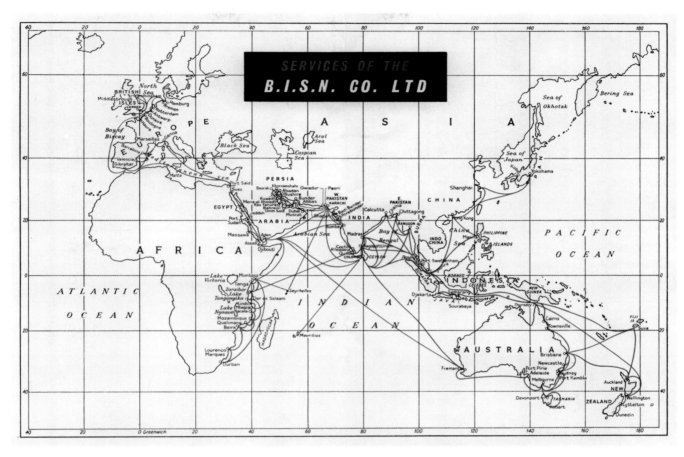

British India provided extensive links amongst the countries of the Empire as can be seen from this company map.
(Clive Harvey collection)

The *Rajula* is an obvious candidate for inclusion in a book called *Favourite British Liners*. Few ships can have been so widely liked. The directors of The British India Steam Navigation Co., Ltd. must have loved her – no other member of their fleet lasted so long and few can have repaid their investment so many times over. Her builders, Barclay, Curle & Co., Ltd., must have been proud of their handiwork and grateful that she so successfully cemented their long relationship with British India. Many of her officers liked her, too: I once asked a man who had been a junior engineer in her last years why this should be. Surely an old ship which was usually so crowded with huge numbers of 'native' deck passengers and whose ancient machinery was so out-dated, must have been a nightmare to keep going? And weren't conditions in the engine room absolutely unbearable during the Hot Season? 'Ah, but she was a happy ship,' he replied as if no other explanation were need-

ed. 'We always did our best for her.' And it seems that she was popular with thousands of her Indian and Malayan passengers: probably better run and certainly cleaner than the competition and so very safe. There is a story that when, in 1966, she finally made it into Madras after surviving a terrifying cyclone in which the winds had dragged her off-course for 30 miles and she had then been forced to inch her way stern first to safety, some of her passengers said prayers of thanksgiving for her on the quayside.

When she entered service in 1926, the British India company, usually known simply as BI, was in its prime. Although it had merged into the P&O group twelve years earlier, it was still a distinct entity and its network of services stretching out from India to the Far East, the Persian Gulf, East and South Africa and the British Motherland made it one of the most important links in the Empire on which the sun never set.

Among its maze of routes, one of the least glamorous – but perhaps most profitable – was the fortnightly service linking Madras, Negapatam and several other ports in southern India with Penang and Singapore. Apart from mail (much of which had crossed the subcontinent to Negapatam by express train from Bombay) and cargo, it carried thousands of poor Indians to work on the Malayan rubber plantations. So when, in September, 1925, British India confirmed their order for two new ships for the service, they specified that each should be able to carry as many as 5,000 deck passengers and a further 92 Indians or Malays who could afford to travel in cabins, quite apart from 30 Europeans in first class and another 30 Europeans in second class.*** Although the new liners were to be mere 8,000-tonners, they would have the largest passenger capacity of any British ships in peacetime. The deck passengers, as on many British India liners, were required to bring their own bedding and camped out, mainly in the 'tween decks. They were certainly not travelling in luxury but on these new ships they did at least have the benefit of mechanical ventilation.

The first of the pair to enter service, the *Rohna*, was built by Hawthorn, Leslie at Hebburn-on-Tyne. The second, the *Rajula*, came from British India's old friends, Barclay, Curle & Co., Ltd. of Whiteinch, Glasgow and was handed over on the 26th November, 1926, just a few weeks after her sister. She had cost £232,700. She was a shapely, rather stately vessel, very much in the steamship style of the times, with a cruiser stern and a single tall funnel, raked and rim-topped. Her enormous passenger capacity required no less than twenty-two lifeboats, some double-banked and all slung from luffing davits. For much of the 'Twenties and 'Thirties, British India had a rather sombre livery – black hull with a thin white line at main deck level; brown superstructure; and a black funnel with two wide and closely spaced white bands. In the mid-'Thirties, the brown superstructure – said to have been adopted by British India and P&O because it did not reflect the glare of the sun and maybe because it was less prone to shew dirt – was replaced by white. Much later, in about 1955, the hull too was repainted white with an encircling black band. About the same time, bunks were erected in the 'tween decks.

The five cargo holds had a bale capacity of 389,230 square feet, a large amount for a passenger liner of this size, and were served by 10 derricks on samson posts and by a single

***This separation of the races may seem shocking to us now but, of course, it is a mistake to judge other times by our own standards – goodness knows what future generations will think of some of our customs.*

Originally *Rajula* had a black hull and, as she carried up to 5,000 deck passengers, she needed many lifeboats which were carried in double-banked luffing davits. *(Author's collection)*

A post-War view of *Rajula* now wearing a white livery. In many ways she was an old-fashioned ship but she survived Out East for 48 years. *(Ambrose Greenway collection)*

heavy lift attached to the foremast. *Rajula* was certainly no express liner: her two 4-cylinder triple-expansion engines, products of her builders, were chosen for economy, simplicity and reliability and, with an output of 5,200 ihp, were sufficient to maintain a service speed of just 12 or 13 knots. In fact, she was able to achieve 15.35 knots on her trials. (*Rohna* had quadruple-expansion engines.) Steam was supplied by five single-ended boilers and the furnaces could be easily converted so that they could burn either oil or coal. James Pottinger tells me that this was quite common at the time, for instance on Clan Line ships. To be frank, the *Rohna* and *Rajula* were intended to be nothing more than sturdy, highly profitable workhorses – which makes it all the more remarkable that *Rajula* in particular became such a favourite.

They came out at a difficult time. In the mid-'Twenties, parts of the British economy were bedevilled by slack trading conditions, particularly in the shipping and shipbuilding industries, and by labour disputes. The order for the two sisters was an absolute godsend to the yards concerned, both of which had virtually no work in hand. The *Rajula* was launched on the 22nd September, 1926, obviously in a fairly complete state since by the 23rd November she was ready to run her trials on the Clyde. She seems not to have attracted a great deal of attention – she got a very perfunc-

tory mention in *Lloyd's List*, for instance. On the 6th December, she left to load cargo at Antwerp, Middlesbrough and London. From there, she worked her way out to India on a voyage slotted into British India's scheduled service to Karachi and Bombay via Suez. She departed the Royal Albert Dock in London on New Year's Day, 1927, never to return to Britain.

Her entry onto her designed route was delayed because when she reached Bombay, she and five other British India vessels, including the *Rohna*, were taken up by the government to carry troops to Shanghai. The civil war between the Chinese Communists and Nationalists had reached that city and it was felt necessary to provide reinforcements for the troops who protected the considerable British interests there. It was not until June that the *Rajula* was able to start her intended service. Although she visited Calcutta and Rangoon at least once, she ran almost entirely between Madras and Singapore throughout the late 'Twenties and the 'Thirties. A typical voyage would take her from Madras down the coast to Pondicherry, Cuddalore and Negapatam (whose English spelling seems to have varied and could, for instance, be Nagappattinam), then across the Indian Ocean to Penang and through the Straits of Malacca to Port Swettenham and Singapore. On the whole, this was an uneventful period for her, apart from a machinery breakdown which caused her to suffer the indignity of being towed into Calcutta in May, 1939.

She emerged from her busy obscurity in September, 1938 when she was requisitioned for a few days for possible troopship duties at the time of the Munich crisis. British India ships were, of course, no strangers to trooping and *Rajula*, with her spaces for large numbers of deck passengers, was an obvious candidate. On the 25th November, 1939, nearly three months after the outbreak of the Second World War, she was again taken up for troopship service. She sailed from Madras and, after calling at Bombay, headed via Suez to Marseilles. From there, she made three trips to Haifa and then headed back to Bombay. Briefly, she was returned to liner service, although now under government control, but in May, 1940 she was assigned to permanent troopship duties. Her capacity was quoted as 80 officers and others in cabins and 1,470 troops in the deck spaces.

Her troopship voyages at this time took her from India to East and South Africa. She also carried troops to the Middle East and in January, 1941 was reported to have 'touched bank' while passing through the Suez Canal. Later that year, she had a spell in a troopship shuttle service between Bombay and Basra. She also visited Australia on a couple of occasions in 1942. In mid-1943, she was sent to the Mediterranean to participate in the Allied invasion of Sicily. Later that year, however, she returned to the East, shuttling for a while between Madras and Chittagong. In March – May, 1944, she was converted at Calcutta in readiness for ambulance transport service during the Burma campaign. In June, 1945, she made the first of a number of visits to Rangoon, which had been liberated from Japanese occupation in the previous month. Two months later, mechanical problems forced her to put back to Rangoon for repairs.

The *Rajula* remained in the Far East for the rest of the War and beyond, before being restored to her peacetime form during a 49-day refit at Calcutta between May and early July, 1946. She was not immediately returned to her owners, however, visiting Batavier, Hong Kong and Kure in government service later that year. She was finally handed back to British India at Singapore on the 28th February, 1947.

She resumed her pre-War service with her 6th March, 1947 sailing from Singapore to Madras. Her accommodation was now quoted as 37 First Class, 133 Second and 1,727 deck passengers. Sadly, she had lost her sister. The *Rohna*, also taken up as a troopship, had been sunk with a big loss of life off Bougie in North Africa in November, 1943 and *Rajula*'s sailings were now co-ordinated with those of the Indian-owned Eastern Shipping Corporation, which eventually became part of The Shipping Corporation of India,

Ltd. (In later years, they used the *State of Madras*, formerly the *Jaljawahar* of the Scindia Steam Navigation Company's Bombay to London service, on the route. After sailing on her, Ted Scull nicknamed *State of Madras* the 'State of Madness'. *State of Bombay* was 'State of Decay'.) *Rajula* sailed on through Indian independence, little affected, it would seem, by anti-British feeling. The weather could be troublesome, however. In January, 1950, she was delayed for about ten days at Negapatam; and, of course, there was her fearsome battle with the elements in November, 1966, already mentioned. Inevitably, there were sometimes health problems among her passengers and in September, 1950 she was quarantined at Penang when she arrived with a smallpox case on board. Then, in May, 1957, she was quarantined again, this time at Madras. There had been an outbreak of influenza in Malaya and by the time *Rajula* reached Madras, many of her passengers had fallen ill. A team of 100 doctors and orderlies boarded the ship, which was detained for 10 days. Again, in May, 1959, she arrived at Penang with a case of smallpox.

Old BI hands often recall the constant routine of cleaning and polishing on the *Rajula* and other ships of the line – very necessarily, 'cleanliness was next godliness'.

Except for these interruptions, *Rajula* maintained an admirably regular service until August and September, 1957 when she was sent to Hong Kong for a lengthy refit. Then, from October, 1961 to January, 1962 she was given a further major refit at the Mitsubishi yard at Kobe, even though she was by now well into her veteran years. The most notable external changes were that she now had fewer but larger lifeboats, on gravity davits, and her heavy lift had been removed. Also, her funnel lost its rimmed top.

In March, 1964, when off Penang, she had a rare mechanical failure – the crankshaft of her starboard engine fractured. She completed her voyage, all the way back to Madras, on one engine, before proceeding to Singapore for repairs.

In January, 1971, she rescued 15 survivors from a Japanese fishing vessel, which had been destroyed by fire. The world of shipping was changing, however, and during 1971-73 the vast and straggling P&O group was in such a precarious state that a brutal re-organisation became necessary in order to save it. In the process, many famous names disappeared. Ownership of the British India fleet was gradually transferred, mainly to the parent Peninsular & Oriental Steam Navigation Co., Ltd., the *Rajula* being officially taken over on the 19th April, 1973. However, like the few other remaining BI passenger ships, she continued in her familiar service for a little longer, happily still wearing her old colours. But it was a temporary reprieve and on the 7th October, 1973 she arrived at Madras for the last time.

She was now more than 47 years old but she had been bought for further trading. The Shipping Corporation of India needed a temporary stopgap to serve the Andaman and Nicobar Islands for a few months. They renamed the old ship *Rangat* and quickly placed her in service. Seven months later, on the 12th May, 1974, she was laid up at Bombay and at the end of August she was sold to the local Maharashtra Shipbreaking Co. Work on the demolition of this favourite old liner started in December.

Throughout her career *Rajula* was renowned for the care and cleanlines with which she was maintained.
(Author's collection)

Arandora Star

Completed as *Arandora*, 1927.   12,847 gross tons.

Length overall: 512 ft. 3ins.   Breadth: 68 ft. 4ins.

Draught: 34 ft. 0ins.

Geared steam turbines. Twin screw.

Service speed: 16 knots.

Rebuilt as cruise ship (14,694 gross tons) and renamed *Arandora Star*, 1929.

Further rebuilt 1934, 1935 (15,305 gross tons) and 1937 (15,501 gross tons).

Torpedoed and sunk, 1940.

The *Arandora Star*, here seen in Stockholm, became a notable cruise ship. *(Author's collection)*

'The World's Most Delightful Cruising Liner' – that is what the brochures said. And, without a doubt, *Arandora Star* was one of the finest cruise ships of her day. Surprisingly, though, she was not born into the British shipping Establishment. Her owners were unwelcome outsiders who had to fight their way into that self-confident, exclusive club. *Arandora Star* and her sisters were the means by which they planned to do so.

The Blue Star Line, privately owned until the end of its days, belonged to the Vestey family. The Vesteys are in the meat and cold storage trades and their interests have ranged from cattle ranches and meat-packing stations in South America and elsewhere to the former Dewhirst chain of butcher's shops in this country. At first, though, they did not own the ships which transported their meat across the oceans. It was natural, therefore, that like the Nelson family a generation earlier, they should set up their own shipping line. They bought their first vessels in 1909 and established the Blue Star Line in 1911. Their early ships were second-hand refrigerated cargo steamers, cast-offs from such companies as New Zealand Shipping and Shaw, Savill & Albion.

The routes between Britain, Brazil, Uruguay and the Argentine were dominated by companies of the Royal Mail group – the Royal Mail Steam Packet Company, Lamport &

Holt, the McIver Line and, after 1913, the Nelson Line. They were part of the huge combine controlled by Sir Owen Philipps, later Lord Kylsant (see the chapter on *Asturias*).

For a time, the UK/River Plate and Brazil Freight Conference, which consisted of the Royal Mail companies and several other established lines, refused to admit Blue Star to membership and was able to inhibit shippers from sending cargo by non-Conference ships. Nevertheless, with its guaranteed homeward cargoes, Blue Star survived.

In May, 1925, the Vestey brothers mounted a daring challenge. Sir Edmund Vestey announced that they would be ordering no less than eight new ships for the route, a number which was soon increased to nine. Four purely cargo vessels of 10 – 11,000 gross tons were to come from Palmers' yard on the Tyne and from Lithgows on the Clyde. Then, in July orders were placed for five 12,000-ton passenger-cargo liners – three from Cammell Laird and two from John Brown. In total, this was a massive £3½ million investment, a welcome boost to the struggling British shipbuilding industry. The Vesteys had struck some hard bargains but, even so, Sir Edmund claimed that building in British yards would cost the family £300,000 more than if they had taken their orders to Germany. (Curiously, the announcement also contained a homily on the evils of drink.)

The five larger ships gave Blue Star its first real presence in the passenger business. They were to run a fortnightly service between London and the River Plate ports and it can have been no coincidence that some months later the Nelson Line also placed orders for five new *Highland* motorships for that route. As *Lloyd's List* commented at the time, these were 'regarded as Lord Kylsant's reply to the Blue Star bid for the River Plate passenger and beef trade'.

There were good reasons for the Vesteys to enter the passenger business. Not only did they hope to establish such a strong presence on the South Atlantic that they could force their way into the freight conference – which they succeeded in doing – but passenger and mail ships could claim priority berthing rights at congested ports. This was very important when they were carrying perishable cargoes such as meat and fruit.

The first of the Blue Star passenger ships was the *Almeda*, which was launched from the Cammell Laird yard at Birkenhead in June, 1926 and, after several delays, started the new service in February, 1927. She was quickly followed by *Avila* from John Brown, *Andalucia* (Cammell Laird), *Avelona* (John Brown) and *Arandora* (Cammell Laird). The choice of these names must have been hugely annoying to the Royal Mail people since their ships on the prestige Southampton – Buenos Aires route also had Spanish names beginning with the letter 'A'. Blue Star seemed to be deliberately trying to confuse potential passengers and shippers. In the end, sense prevailed and the Blue Star ships had the suffix *Star* added to their names.

When seen in profile, the Blue Star liners were not particularly handsome, despite their modern cruiser sterns. Since they carried only first class passengers, and in fairly limited numbers, they had quite short superstructures. Intended to sail through the tropics, they had long open promenades. Two funnels, the second a dummy, initially had rimmed tops but these were soon removed. Those funnels were painted in the line's rather complicated colours – red with a black top beneath which were narrow white and black bands and, lower down, a white disc bearing a five-pointed blue star.

First class passengers on this route – who might, for instance, include wealthy polo-playing Argentine sybarites heading for the pleasure spots of Europe – would certainly expect to travel in luxury and the Blue Star Line spared no expense in fitting out their new ships. In his book *Liners of the Ocean Highway*, published a few years later, Alan L. Carey commented that 'the luxury and refinement of the artistic decorations and furnishings [...] are unsurpassed' and that the sisters offered 'as beautiful public rooms and large and luxurious staterooms as have ever been provided on ships of their size.' It has been said that the original intention was that each ship should have accommodation for 400 passengers but, in the event, the same amount of space, spread over four decks, was devoted to just 160.

All staterooms were outside and, notably for the time, some had private bathrooms. Waring & Gillow were responsible for fitting out the public rooms in a style which owed much to the eighteenth century. The forward-facing, domed dining room was particularly attractive and the lounge and smoking room were also extremely pleasant. But, despite the facilities they provided for their passengers, the Blue Star liners were primarily cargo-carriers. They had long fore and after decks, each with a short well, and there were eight kingposts in addition to the masts. Each ship had six holds, mainly divided into a large number of refrigerated compartments. *Arandora*, for instance had 49 such chambers, with a total refrigerated capacity of no less than 415,574 cubic feet. On each ship, four sets of steam turbines – in the case of *Arandora*, built by Cammell Laird – were single-reduction geared to twin shafts and were rated at 2,078 nhp.

Arandora was launched on the 4th January, 1927 by Lady Vestey, the wife of Sir Edmund. It was a fraught occasion – the tide and a strong wind carried the ship up-river and caused her to collide with a hopper barge, fortunately with only slight damage. By the end of May, *Arandora* was ready to

head for the Clyde for her trials. She then made for the Royal Albert Docks in London, where she arrived on the 3rd June. She set sail on her maiden voyage on the 22nd June, calling at Boulogne, Lisbon, Funchal, Rio de Janeiro and, finally, Buenos Aires. On later voyages, she would often put in at Santos or Montevideo. Since, unlike most liners on the South American routes, she was not intended to carry migrants, her Lisbon calls were purely for touristic purposes and maybe to pick up more cargo. On the return leg, she usually put in at Plymouth to land her passengers.

Her stint in the liner service was short, however. It may be that Blue Star had over-egged the pudding and that there was insufficient passenger trade to support five ships. In 1934, in the depths of the Depression, one of the sisters, *Avelona Star* as she was by then called, was converted into a purely cargo-carrier but long before that the *Arandora* had become a full-time cruise ship. On the 13th December, 1928, she had reached London at the end of her eighth round voyage to South America and on the 5th January, 1929 she arrived in the Clyde where she was placed in the hands of the Fairfield Shipbuilding &Engineering Co., Ltd. of Govan. There she was given a £200,000 conversion which involved closing off the cargo spaces, extending the superstructure both fore and aft, enlarging some of the public rooms and adding such facilities as a gymnasium, a children's playroom, a ballroom and a verandah café looking out over the stern. Outside, there was a large sports deck. Extra cabins were built, which increased the passenger capacity to 354.

The work was completed by the end of May and the *Arandora* emerged with a new name, *Arandora Star*. In the same month, her former sister ships also gained the *Star* suffix. After arriving in London docks on the 4th June, *Arandora Star* was briefly dry-docked and made a one-day promotional cruise down the Thames into the Channel. Her new career began in earnest on the 14th June, when she sailed from the Lincolnshire port of Immingham on the first of several cruises to Norway. In those days, Immingham, which had rail connections with many northern cities, was fairly often used as a home port for cruises, particularly by the Orient Line. In September, *Arandora Star* made her way to Southampton from where she embarked on three long cruises into the Mediterranean.

In most years, she would spend some weeks in November and December either in lay-up or undergoing one of her many refits. Like so many cruise ships, she established a regular annual schedule. In her case, this would begin with a single long cruise to sunnier parts, starting in January: the first of these left Southampton on the 22nd January, 1930 for Madeira, Barbados, La Guaira, Curaçao, Kingston, Havana, Nassau, Bermuda, St. Michaels, Lisbon and home again. From March onwards there would be several long

Mediterranean jaunts and then, in July, it was back to Immingham for a short season of Norwegian and Baltic cruises, perhaps including – adventurously, in those days – a visit to Spitsbergen. September would see her return to Southampton for a few more Mediterranean voyages.

In August, 1930, at the end of one of her calls at Bergen, the tug assisting her to pull away from the quay became entangled in the hawser and sank, fortunately without casualties. In December, 1931, *Arandora Star* emerged from her latest winter lay-up with her hull painted white. It may have been at this time, too, that provision was made to floodlight her funnels at night. She was, in fact, becoming a rather spectacular cruise ship. Her January, 1932 voyage to the Caribbean included a call at Miami, then an insignificant port which gave no hint of the importance it would later achieve as 'the World's cruise capital'. (*Arandora Star* marked the occasion by striking her pier, but with only slight damage.)

Almost every November and December between 1933 and 1937, she underwent more reconstruction. The first major change, carried out at her builders' yard at Birkenhead, was the addition of a further deck containing 50 single cabins

above the forward extension to her superstructure which had been part of the 1929 conversion. Despite the effects of the Great Depression, which was reducing the passenger lists of ships everywhere, her cruises were proving sufficiently popular to encourage her owners to increase her capacity. Unfortunately, without the bottom weight once provided by cargo and with greater top weight as a result of successive additions to her superstructure, she gradually lost the reputation for steadiness which was still enjoyed by her former sisters. So, in an attempt to improve her stability, her mainmast was eventually removed. In 1935, again at Birkenhead, and in 1937 at Southampton, further extensions were made to the superstructure both fore and aft and, over the years, the facilities enjoyed by the passengers were improved, notably by the addition of a swimming pool.

In January, 1934, *Arandora Star* sailed on her most exciting cruise yet – from Southampton to the Caribbean, then through the Panama Canal and into the Pacific for calls in Hawaii and then north to San Francisco and Los Angeles before returning via the Panama Canal again. One change that year was that Immingham was abandoned in favour of

Arandora Star anchored off Dakar during one of her long cruises. *(Author's collection)*

Above, as the passenger-cargo ship *Arandora*. Below, after her 1929 conversion to the cruise ship *Arandora Star*. (*Author's collection*)

Tilbury as the departure port for the summer cruises to Norway and the Baltic.

Over Christmas, 1934, *Arandora Star* made a cruise to West Africa and then, on the 26th January, 1935 she left Southampton for her annual long cruise, which this time took her to Tenerife, St.Helena, Cape Town, Port Natal (or, as we would now say, Durban), Port Louis in Mauritius, then across to Bali and Batavia, Singapore, Penang, Colombo, Aden and home via Suez, arriving back in Southampton after a voyage which had lasted 75 days. For the equivalent cruises in 1936 and 1937 she again visited Panama, Honolulu, San Francisco and Los Angeles.

1938 was not an entirely fortunate year for the ship. In January, at the beginning of her annual long cruise – this time to the Caribbean – she had to return to Southampton with slight turbine trouble. She finally set off 21 hours late. In

May, she had a minor collision with the American destroyer *Claxton* at Villefranche. Then in June she was delayed at Southampton by a lightning strike of deckhands.

On the 26th August, 1939, she arrived back at Southampton having cut short what proved to be her last cruise. From midnight on that day, with war looming, the British government took control of the movements of all the nation's merchant ships.

Arandora Star did make one more civilian voyage, however, leaving Southampton for Cherbourg and New York on the 1st September. It may be that she was one of the ships rushed into service to carry home anxious Americans who were stranded in Europe. On her return, she was temporarily laid up and later she was taken to Avonmouth to be adapted to test experimental anti-torpedo nets. That duty completed, she was then sent to Liverpool to be pre-

The two final stages in the evolution of the cruise ship *Arandora Star*. (*Author's collection*)

pared for troopship service. While there, she had a narrow escape during an air-raid. In May, 1940, she returned to Norway – not now in her familiar rôle as a cruise ship but as one of the converted liners rescuing Allied troops after the unsuccessful Narvik landing. Immediately afterwards, she made several perilous voyages across the English Channel during the evacuation from France.

Then, on the 1st July, 1940, she sailed from Liverpool bound for St. John's, Newfoundland. It proved to be her final assignment and one of the most tragic episodes in the War. She was carrying German prisoners of war and internees and many Italians who had been living in Britain and had been interned following Italy's entry into the War. One day out, while some way off the coast of Donegal, she was torpedoed by the German submarine *U-47* which was, of course, quite unaware that her victim was carrying so many Axis subjects. *Arandora Star*, which had been sailing alone, sank within an hour. There was panic onboard and many lives were lost, including that of her captain. The exact figure is uncertain – either 761 or 805. Some hours later, the Canadian destroyer *St. Laurent* rescued the 868 survivors.

The following month, one of the lifeboats drifted ashore off the coast of Galway. The locals soon found a use for it and in 1968 Laurence Dunn travelled in it while he was attending the opening of the Bantry Bay oil terminal where it was being used as a service boat (see the chapter on the *Avalon*).

The Blue Star fleet was particularly hard hit during the War, losing 29 of its 38 ships, with a commensurate loss of life. Sadly, the casualties included not only *Arandora Star* but also all four of her original sisters.

Duchess of Bedford / Empress of France

Completed 1928. 20,123 gross tons.

Overall length: 601ft. 0ins.

Breadth: 75ft. 2ins. Draught: 41 ft. 8ins.

Twin screw. Geared turbines.

Service speed: 17½ knots.

Became *Empress of India*, 1947

and *Empress of France*, also 1947.

20,448 gross tons.

Scrapped 1960.

The Canadian Pacific intermediate liner *Duchess of Bedford*. *(Author's collection)*

Canadian Pacific's *Duchess*-class liners were by no means the most glamorous ships on the North Atlantic but they could certainly claim to be outstandingly modern vessels for their day. At the time, Canadian Pacific Steamships' Chief Superintendent Engineer, Mr. John Johnson, came in for much praise for his forward-looking attitude to ship design. The new liners were, for instance, among the earliest to have their lifeboats handled by gravity davits.

More importantly, they were also the first British deep-sea passenger ships to be fitted with water-tube boilers. (British merchant shipbuilders and owners had been slow to adopt these boilers, although they had been used very successfully by the Royal Navy for many years. H.M.S. *Hood*, for instance, is said to have reached a speed of 32 knots. But as far as passenger vessels were concerned, the British had lagged behind the French and the Germans in this respect. The Germans had specified water-tube boilers in several express liners before the First World War, including Hamburg America's colossal *Imperator*, *Vaterland* and *Bismarck*.) It was not until June, 1926 that the Canadian Pacific Railway ordered two passenger liners with Yarrow-designed boilers of this type for its Canadian Pacific Steamships, Ltd. subsidiary. A few days later, the railway company's president, Mr. E. W. Beatty, went on to announce an order for a class of freighters which, it was eventually decided, would also be fitted with water-tube boilers. (He seems to have taken a delight in coming over to Britain to negotiate, place the orders and then announce all the group's most important ships.) Working at a much higher pressure (350 lbs) than the old cylindrical boilers, the new water-tubes proved to be very economical and the *Duchesses* were said to consume between 25% and 30% less fuel than conventional ships.

Subsequently, two more passenger liners of the *Duchess* class were also ordered. There is some uncertainty over whether the company intended to build a fifth ship. This may arise from the decision to change the proposed name of the fourth member of the class from *Duchess of Cornwall* to *Duchess of York*. However, there can be no doubt that Canadian Pacific were making a huge investment in new tonnage and in the space of just over a year British yards launched no less than 11 ships for them, totalling nearly 135,000 gross tons.

The *Duchesses* were intended for the company's secondary Atlantic service. Whereas the more prestigious *Empresses* worked out of Southampton, the secondary ships sailed from Liverpool and often called at Greenock. They thus maintained the service out of the Clyde originally run by the old Allan Line, which Canadian Pacific had absorbed in 1916.

They also often called at Belfast. At the Canadian end of their route, the new 20,000-tonners were the biggest liners able to go beyond Quebec and reach Montreal. In the winter months, when the St. Lawrence was frozen over, their Canadian terminal port was St. John, New Brunswick. The main competition came from the Cunard Line's 'A'-class ships of 1922-25 which, at 14,000 tons and a knot or two slower, must have seemed somewhat inferior. In fact, the new Canadian Pacific liners proved very successful, despite acquiring a reputation for rolling in rough seas. Kevin Griffin reminds me that they were known as the Dancing Duchesses. At first, it was thought that they would have names beginning with the letter 'M', a tradition which sprang from another Canadian Pacific acquisition – in 1903 they had taken over the North Atlantic services of Elder Dempster. In the end, however, it was decided to give them *Duchess* names. These were no doubt thought to have a more prestigious ring about them, although not as grand-sounding as those of the *Empresses* or, for that matter, the *Princesses* which ran the Canadian Pacific coastal services out of Vancouver.

The *Duchesses* were in some respects a development of the *Montcalm*, *Montrose* and *Montclare* of 1922. Also like them, they were cabin liners (i.e.: their best accommodation was called cabin class, was perhaps slightly less luxurious than first class on more traditional ships and, under the rules of the North Atlantic Passenger Conference, could be sold for rather lower fares). The orders for three of the ships, the *Duchesses of Bedford*, *Richmond* and *Cornwall* (later *York*), went to the John Brown & Co., Ltd. yard at Clydebank, where they were built side by side, while that for the *Duchess of Atholl* was awarded to William Beardmore & Co., Ltd. of Dalmuir.

Each sister was powered by two sets of Parsons-type turbines constructed by her builders, those on the *Duchess of Bedford* developing 3,557 nhp. They drove the propellers through single-reduction gearing, the more complicated double-reduction mechanism on the *Montcalm* class having proved troublesome. The boilers were also products of the ships' builders and were oil-fired, whereas the furnaces on some of the new freighters burned pulverised coal – another example of Canadian Pacific's willingness to try out innovative technology. Each *Duchess* had seven holds, four forward of the engine spaces and three aft, with a total capacity of 390,000 cubic feet (including 67,000 cubic feet of refrigerated space).

The *Duchess of Bedford* could accommodate 580 passengers in cabin class, 486 in tourist-third class and 500 in third. Although they may have been a little less grand than first class on the *Empresses*, her cabin class quarters were said to be the

The "*Duchesses*" were built with an eye to economy of operation and maintenance. Nevertheless the *Duchess of Bedford*'s dining saloon had a certain modern elegance. *(Author's collection)*

finest of their kind on the Atlantic. Passengers in that class could, in fact, enjoy some of the amenities usually reserved for first class – they took their evening meals, for instance, to the sound of the ship's orchestra playing in a gallery overlooking their dining room.

Interior design, as often on Canadian Pacific ships, was the work of the London firm of Staynes & Jones and the furnishings for the cabin class public rooms were made by H. H. Martyn & Co., Ltd. of Cheltenham. Styles were changing in the late 'Twenties and, although it can hardly be claimed that the *Duchess of Bedford* was furnished in the emerging Art Déco manner, *Shipbuilding & Shipping Record* did comment that, 'A distinctly new note has been struck...... Besides possessing an air of novelty, very pleasing to those who have become accustomed to the usual type of decoration on board ship, it has the additional advantage that the basic idea has been to avoid the heavy expense of upkeep associated with the renewal of extensive areas of painted and enamelled surfaces. In giving effect to this principle, natural woods have been used and these are polished in varying degrees.' This concern with the cost of upkeep may sound like penny-pinching – and, indeed, in several respects the ship had been specifically designed with an eye to economical operation – but many people found the lighter, less imposing style very pleasing. Colourful artworks added to the stylishness of several of the cabin class public rooms, with the dining room, for instance, having touches of chinoiserie. Much use was made of indirect lighting and several of the rooms were given extra height and natural light by extending them several feet upward to penetrate the boat deck above.

The introduction of an intermediate category (tourist-third), which had hitherto been lacking in the *Montcalm*-class ships, meant that there was now the opportunity for passengers who could not afford cabin class fares to experience more comfort than was provided in third. *Shipbuilding and Shipping Record* commented that in tourist-third 'the cabins are remarkably comfortable and the public rooms are almost up to the standard of those assigned to first class in liners of pre-War days'. That may have been something of an exaggeration but, while clearly lacking the spaciousness and style of the cabin class public rooms, those in tourist-third seem to have been pleasant enough. And there was even a colourful nursery for tourist-third children, who would have been unlikely to enjoy such a facility a very few years earlier. The third class rooms were more on a par with traditional third class standards, with, for instance, meals being taken at long tables. But even there, deckhead panelling covered the bare steel beams and pipework which would once have formed the décor.

As for cabins, most of those in cabin class were rather plain and some of them seem to have been somewhat cramped but they had hot and cold running water. As usual in those days, other facilities were communal and required passengers to don their dressing gowns and pad down the passage. Tourist-third cabins had cold water only. Some of the third class passengers were accommodated in portable cabins of the Blaco type (a name derived from that of the makers, F. C. Blackwell & Co., Ltd.) which could be disassembled when not required, so as to provide more cargo space.

Although they were soon to be outshone in the Canadian Pacific fleet by bigger and more glamorous liners, the *Duchesses* were considered to be extremely important ships – just how important can be gauged from the fact that the *Duchess of Bedford* was launched on the 24th January, 1928, 'in the glorious sunshine of a break in the weather', by Mrs. Stanley Baldwin, the wife of the British Prime Minister. Mr. Baldwin himself was also present and spoke at the lunch which followed the ceremony. And in September, the *Duchess of York* became the first merchant ship to be launched by a member of the British Royal family – the future Queen and Queen Mother, who was then still Elizabeth, Duchess of York. Unexpectedly, the *Duchess of Bedford* was the first of the quartet to enter service as completion of the *Duchess of Atholl* was delayed by an accident at Beardmore's yard as one of her main turbines was being lowered into place. Thirty tons of machinery crashed into the engine spaces, causing huge damage. Consequently, John Brown were asked to speed up the completion of the *Bedford* and succeeded in installing her machinery and fitting her out in no more than four months. She ran her trials in the Clyde between the 12th and 15th May, 1928, was handed over to her owners at Liverpool on the 29th May and left on her maiden voyage just three days later. She had cost roughly £1 million.

While she spent most of her time on the Canadian run, every year until 1934 she would make two or three long and leisurely Caribbean cruises out of New York during the months of deepest winter. Cabin class liner though she was, she was obviously sufficiently comfortable to satisfy the demands of Canadian Pacific's New York cruise passengers who were used to the splendour of the *Empresses*. Typically, these cruises would include calls at Hamilton (Bermuda), San Juan, Barbados, Trinidad, La Guaira, Curaçao, Cartagena (Columbia), Cristobal, Kingston, Port au Prince, Havana and Nassau. In Summer, 1933, she ran a few much cheaper and less prestigious cruises from Montreal to New York. And, in the spring of both 1932 and 1933, she was chartered by the Furness Bermuda Line for several voyages on the New York to Bermuda 'honeymoon route', taking the place of their luxurious but twice fire-damaged liner *Bermuda*.

The *Duchess of Bedford*, too, was prone to mishap, but usually of a minor kind. 1933 was a particularly ill-starred year for her. In May, she had a slight brush with wreckage in the Mersey; in July, she struck an iceberg while navigating the

Straits of Belle Isle in thick fog, fortunately without great injury to herself; and also in July she damaged a propeller while leaving New York on one of her cruises from Montreal and had to be drydocked at Quebec. Then in November she was delayed by exceptionally early winter conditions at Quebec. *Lloyd's List* commented on 'the most serious shipping hold-up in the history of navigation in the St. Lawrence'. It was so cold that two steamers lying alongside each other were said to have frozen together. There was concern that the *Duchess of Bedford* and many other vessels would be trapped for the Winter but, after several days' delay, most of them were able to escape down the river with the help of ice-breakers.

Thus the *Duchess of Bedford* and her sisters sailed on through the 'Thirties, difficult times for almost all liners but perhaps the Canadian Pacific ships were more successful than most.

On the 30th August, 1939 – four days before the declaration of war – the *Duchess of Bedford* started a trooping voyage from Liverpool, Belfast and Glasgow to Bombay under charter to the British government. After that, she briefly returned to her owners' Liverpool – Canada service but after February, 1940 her crossings were made under government auspices. Then, on the 14th August, she was taken up for hasty conversion into a troopship with a capacity of 271 officers and 2,880 troops. On the 20th August, she left Liverpool for Durban and Cape Town via Suez, returning via Freetown in West Africa. Thereafter, she made several long voyages which took her to South Africa and up the coast to Suez; to New York; and to Iceland. Perhaps her most notable trooping voyage, however, started from Liverpool in 12th November, 1941 and lasted five months, during the course of which she took rein-

forcements from Bombay to Singapore and then civilian evacuees from there to Batavia. She was attacked several times but damage was fairly slight. A more serious attack took place on the 9th August, 1942 soon after she had left Liverpool for an Atlantic crossing. It was made by the *U-704*. The *Duchess of Bedford* opened fire with her scanty armament to such effect that it was thought that she had sunk the German submarine – although it later emerged that this was not the case. Nevertheless, it was a gallant exploit.

In September, 1942, she was fitted out as an L.S.I (Landing Ship Infantry) to take part in the North African campaign and, later, in the Italian landings. By now, her boilers were requiring occasional repair but she continued in service, surviving many attacks. Her gunners shot down an enemy aircraft off the Algerian coast. By 1944, she was back in trooping service and was soon making repatriation voyages. She made a couple of visits to Basra in the Persian Gulf and, in February, 1945, to Odessa in the Black Sea carrying Cossacks back to the Soviet Union. Most of these men most certainly did not wish to return, fearing that the Soviet authorities would either imprison or execute them – and such, unfortunately, proved to be the case.

The *Duchess of Bedford* was not released from government service until the end of February, 1947, in the meantime making further trooping voyages to Canada and to West Africa but mainly to Bombay, Rangoon and Colombo. (She seems to have been rather prone to touching bank during her transits of the Suez Canal.) By the end, she had covered more than 400,000 nautical miles as a troopship, carrying 179,000 men and women.

Looking worn, *Duchess of Bedford* at Aden in early 1947, during her final days as a troopship. *(Sheila Bourne collection)*

Ariving at Liverpool on the 26th February, 1947 and in the Clyde on the 3rd March, she was soon afterwards taken in hand by Fairfields for conversion back to a civilian liner. They were already doing similar work on the former *Duchess of Richmond*, which had now been promoted to *Empress of Canada*. The *Duchess of Bedford*, too, was given an imperial name – initially *Empress of India* but, with that country about to achieve independence, it was decided in October, 1947 to call her *Empress of France* instead. What the touchy, French-speaking Québequois thought of a London-registered ship claiming to rule their beloved motherland is a matter for conjecture.

Canadian Pacific's Atlantic passenger fleet had been badly hit during the War, losing not only the great *Empress of Britain* but also the *Montrose* and the *Duchesses of Atholl* and *York*. The *Montcalm* and *Montclare* had been bought by the Admiralty and were now naval depot ships and the *Empress of Australia* remained in trooping serv-

ice. As we shall see in a later chapter, it was not until 1950 that the former *Empress of Japan*, now *Empress of Scotland*, could be brought in to strengthen Canadian Pacific's presence on the North Atlantic and in the meantime the company had to make do with what remained to it.

After the post-War conversion, the first class cocktail bar and lounge both retained their former warmth. *(Clive Harvey collection)*

When the *Empress of France* emerged in August, 1948 – several weeks ahead of schedule – she had not merely been thoroughly re-conditioned but she had been somewhat changed. In particular, the open promenades along each side had been enclosed and the superstructure had been extended at the stern. Her hull, originally black, was now painted white and the company's chequered flag logo was added to the traditional buff funnels.

She carried fewer passengers than in pre-War days: 400 in what was now called first class and 482 in tourist class. C. M. Squarey seems not to have been utterly convinced that, by then, her first class was really worthy of the name: 'If the express service ships' (i.e.: presumably the prestige Cunarders and French liners on the New York route) 'rank as four star ships, this one ranks as three star. There is an atmosphere of sedateness…. which blends well with her democratic appointments that are splendidly suited for the Canadian trade.' In what was now first class, he still admired the forward-facing cocktail room, the main lounge and the dining room but regretted that the former smoking room was now the Empress Room which – at separate times, of course – was allocated to both classes for film shows, dancing, horse racing and other socialising. (The dual class Empress Room became a feature of all post-War Canadian Pacific liners.) 'The space for deck games, whilst adequate, is not bountiful but it must be remembered that this ship is now over twenty years old, that she has two funnels and was built at a time when naval architects gave their minds much more to ventilation plant on deck than to space for deck games.' He did remark, however, on 'the complete absence of vibration, even right aft' and that 'the fine and long-established tradition of this line for good service and reliability of schedules' was being well-maintained.

A comfortable tourist class two berth cabin. *(Clive Harvey collection)*

There were also some less obvious changes. She could now carry slightly more refrigerated cargo and the work on her turbines had raised their power output by 5%, so that her service speed was increased slightly, to 18 knots.

In 1947, Mr. Neal, the then president of Canadian Pacific, had told *Lloyd's List* that he was in the market for a new passenger ship for the Atlantic route and another for the Pacific – if British shipyards could quote an affordable price. However, it was not until well into the 1950s that the company finally ordered a new liner, reviving the famous name *Empress of Britain*. In the meantime, the two former *Duchesses* and, eventually, the *Empress of Scotland* soldiered on, sailing out of Liverpool. The pre-War express service from Southampton was not revived.

The *Empress of France* started successful trials in the Clyde on the 23rd August, 1948 and arrived in her home port of Liverpool on the 26th. She left on her maiden voyage in her new guise on the 1st September, carrying about 700 passengers, and arrived in Quebec on the 7th and in Montreal on the 8th. Those were serious, even grim, times and there was no question of diverting the two sisters to cruising, even in the winter season. As in pre-War days, their winter transatlantic sailings were to St. John, initially with a call at Halifax. Twice, the *Empress of France* put in at Greenock but the regular pre-War calls there were not revived until the advent of the speedier *Empress of Scotland*.

In September, 1951, Princess Elizabeth (the future Queen Elizabeth II) and the Duke of Edinburgh were due to embark on a tour of Canada. As in pre-War days, Canadian Pacific ships were chosen to carry Royalty to and from the Dominion. On the outward voyage the Princess and her husband would sail on the *Empress of France* and they would return on the *Empress of Canada*. Whereas the pre-War *Empresses* would already have had a suite fit for a Princess, it would be necessary to create one on the *Empress of France*. Between the ship's arrival in Liverpool on the 21st September, at the end of her previous voyage, and the Royal departure on the 25th September, three cabins were to be converted into a suite consisting of a room for the Princess, a room for the Duke and, between them, a combined dining room and lounge. They would all, of course, be completely refurnished. In the event, the Princess's father, King George VI, became seriously ill and the arrangements had to be changed. It was announced that the Royal party would now fly out some days later and would return on the *Empress of Scotland*. Thus the *Empress of France* lost the honour of playing host to the future monarch. It must have been particularly disappointing for Captain B. B. Grant, who was about to retire and would have ended his career on this high note.

On the 2nd January, 1952, the *Empress of France* struck a dock wall at Liverpool while under tow but this did not prevent her making her scheduled departure for Canada later that day. Slightly more disruptive was a bout of engine trouble which forced her to put back shortly after leaving Liverpool on the 8th July, delaying her by a single day. (The following year, the *Empress of Canada* was terminally damaged by fire and had to be temporarily replaced by the hastily purchased *De Grasse*, formerly of the French Line and now called *Empress of Australia*.) By the mid-'Fifties, frequent labour disputes were disrupting British shipping services. The *Empress of France* was less troubled than many of her contemporaries but she was delayed at Liverpool by a strike among her catering staff in June, 1955. Repairs to her turbines detained her at St. John in March, 1957. Towards the end of 1957, she made three, presumably experimental, voyages from Rotterdam to Canada. She made two more in late 1959.

Times were changing on the Canadian run. Cunard had introduced the first of their four *Saxonia*-class ships in 1954. Home Lines had entered the fray – outsiders maybe, but their *Homeric* was a speedy and comfortable liner. Canadian Pacific's new *Empress of Britain* arrived in 1956 and was followed by the *Empress of England* in 1957. All of these were predominantly tourist class vessels, with the *Empress of Britain*, for instance, accommodating 900 in tourist class, as against just 150 in first. The somewhat less splendid ships of Polish Ocean Lines, Arosa Line, the Greek Line and the Europa-Kanada Line were devoted almost entirely to tourist class passengers. That was the new reality and the *Empresses of France* and *Scotland* were out of tune with it. The *Empress of Scotland* was

withdrawn at the end of 1957 and was sold to the Hamburg Atlantik Line but the *Empress of France* was retained for a while longer. She was given a substantial, month-long refit. Her funnels were re-modelled and now had domed tops. One reason was, no doubt, to modernise her appearance but, in many people's opinion, she now had a 'mutton dressed as lamb' look about her. More importantly, her accommodation was re-arranged to 218 in first class and 482 in tourist. It was surprising that Canadian Pacific were prepared to spend on what must have been a fairly expensive refit at this late stage in her career - the keel of their new flagship, the *Empress of Canada*, was laid in January, 1959 and, in the event, the *Empress of France* lasted for only two more seasons.

In her final year, she suffered engine and boiler problems but, much more seriously, 1960 was also a year of crippling labour disputes in the British shipping industry – although Canadian-owned, the Canadian Pacific liners were registered and crewed in Britain. Like many other ships, the *Empress of France* was strike-bound at Liverpool for several days in July and again the following month. She made one final call at Rotterdam (and two at Southampton) in November but her final transatlantic voyage ended at Liverpool on the 7th December. Even in her last year, she had retained her immaculate appearance.

On the 19th December, she left for Newport, having been sold to the shipbreakers J. Cashmore & Co., Ltd. So ended the long career of a liner which had been a good servant of a distinguished shipping company.

In her last years, *Empress of France* was given streamlined funnels in a misguided attempt to modernise her appearance. *(Author's collection)*

Empress of Japan / Empress of Scotland

Completed 1930. 26,032 gross tons.

Length overall: 666 ft. 6ins. Breadth: 83 ft. 10ins.

Draught: 31 ft. 7¾ ins.

Twin screw. Geared steam turbines.

Service speed: 21 knots.

Became *Empress of Scotland*, 1942. 1951 after refit:

26,313 gross tons. Became *Scotland*, 1958.

Refitted and became *Hanseatic*, 1958. 30,030 gross tons.

Length overall: 673 ft. 0ins.

Scrapped 1966.

The *Empress of Japan* was the largest and fastes liner on the Pacific. *(Maurizio Eliseo collection)*

Canadian Pacific's *Empress of Japan* was a beautiful elder sister, rather overshadowed by her even more glamorous younger sibling, the *Empress of Britain*, which was one of the most sensational ships of the 'Thirties – a decade certainly not short of stylish liners – and, in the end, one of the most tragic. But the *Empress of Japan* should not be forgotten either. She too has very strong claims to fame.

She was one of the finest liners on the trans-Pacific run, where competition was almost as intense as on the North Atlantic. Her interiors, too, were pretty amazing, as the accompanying illustrations shew. And, unlike the extravagantly designed *Empress of Britain*, she was profitable for most of her commercial career. During the War, she was a hugely successful troopship and then, once again in peacetime service, she ran to great acclaim on Canadian Pacific's Atlantic route and later, as the *Hanseatic*, for German-flag owners. Particularly in that very last phase of her life, she was an especial favourite.

Canadian Pacific Steamships, Ltd., registered in London, was part of 'The World's Most Complete Transportation System', which included not only the famous trans-continental Canadian Pacific Railway, but also hotels, shipping lines on both the North Atlantic and the Pacific and, in later years, an airline. (The plans for the development of Canadian Pacific Airways after the War were perhaps one of the factors which persuaded the parent board in Montreal not to revive the trans-Pacific passenger liner service.)

In the late 'Twenties, Canadian Pacific felt the need to upgrade their service from Vancouver and Victoria to Yokohama and further into the Far East. It was being maintained by the *Empress of Canada*, completed in 1922, and the sisters *Empress of Russia* and *Empress of Asia*. They were all fine ships and, when built, had been outstandingly modern but the last two dated back to pre-First World War times. And the rival lines were known to be planning new ships. In 1929-1930, the Japanese company Nippon Yusen Kaisha introduced the new motorliners *Asama Maru*, *Tatsuta Maru* and *Chichibu Maru* on their route from the Far East to Los Angeles and San Francisco and the Dollar Line of San Francisco brought out the turbo-electric *President Hoover* and *President Coolidge* in 1931. These were all wonderful ships but many would say that, with the *Empress of Japan*, Canadian Pacific trumped their ace.

The order for the new liner was placed with the Fairfield Shipbuilding & Engineering Company, Ltd. of Govan, Glasgow on the 27th June, 1928. Fairfield had long been one of Canadian Pacific's favourite builders and, indeed, had been responsible for the *Empresses of Russia*, *Asia* and *Canada*. For this latest order, they had been in keen competition with the John Brown yard. In the event, the spoils were shared: the President of Canadian Pacific, Mr. E. W. Beatty, who was on a visit to Britain, announced that Fairfield had won the order for the new ship for the Pacific route – she would be the biggest liner the yard had yet built – and that John Brown would be responsible for an even larger vessel for the Atlantic express service. (This was, of course, the *Empress of Britain*.) The Pacific ship, yard no. 634, was to be called *Empress of Japan* and would be a true luxury liner. She would also be speedy, a full three knots faster than her predecessors and, as it turned out, slightly quicker than her competitors. In fact, Canadian Pacific used this extra speed – and that of the *Empress of Canada* which, at the same time, was sent to Fairfield's to be fitted with more powerful turbines – not so much to accelerate the existing service, which continued to be maintained mostly by the two older *Empresses*, but to tap the newly fashionable Hawaiian trade. The Matson Line of San Francisco, with its splendid *Malolo* of 1927 and the later *Lurline*, and the Los Angeles Steamship Company, with luxuriously refitted pre-War ex-German tonnage, were developing Honolulu as a holiday destination. Canadian Pacific now set out to compete with Matson in attracting Hawaii-bound passengers living in northern California.

1930s magnificence. The first class main staircase and (facing page) the dining saloon on the *Empress of Japan*. (Author's collection)

PROMENADE DECK

Canadian Pacific publicised the stylish *Empress of Japan* and her running-mates on the Trans-Pacific route with some suitably striking brochures. *(Paolo Piccione collection)*

The *Empress of Japan* was a particularly spacious ship and many of her first class passengers travelled in some state; here we see a luxury two-bed cabin. *(Paolo Piccione collection)*

This involved the *Empress of Japan* and the *Empress of Canada* in making a long, 1,500-mile diversion via Honolulu while en route from Victoria to Yokohama but it seems that the move was successful.

At over 25,000 tons, the *Empress of Japan* was a big ship by the standards of the day and she looked it. In some ways, her profile was rather traditional, with a sharp bow, three substantial funnels (the final one a dummy), two masts and conspicuous ventilating cowls. But that bow was slightly raked, her white hull had a spoon stern and the lifeboats were on gravity davits, all of which added to the modernity of her appearance. She was a development of the *Empress of Canada* but her design was also influenced by that of the *Duchess*es, whose combination of single-reduction-geared Parsons turbines and Yarrow water-tube boilers was proving very economical. The *Empress of Japan* had six sets of turbines, built to Parsons' design by Fairfield and developing 33,000 shp. They quickly enabled her to establish her credentials as the fastest ship on the Pacific.

Six cargo holds, served by 29 derricks, had a capacity of 304,000 cubic feet, including 33,000 cubic feet of insulated space. There were also secure silk rooms since the silk trade from China and Japan had for years been an important revenue-earner for Canadian Pacific. It is said that silk traders usually chose to transport their precious fibres by the fastest ship available because the cost of insurance was so high that even a day or two saved was worthwhile. By the 'Thirties, the trade was declining but presumably the *Empress of Japan* still carried quantities of the fibre on those voyages on which she returned directly to Victoria and Vancouver without making the diversion to Honolulu.

As built, the *Empress of Japan* had accommodation for 298 first class passengers plus 82 in cabins which were interchangeable between first and second, 164 in second class, 100 third class and, in the eastbound direction only, up to 548 Chinese and Japanese migrants travelling steerage. The first class accommodation included several truly de luxe suites. Each consisted of a bedroom, a sitting room, a verandah, a bathroom with tub, a separate toilet, a boxroom and entrance hall. Attached was a single cabin for one's servant.

The first class public rooms were particularly spacious. To a large extent they were the work of P. A. Staynes and A. H. Jones, Canadian Pacific's usual designers. The facilities included a dining saloon with two small private dining rooms adjacent; a verandah café; an impressive domed lounge (with stage); a smoking room (also domed); a full-width Palm Court with dance floor and fountains; a Long Gallery; a card and writing room; nursery; shop; gymnasium and indoor swimming pool. The latter two, although on different decks, were linked by a lift. The swimming pool was said to include 'an electric bath' – one hopes that it was not as dangerous a device as it sounds.

In 1927, the *Ile de France* had caused a sensation with her 'modern' or 'contemporary' décor (a style which much later became known as Art Déco) and had immediately become the liner above all others which was patronised by the smart set when they crossed the Atlantic. Canadian passengers were known to be rather conservative in their tastes and the décor of the *Empress of Japan* was, perhaps, not so extreme but she it was who now introduced the new style to the Pacific run.

She was launched by Mrs. Edward R. Peacock, the wife of a Canadian Pacific Railway director, on the 17th December, 1929, a particularly misty day. By the 12th May, 1930, the new liner was able to run her trials, achieving more than 23 knots over the measured mile. A month later, after being drydocked at Belfast – there were then no drydocks of sufficient size on the Clyde – she was ready to enter service. Cautiously, Canadian Pacific tried her out on the Atlantic route so that, if there were teething problems, they could be conveniently sorted out by her builders before she left for the other side of the World. Her maiden voyage, starting on the 14th June, was therefore from Liverpool to Quebec, returning to Southampton. At Quebec, she had a minor brush with a quay, the first of a number during her long career. On the 12th July, she left Southampton for Hong Kong via the Suez Canal. Her first trans-Pacific voyage started on the 6th August and she arrived at her home port of Vancouver on the 22nd.

Her initial departure from Vancouver took place on the 4th September. Outward, she visited Honolulu, Yokohama and Hong Kong, from whence she returned direct to Vancouver. Occasionally on later voyages, she would go beyond Hong Kong to Shanghai. With her 9th April, 1931 eastward crossing from Yokohama, she broke the trans-Pacific record, taking 7 days, 20 hours and 16 minutes to reach Victoria and averaging 22.27 knots. Among her passengers on that voyage were the King and Queen of Siam. There were no further record attempts, however, since from then onwards she took to making the diversion to Honolulu in both directions. This was a long route, 5,800 miles each way, and the voyage usually took about 20 days, enabling her to make six trips a year. In the late-'Thirties, she sometimes included Manila in her schedule on the return leg.

Inevitably, there were incidents. At Vancouver in July, 1932 and at Honolulu in March, 1939, the authorities found opium on board, an almost inevitable risk with a ship carrying Chinese passengers and crew members. In April, 1938 she arrived at Yokohama with a case of typhus on board.

When the Second World War broke out on the 3rd September, 1939 the *Empress of Japan* was at Shanghai, by then occupied by the Japanese – but as yet the Sino-Japanese war was a quite separate conflict from that which had just erupted in Europe. Nevertheless, her career as a Pacific liner was almost at an end. She made her final arrival at Vancouver on the 20th November and by the 27th she had been commandeered for duties as a troopship. After a hasty conversion at Esquimault, she could carry up to 3,265 service personnel – 857 officers in the former first and second class cabins, 1,791 men in other cabins and spaces and 617 in the areas formerly occupied by the steerage passengers but which now became troop decks.

Painted grey, she left Victoria on the 22nd December and by the 2nd January she was at Sydney, embarking Australian troops for the Middle East. Thereafter, she roamed widely. In the famous convoy US3, she was in company with the *Queen Mary*, *Aquitania*, second *Mauretania*, *Andes*, *Empress of Canada* and *Empress of Britain*, bringing Australian and New Zealand troops to Britain. However, when this parade of great liners reached Cape Town, Chinese crew members on the *Empresses of Japan* and *Canada* refused to risk the voyage through the submarine-infested Atlantic and the *Empress of Japan* was chosen to turn back and repatriate them to Hong Kong. From there, she carried Europeans to, it was thought, the safety of Manila.

On the 9th November, 1940, on her way from Australia to the Clyde, again laden with troops, she was attacked by a German bomber off the Northern Irish coast, not too far from where the *Empress of Britain* had met her fate a fortnight earlier. Fortunately, the *Empress of Japan*'s evasive action was partly successful. She was damaged but managed to make her escape and reached the Clyde the following day. After repairs at Belfast, she was back in service carrying troops for the defence of Singapore; bringing Canadian forces to Britain from her old home port of Vancouver and from Halifax; and by 1943 taking part in the massive shuttle of American troops from New York and Newport News to Britain and to Casablanca.

In February, 1942 she had suffered another air attack, sustaining damage above the waterline, and in October she had been renamed *Empress of Scotland*. Obviously, with Japan having entered the War on the Axis side in the previous year, her old name was unsuitable. It is said, though, that some members of her crew disliked the change – not through any lack of patriotism but because they were fond of her and to them she was still the *Empress of Japan*. In late 1944 and 1945, she made a couple of voyages from Liverpool to Sydney and

Wellington and then, with the War over, began returning troops to India and to South Africa.

During her period on the Atlantic shuttle, she had received regular maintenance in the Todd shipyard in New York. In November, 1945, Todd's placed advertisements in *Lloyd's List* headed 'Waiting on an Empress' and showing a pre-War picture of her. The text ran 'Hail to the *Empress of Scotland*! This far-travelled lady has behind her three complete globe-girdling trips and approximately one half-million miles of wartime steaming as a converted merchant ship. Truly an amazing Amazon of the deep!' At the time, neither they nor anyone else could know that she would remain in government service for another two and a half years. Based in Liverpool, she made regular trooping voyages to India and later to Hong Kong and Japan. Her final assignment was a voyage from Haifa, evacuating troops from Palestine, where the British Mandate was ending.

She docked at Liverpool on the 2nd May, 1948 and the following day *Lloyd's List* said that she had been in 'war service' longer than any other merchant ship – 8 years, 5 months and 7 days – during which time she had steamed 712,689 miles and had spent only 125 days in repair yards. She had carried 292,000 persons, 92% of whom were troops.

Now, stripped of her troopship fittings, she was worked on in the Canada Dry Dock, Liverpool before, in November, steaming up to the Clyde for a lengthy overhaul and refit by her builders. Eighteen months later, she emerged as the new flagship of Canadian Pacific's Atlantic fleet – once again with a white hull, but with a green band round it rather than the previous blue one. Conforming to the company's new livery, her buff funnels were now adorned by the red and white chequered Canadian Pacific flag. To fit her for her new trade, her long open promenades had been enclosed and, in the Winter, they were heated. They had deep windows so that the occupants of the deck chairs could have a clear view of the sea.

The passenger accommodation was almost completely reconfigured and now totalled 663 berths. 458 first class passengers travelled in 63 two-berth cabins, 76 with three berths and 26 with four berths. All were outside-facing and 84% had either a bath or a shower. Perhaps because the post-War trade between Britain and Canada did not have the sort of select upper crust of passengers who had crossed the Pacific in such great state before the War, those huge suites had been dismantled. However, one group of cabins could be 'unitised' to form a suite if required. Tourist class passengers numbered up to 205 and were allotted 26 two-berth cabins, 7 with three berths and 33 with four berths. Notably, they too were all outside. 22 of the tourist class cabins had their own private toilets.

Two of the public rooms – the glass-domed Empress Room (the former first class smoking room, now restyled and also serving as a cinema) and the ballroom – were to be used by

Now the *Empress of Scotland*, the former liner served for over 8 years as a troopship. Note the guns with which she had been equipped. *(Maurizio Eliseo collection)*

both classes, but not at the same time since in those days the separate levels of shipboard society did not mix. The first class dining room was considered particularly handsome, retaining its pre-War green-veined Cipolini marble walls, framed by teak. But it seated only 294 passengers and, with the ship now carrying more first class passengers, two sittings were necessary. According to one newspaper correspondent, the attractive new cocktail room might well have been called an observation lounge since it had windows on three sides. Tourist class public rooms included a full-width dining room, a lounge and a smoking room decorated in Tudor style and with an imposing fireplace. The only real criticism I have seen of her among the contemporary reports was that she was "perhaps thin on deck-games space if she goes cruising out of New York". That comment came from C. M. Squarey in his revealing book *The Patient Talks* but, having known her before the War, he felt impelled to write, "It thrilled me to see this romantic ship again [...]. She looked now as impressive (or should I say 'empressive'?) as ever [...]. Much that was good about her still remains; she retains a strong sense of spaciousness."

At last, on the 9th May, 1950, the *Empress of Scotland* left Liverpool on her first post-War Atlantic crossing. Her running-mates in the company's war-depleted passenger fleet were the former *Duchess of Bedford*, now elevated to *Empress of France*, and the *Duchess of Richmond*, now called *Empress of Canada*. Good ships though they were and faithfully though they had maintained the service during the early post-War years, they were perhaps not quite up to *Empress* standards. The *Empress of Scotland* was altogether bigger, more luxurious, faster. Her extra speed enabled Canadian Pacific to reinstate their pre-War calls at Greenock in both directions, a move which was welcomed since many Canadians had Scottish roots. On the other hand, as with the *Empress of Britain* in pre-War days, her tall masts made it impossible for her to proceed up the St. Lawrence beyond Quebec – she could not pass under the Jacques Cartier Bridge. It was thus left to the two smaller ships to serve Montreal until, in 1952, the *Empress of Scotland*'s masts were shortened and she was at last able to cover the full route. Liverpool to Quebec had been taking six days and the ship would remain in port for four days at each end of the voyage.

In pre-War years, several of the company's Atlantic liners had achieved a fine reputation for their cruises out of New York and now the *Empress of Scotland* took up their mantle. Her 12th December, 1950 departure from Liverpool was therefore to New York and on the 22nd December she left her Manhattan berth on a 12-day Christmas cruise to Kingston, La Guaira and Havana. Other, similar Caribbean cruises followed and at the end of each of them she would lie in New

Wearing Canadian Pacific's post-War livery, the *Empress of Scotland* was transferred to the North Atlantic. Here we see her after the masts have been cropped in order to enable her to reach Montreal. *(Maurizio Eliseo collection)*

York for three days being stored and serviced – a sharp contrast with the hasty turn-rounds of to-day's cruise ships. That first New York cruising season lasted until April, 1951, when she returned to Liverpool and resumed her summer and autumn transatlantic service.

An eastbound crossing in November, 1951 was particularly special. The *Empress of Scotland* had been chartered to bring Princess Elizabeth and the Duke of Edinburgh home from a visit to Canada and the United States. She anchored briefly four miles offshore in Conception Bay, Newfoundland and the Royal couple embarked in a gale after enduring half an hour being tossed around in a small local ferry. When, five days later, the *Empress of Scotland* reached home waters, she and her Royal passengers were escorted into the Mersey by two naval vessels.

The 1951-52 Christmas and New Year cruise was a month-long jaunt to the West Indies from Southampton after which it was across to New York for another season of Caribbean cruises, before returning to the Atlantic run in May. This pattern was repeated in subsequent years. 1953, Coronation Year, was expected to be a very busy one for the Canadian Pacific liners and it was particularly unfortunate that in January the *Empress of Canada* was badly damaged by fire and capsized while in Liverpool. She was eventually found to be beyond repair but meanwhile the company had purchased the French Line's *De Grasse* – with her modest speed, she was not the most suitable ship for their purposes but she was the best they could find at short notice. The famous name *Empress of Australia* was revived for her. Already, however, plans were being made for a new *Empress of Britain* which would be quickly followed by a near-sister, the *Empress of England*. The advent of these two liners would eventually spell the end of the *Empress of Scotland*'s service with Canadian Pacific. As Clive Harvey persuasively points out in his book *The Last White Empresses*, the new ships were excellent vessels but in those egalitarian times they catered for many more tourist class passengers than first class. The days of the magnificent luxury liners of old were almost over.

In the meantime, the *Empress of Scotland* soldiered on and continued to be very popular with her passengers. However, by September, 1957 she was being offered for sale and her arrival at Liverpool on the 26th November marked the end of her career with Canadian Pacific. Five weeks later, she sailed for Belfast to be dry-docked 'for inspection by possible purchasers' and on the 9th January, 1958 she was sold to the newly-formed Hamburg Atlantic Line. In an attempt to obscure her true identity during the delivery voyage, she was temporarily renamed *Scotland* – memories of the Second World War were still raw and news of the sale of a great British liner to a German company had not been happily received in some quarters. According to Nils Schwerdtner, there were

also questioning voices in Germany, who doubted the wisdom of purchasing such an elderly ship. Her subsequent career was to prove the sceptics very wrong indeed.

The Hamburg Atlantic Line (Hamburg-Atlantik Linie) was the brainchild of Axel Bitsch-Christensen. He was an executive with Home Lines, in charge of the Cuxhaven – Halifax – New York service which they had established to participate in the hectic emigrant trade from Northern Europe to Canada and America, which the big German lines had been precluded from sharing in the early post-War years. Home Lines proved to be a seed bed for future shipowners: after some years as Home Lines employees, Charalambos Keusseoglou set up his Sun Lines and Pericles Panagopoulos formed the Royal Cruise Line. Bitsch-Christensen too branched out on his own. The Home Lines service from Cuxhaven was being maintained by the *Italia* (ex-*Kungsholm*), for which the Hamburg America Line (HAPAG) were acting as general agents and were providing the crew. In the mid-'Fifties, Nicolo Vernicos Evgenides, the new owner of Home Lines, offered to sell the ship to HAPAG but they declined, whereupon Bitsch-Christensen, though a Dane, decided that he would try to re-establish HAPAG's pre-War German-flag transatlantic passenger service himself. With financial support from the city of Hamburg and from Mr. Vernicos Evgenides, he formed the Hamburg-Atlantik Linie.

His choice of ship fell on the *Empress of Scotland*, old enough to be affordable but a true ocean liner – big, solid, still quite speedy. The contract for her conversion, which was said to have cost the equivalent of £2¾ million, naturally went to a Hamburg yard, the Howaldtswerke. When she emerged as the *Hanseatic* in June, 1958, the former Canadian Pacific liner had been transformed. Her third, dummy, funnel had gone and the other two had been replaced by broader ones painted red with a black top and bearing the three-pronged Hanseatic cross in white. Their placing, well forward, gave the ship the kind of eager look which had once characterised the *Rex* and the *Conte di Savoia*. The hull now had a shapely new bow and the front of the superstructure had been largely rebuilt with a much more rounded appearance. The enclosed promenade was extended a little nearer the stern and an additional deckhouse was built above part of the superstructure.

There were also internal changes. The ship now carried no more than 85 first class passengers but up to 1,167 in tourist class, where there was the choice of one-, two-, three- or four-berth cabins, about 90% of which had private facilities. All passenger spaces were air-conditioned. The public rooms were re-furnished in modern style by the German architect Georg Manner. Ted Scull crossed twice in her and in his book *Ocean Liner Odyssey* he comments on the entire deck of lounges and bars available to tourist class passengers, particularly the forward-facing observation bar, called the Alster

Club, with its huge windows and heavy curtains; and the St. Pauli Tavern, 'a noisy, crowded and smoky German pub'. And there were 'lots of good places to read other than the main public rooms'. He managed to peep into the dining room reserved for the limited number of very separate first class passengers, which was 'all the way aft, not unlike the position of the *Queen Mary*'s Verandah Grill, with windows looking over the stern'. The ship now had two swimming pools, one still indoors, and a cinema equipped to show the new Cinemascope films.

The *Hanseatic*'s transatlantic crossings seem to have been very sociable affairs and proved popular. She was also very well-liked by her crew. Years later, I met the then Chief Engineer of Peter Deilmann's *Berlin*, who was very nostalgic about his days on the old liner. And, in the 1990s, the charterer of the former *Society Adventurer* took the name *Hanseatic* for both his company and the ship and decorated her funnel with the three-armed cross. He too had served on the previous *Hanseatic*.

The Hamburg Atlantic Line service started with the 21st July, 1958 sailing from Cuxhaven to Le Havre, Southampton, Cobh and New York. On a few of her later outward voyages, the *Hanseatic* also called at Halifax, where she disembarked quite large numbers of emigrants. In later years, she would sometimes have passengers tendered to and from her in Cowes Roads, so as not to have to dock expensively and time-consumingly at Southampton. Eventually, Cherbourg was substituted for Le Havre and the Cobh call was dropped. Like the Home Lines' *Italia*, she was managed by the Hamburg America company and, until the *Italia* was switched to a Cuxhaven – Quebec – Montreal service in 1959, the two ran in conjunction. *Hanseatic*'s first master was Captain Walter Pabst, who had previously commanded the *Italia*.

The *Hanseatic*'s first few voyages were not trouble-free and in both January and March, 1959 she had to be taken out of service for brief repairs to her turbines. Thereafter, she seems to have run very reliably. She was intended primarily as a transatlantic liner but she was also well-suited for pleasure voyages and in February, 1959 she made a Caribbean cruise

In 1958, the *Empress of Scotland* was sold to the newly formed Hamburg Atlantic Line, for whom she became the *Hanseatic* after being partially rebuilt. *(Clive Harvey collection)*

from New York. A further expensive refit in the winter of 1959-60 improved many of her cabins, making her even more competitive as a cruise ship. More Caribbean jaunts from New York followed, but by October, 1960 Port Everglades had become her main American cruise port. On the 27th December, she left Cuxhaven on her first cruise for the German market. It took her to Lisbon, North Africa and the Atlantic islands. Thereafter, a Christmas and New Year cruise from Cuxhaven became a regular feature of her schedule before she started her American cruise season. In the summer months, she still interspersed some transatlantic voyages between cruises and, indeed, hers may have been one of the more successful liner services in those days when the jet aeroplanes were sweeping all before them.

In 1961, her appearance was changed – and not for the better. Extension pipes now emerged from the top of her funnels, each surrounded by a network dome. She had been in the habit of spewing out a great deal of thick black smoke and this modification was an attempt to keep it off the after decks. In 1963, she ran aground at San Juan and had to head for Newport News for repairs.

She was proving sufficiently popular to encourage Mr. Bitsch-Christensen to contemplate a running-mate – this time a newbuilding. To finance it, in 1965 he formed a separate company and was able to persuade over 200 of the *Hanseatic's* wealthiest First Class passengers to subscribe for shares – a tribute to the loyalty which the old ship had engendered.

Unfortunately, nearly a year later, on the 7th September, 1966, his plans began to unravel. While the *Hanseatic* was preparing for a morning departure from Pier 84 in New York, she suffered a devastating engine room fire, caused by a leaking fuel line. The passengers and crew were safely evacuated but it took nine hours to extinguish the blaze. Perhaps remembering the lessons learned when the *Normandie* caught fire at her New York pier, the 200 firemen mainly used chemicals to staunch the blaze rather than water. But much of the ship's interior was damaged by fire and smoke and had to be ripped apart by the firefighters. The pathetic hulk of this great liner was taken to the Todd yard, where she had once been so admired. The verdict was gloomy but nevertheless she was towed back to Hamburg. She broke away from one of her tugs during a storm off the Azores but finally arrived at Hamburg on the 10th October. There she was greeted by a fireboat welcome, so fond had the local maritime community become of her. But there could be no denying the bitter truth – the *Hanseatic* was declared a Constructive Total Loss and on the 2nd December, after negotiations with Italian shipbreakers had failed, she was sold to a local firm to be demolished.

Mr. Bitsch-Christensen formed yet another company to buy a replacement, the Israeli flagship *Shalom*, which assumed the favourite name of *Hanseatic*. In 1969, she was joined by the new *Hamburg*. But, although both were fine modern liners, costs were too high and the dollar/deutschmark exchange rate moved unfavourably. In 1973 the operation was forced to close down.

Now with just two funnels, a new bow and a curved bridge front, she became extremely popular, carrying mainly tourist class passengers. *(Maurizio Eliseo collection)*

Britannic

Completed 1930.

26,943 gross tons.

Length overall: 711 ft. 9ins.

Breadth: 82 ft. 5ins.

Draught: 35 ft. 0¼ ins.

Diesel engines. Twin screw.

Service speed: 18 knots.

Scrapped, 1960.

The *Britannic* was the height of 1930s motorship modernity. *(Maurizio Eliseo collection)*

The last years of the White Star Line were very sad. One of the really great transatlantic lines and tracing its roots back to the mid-nineteenth century, it was in decline in the late 'Twenties. By the early 'Thirties it was teetering on the brink of bankruptcy. Finally, in 1934 it was effectively absorbed by its old rival Cunard. True, for nearly a decade and a half thereafter the combined Atlantic services of the two lines were operated by a Cunard subsidiary called Cunard-White Star Line, Ltd. in which White Star's principal creditors retained a minority stake. However, in 1947 the arrangement was unravelled and Cunard took over the Atlantic services completely. Soon, the once-prestigious White Star name was dropped, presumably because it was no longer thought to be of value. (To-day, Cunard take a different view and boast that they offer their passengers what they describe as White Star service.)

Although often considered to be thoroughly British, White Star had in fact been taken over by a huge American combine in 1902. The International Mercantile Marine, usually referred to as the IMM, was the brainchild of the powerful Wall Street banker J. Pierpoint Morgan who hoped to dominate the transatlantic shipping trade. In fact, the IMM was not successful and by the mid-'Twenties

Morgan's successors were either disposing of its non-American subsidiaries or simply closing them down. On the first day of 1927, they sold White Star to companies in the Royal Mail Steam Packet group, presided over by another great mogul, Lord Kylsant. There was rejoicing on this side of the Atlantic that such an important shipping line had been returned to British ownership but the purchase became one of the factors which eventually precipitated the collapse of the Kylsant empire. (There is more information on that subject in the chapter on the *Asturias*.)

Both Cunard and White Star had foreseen the need for new express ships to meet the competition of the spectacular new Atlantic liners being planned by their French and German rivals and, albeit for a more southerly route, by the Italians. Cunard had responded with plans for the huge ship which eventually emerged as the 80,000-ton *Queen Mary*. And in August, 1926, while still owned by the IMM, White Star had placed a provisional order with Harland & Wolff for a 60,000-tonner to be called *Oceanic*. If built, she would have been the World's first 1,000 feet long liner.

It has sometimes been said that the worsening economic conditions later prompted a decision to cancel the building of the *Oceanic* and to substitute orders for two smaller, slower and more economical ships, *Britannic* and her later sister *Georgic*. That cannot be true since *Britannic*'s keel plates were laid at Harland & Wolff's North Yard in Belfast in April, 1927, some months before those of *Oceanic*. However, hardly any work was actually done on *Oceanic* (while a decision was made on her propulsion system, so it was claimed). It seems that progress had ceased long before the end of July, 1929, although the order for her construction was not formally cancelled until September, 1929 and her scanty beginnings were not removed from the slipway until some months later.

Advertisements sometimes called the White Star Line transatlantic service 'The Biggest Ship Route'. Just how daring a project the 60,000-ton three-funnelled motor ship *Oceanic* would have been can be judged from the fact that in 1927 the World's largest motorliner was the Italian *Augustus* of 32,000 tons.

Britannic and *Georgic*, intended not for the prime express service between Southampton and New York but for the secondary Liverpool – New York route, were also motor ships but with the power of their diesel engines transmitted by conventional gearing rather than by the still somewhat experimental system of electric drive which had eventually been chosen for *Oceanic*.

Even more than White Star's Southampton service, the one from Liverpool was in need of new and more up-to-date tonnage. The 'Big Four' – *Celtic*, *Cedric*, *Baltic* and *Adriatic* – were extremely fine ships noted for their steadiness in rough conditions but they variously dated back to between 1901 and 1907. The loss of *Celtic*, wrecked off Cobh in 1928, added extra urgency to the work on *Britannic* and for a while it proceeded round the clock on a three-shift basis. She was launched on the 6th August, 1929 without ceremony.

Britannic left Belfast on the 26th May, 1930 for trials in the Firth of Clyde, returning for final titivation on the 28th. Later, there were indeed celebrations when, on the 21st June, a large number of guests arrived in Belfast on a ship belonging to the Belfast Steamship Company, another Kylsant-controlled concern, and embarked on *Britannic* for a two-night cruise which ended at her new home port of Liverpool. A correspondent from *Lloyd's List* was one of the party and described how *Britannic* made 'a fine spectacle of graceful strength'. In fact, with her straight bow, two low motor ship funnels (raked but with horizontal tops) and her cruiser stern, she had a somewhat similar profile to those of the liners which Harland & Wolff were building for other companies in the group: the Royal Mail Steam Packet Company itself, Nelson Line, Union-Castle and Elder Dempster. Her forward funnel, by the way, was a dummy.

Britannic was the biggest British motor ship so far and, at the time, the largest vessel of any kind to sail regularly from Liverpool. With her service speed of 18 knots, she was by no means an express liner and, indeed, she was very much in the old White Star tradition of offering comfort and steadiness rather than the ultimate in speed. It was a sign of the straitened times that she was a 'cabin ship' – her highest grade of accommodation was not called first class but rather cabin class, thus enabling the line to charge lower fares while still abiding by the rules of the North Atlantic Passenger Conference. She was far from unique in this – very controversially, even the hugely prestigious and luxurious *Queen Mary* was designated a 'cabin ship' when she came out in 1936.

'Cabin ship' though she may have been, *Britannic* was a liner of the highest standards and her accommodation and public rooms would not have been out of place on the premier route out of Southampton . As one speaker said at the lunch to celebrate her commissioning: "Here is a ship which offers the man of middle station in life the dignities of travel" – a remark redolent of that class-conscious era.

A 1930s postcard using a picture by James S. Mann, a well-known Liverpool maritime artist. *(Maurizio Eliseo collection)*

Passenger capacity was 504 in cabin class, 551 in tourist and 493 in third. Tastes were changing and, while the designers of *Britannic*'s cabin and tourist class interiors did not plunge headlong into the new style, they did produce a pleasing compromise between the traditional and the modern. (The sister, *Georgic* which came out in 1932, was more overtly modernistic, not only inside but also, with her slightly rounded bridge front, outside.)

Perhaps *Britannic*'s most modern-looking room was her imposing two deck-high cabin class Lounge. However, the attention of the man from *Lloyd's List* was particularly caught by the Long Gallery, a combined lounge and indoor promenade which ran along the port side, and he was impressed by the full range of facilities enjoyed by the cabin class passengers – swimming pool, gymnasium, tennis courts, 'talkies', shops and 'band repeaters in all public rooms' (in other words, a public address system). She did not, though, have bridal suites which, he told his readers, had been a feature of the first *Britannic* in 1874. He was also struck by the 'remarkable standard' enjoyed by passengers lower down the social scale, commenting on the 'homogeneity of accommodation' between the classes. As far as the third class cabins were concerned, he was perhaps stretching a point but it was notable that even in that class there were elevators and a children's playroom.

Modernity extended to the ship's equipment. Cooking was by electricity and it was claimed that, for the first time on the North Atlantic, electric heaters were used in the passenger quarters. Electricity also powered all the auxiliary machinery, both in the engine department and on deck, with cargo being handled by 16 electric winches. *Britannic* was, in fact, a considerable cargo-carrier whose eight holds had a bale capacity of 654,480 cubic feet, with 72,440 cubic feet of refrigerated space. She was driven by two Harland & Wolff/Burmeister & Wain 10-cylinder double-acting diesel engines developing a total of 20,000 bhp.

Britannic left Liverpool on her maiden voyage on the 28th June, 1930, an occasion sufficiently important to merit a special broadcast by the BBC. She called in the Clyde to pick up more passengers the following day before striking out across the Atlantic, arriving off Quarantine in New York harbour in the very early hours of the 7th July. Her return voyage, via Boston and Cobh, began on the 12th July and she was back at the landing stage at Liverpool on the 21st. Her master, Captain F. F. Summers, told the press that he had

By July, 1934 when the first of these cruises was due to take place, the merger between White Star and Cunard had already happened. *(Clive Harvey collection)*

been impressed by her lack of vibration and that she was a very steady ship.

These were already difficult times. On the day *Britannic* made her first departure from New York, figures were published which demonstrated that even in 1929, before the Great Depression had set in, there had already been overcapacity in the passenger trade between Europe and the United States. That year, the British ships had, on average, travelled 42.9% full in the eastward direction and only 32.1% full westward. The Germans did better (86.7% and 50.1%) and the French achieved 51.8% and 51.1%. Bottom of the league came the Swedes with 38.6% and 18.6%. As the 'Thirties progressed, things became far worse but *Britannic* and *Georgic* did better than most Atlantic liners and, being much less fuel-thirsty, almost certainly produced more favourable financial results for their owners.

For much of each year, *Britannic* ran a regular Liverpool – Cobh – New York schedule, usually with a call at Boston in one or both directions.

The first class long gallery (above) was a compromise between the traditional and the modern, as was the less ornate tourist class lounge. *(Author's collection)*

Pre-War and post-War vews of *Britannic*. She was easily distinguishable from her sister *Georgic* by the square front to her superstructure. *(Ambrose Greenway collection and Maurizio Eliseo collection)*

While in Liverpool, she would lie in Gladstone Dock. However, like many other Atlantic liners, she was sent cruising during the slack winter months. In her first season, this occupied her from Boxing Day, 1930 until the following April. Her first cruising voyage was a trip from New York to Bermuda and this was followed by a long cruise to the Mediterranean (New York, Madeira, Gibraltar, Algiers, Monaco, Naples, Piraeus, Istanbul, Alexandria and Syracuse, calling again at Naples, Monaco and Gibraltar on the return leg to New York). She rounded off the season with two Caribbean cruises calling at Kingston, Colon and Havana and at Nassau, Port au Prince, Kingston, Vera Cruz and Havana. She then returned to her Atlantic service.

Her 1931-32 cruise schedule was less ambitious, consisting entirely of a series of New York-based Caribbean cruises of between one and two weeks. In 1933, she made just two cruises – a 40-day trip out of Liverpool, taking her passengers to Trinidad, Barbados, La Guaira, Colon, Kingston, Havana, Nassau and Madeira; and, in May, a brief New York – Bermuda spin. Also that year, in an attempt to drum up more Irish trade, she began calling at Galway as well as Cobh during some of her transatlantic crossings. As time went on, there were also occasional calls at Halifax. In 1934, she made another long cruise from Liverpool which this time took her to various Mediterranean ports including Beirut and Haifa; and later that year there were two more New York – Bermuda cruises.

In the words of a 1949 brochure: "The unique blending of tapestried old English charm and bright modernity so delightfully typical of the *Britannic*".
(Clive Harvey collection)

In May, 1934, after long negotiations, Cunard finally took over the Atlantic services and fleet of White Star. It was a move forced on them by the British government as a quid pro quo for loans to finance the resumption of work on the partly-built *Queen Mary* – construction of which had been halted when Cunard had run out of money due to the effects of the Great Depression. In the painful reorganisation which followed, there was a cull of the White Star fleet and within two years only three remained – *Britannic*, *Georgic* and the 18,000-ton steamer *Laurentic*. However, although they were now effectively Cunard ships, they continued to wear the old White Star livery including the buff-painted funnels with broad black tops. The combined fleet now flew both companies' flags, with the Cunard ensign fluttering above the White Star Line burgee on the ex-Cunarders but with the positions reversed on the former White Star ships.

After completing her 1935 winter cruise season out of New York, *Britannic* was transferred to a service from London (King George V Dock for cargo) and Southampton (for passengers) to New York with calls at Le Havre, Cobh and occasionally Boston. With her sister *Georgic*, she maintained a fortnightly schedule but with the usual annual interval for winter cruising from New York. Apart from a few Liverpool voyages, she spent the rest of the pre-War period on the London route and was a great success.

Then, on the 25th August, 1939, with Europe overshadowed by the looming war, the direction of *Britannic's* career changed abruptly. She was en route from New York to London when her owners received notice that she was being taken up for government service. After putting in to Southampton to land her passengers, she made for Liverpool where she arrived with her funnels already painted dark grey. By the time she had unloaded her cargo and had been quickly readied for trooping duties, the Second World War had already begun. She was sent to the Clyde, from where she sailed on the 5th September bound for Bombay carrying British personnel belonging to the Indian Army. On her return in November, she was temporarily handed back to her owners and made a few very dangerous voyages between Liverpool and New York. However, on the 15th August, 1940 she was once again requisitioned and was now thoroughly converted into a troopship. (By the end of the War, after several number-expanding refits, she was able to accommodate and provide the necessary facilities for as many as 4,076 men – 2,792 of them sleeping in bunks erected on what had become the troopdecks.)

She left Liverpool for Suez on the 10th September, 1940. The Mediterranean was no longer passable and so the voyage involved a long trek round the Cape of Good Hope. Voyages to India, to Canada and to West and South Africa followed and on one occasion in 1941 she returned from the Cape via

Trinidad. She mainly sailed out of Liverpool but with some calls at the anchorage in the Clyde where thousands of troops were disembarked and embarked by some of the most famous liners in the World, including *Queen Mary* and *Queen Elizabeth*. By 1943, the War was beginning to swing in the Allies' favour and when she went Out East she was able to sail by way of the Mediterranean and the Suez Canal. In November of that year, however, she joined the 'G.I. Shuttle' bringing thousands of American and Canadian troops to Britain and returning with wounded men and prisoners of war. By 1945, with fighting no longer raging in Europe, the flow was in the opposite direction and she was taking part in 'Operation Magic Carpet', returning battle-weary men to America and Canada. During her troopship service, she had several times been drydocked for repairs – including fitting new tail shafts and propellers in 1944 – and periodically she had undergone a no doubt very necessary fumigation.

The end of the War in 1945 did not immediately trigger her return to civilian service. By the end of January, 1947 the British government had released 121 passenger vessels back to their owners but still had 111 under requisition and *Britannic* was still making trooping voyages to Bombay and Singapore and to Malta and Port Said. She made her final arrival in Liverpool on the 13th February carrying over 3,000 returning servicemen and civilians. In all, during her time as a troopship she had travelled 376,000 miles and carried 180,000 'passengers'.

She had been lucky and had come through the War more or less unscathed, in contrast to her sister *Georgic* which was badly damaged by fire after being bombed at Port Tewfik in Egypt in 1941. (Although bought by the British government and partially restored, *Georgic* was never again fit to operate as a top-notch Atlantic liner. Instead, she was used for trooping, for carrying emigrants to Australia and for a few cheap 'austerity' voyages between Southampton and New York.)

On her release, *Britannic* was taken in hand by Harland & Wolff's Liverpool establishment for repairs and restoration to her pre-War splendour and then for drydocking. In the process, her open-sided promenades were enclosed. Her passenger cabins were thoroughly modernised and numbers were reduced so that she could now carry up to 429 in what was at last called first class and 564 in tourist class. It was all a huge task, hindered by a four week strike of shipyard workers. It had originally been announced that the work would occupy 1,000 men for seven months but in the end it took fifteen months and it was not until the 22nd May, 1948 that *Britannic* left on her post-War maiden voyage.

She returned to her original route between Liverpool and New York via Cobh. In this service she joined the newly built 13,000-ton *Media* and *Parthia*. They made a some-

what ill-matched trio. *Britannic* was once again a decidedly grand liner, whereas her running mates were much more modest vessels. Like her, they were very large cargo-carriers but they could accommodate no more than 250 passengers, all in a first class which was extremely pleasant but lacked the scale and glamour of that on *Britannic*.

These were busy years for transatlantic liners and *Britannic* quickly regained her pre-War popularity and prestige. Unfortunately, this was also a time when labour disputes were rife in ports on both sides of the Atlantic and twice she was forced to head for Halifax rather than New York. On the 1st February, 1949, however, it must have seemed to her crew as if the good times had returned at last when she set off on her first post-War cruise from New York, a voyage to wonderful places – Bermuda, Barbados, Rio de Janeiro, Buenos Aires, Montevideo, Rio again, Bahia, Trinidad, Cristobal, Kingston and Havana. She also called at Bermuda on several of her transatlantic crossings during the following years and made a few calls at Greenock on the Clyde.

Britannic had once been a remarkably trouble-free ship but now she began to be more incident-prone, with dropped anchors, fires (including quite a serious one in April, 1955) and slight collisions, and towards the end her diesels became rather troublesome and demanded careful attention from the engine room crew. As early as January 1950, at the start of her annual cruise, she had been forced to put

The first class smoking room had a hint of "Odeon" style as in the light fittings and the fireplace. Typically of the times, it was one of the largest rooms in the ship.
(Clive Harvey collection)

Britannic at Palermo during one of her popular post-War Mediterranean cruises. *(Maurizio Eliseo collection)*

back to New York for brief engine repairs before setting off on her long journey to a whole succession of Mediterranean ports. As planned, the cruise terminated at Southampton where her passengers were transferred to one of the company's express liners for the final leg of the trip back to New York. This lengthy Mediterranean winter cruise became an institution – she repeated it every year for the rest of her career, except in 1957 when it had to be cancelled because of the Suez crisis.

Barbara Peden was a lady purser on board *Britannic* during the mid-1950s. (Unlike Union-Castle, Cunard did not adopt the condescending title of purserette for the female members of that department.) She remembers that *Britannic* was an extremely happy ship which was very popular with passengers travelling to and from the North of England, such as the singer and comedienne Gracie Fields who famously came from Rochdale. As the ship spent five or more days in port at either end of her transatlantic crossings the demands upon the purser's department were not excessive. And the annual long Mediterranean cruise was always exceptionally pleasant. But, under Cunard's house rules, Barbara had to leave the company's service when she got married.

On the 7th May, 1960 *Britannic* limped into New York with one engine disabled by a broken crankshaft. She remained at her pier for nearly two months while repairs were made. Following trials, she finally resumed sailings on the 7th July. Despite this blot on her record, she remained one of the best-loved liners on the North Atlantic. Like her Italian motorliner contemporaries *Saturnia* and *Vulcania*, she may not have been the biggest or fastest ship in her owners' fleet but she was steady, extremely comfortable, full of character and very popular.

Nevertheless, it was announced that she would be withdrawn at the end of 1960, despite the fact that the published schedule for 1961 had included a full series of *Britannic* sailings. Cunard replaced her by transferring the 1957-built *Sylvania* from the Canadian service but, with the jet aeroplanes making deepening inroads into the liners' passenger lists, *Sylvania* spent more time cruising until she was finally withdrawn in the fearsome 1967-68 purge of the Cunard fleet. As for the *Britannic*, she left New York for the last time on the 25th November, 1960, escorted out of the harbour by a fireboat sending up a plume of water in her honour and with the *New York Times* publishing an affectionate tribute to this last White Star liner. She arrived back at Liverpool on the 4th December, 1960. A few days previously, she had been sold for scrap and after de-storing she sailed for the breaker's yard at Inverkeithing where she arrived on the 19th.

Isipingo

Completed 1934.

7,069 gross tons.

Length overall: 420 ft. 0ins.

Breadth: 57 ft. 3ins.

Draught: 25ft. 0ins.

Twin screw. Diesel.

Service speed: 15 knots.

Scrapped, 1964.

Bank Line's modestly sized motor ship Isipingo. *(Ian Shiffman, Table Bay Underway collection)*

When the *Isipingo* and her two sisters came out in 1934, they were hailed as 'Empire Ships' and as symbols of hope for better times. They were built for the route between Burma, India and South Africa at a time when trade between the countries of the British Empire was being promoted as a remedy for the crippling slump which by then was being called 'the Great Depression'.

The shipping industry and, as a result, the shipbuilding trades, had suffered more than most. Just how bad things were can be seen from the fact that, when she ran her acceptance trials in Belfast Lough in January, 1934, *Lloyd's List* claimed that the *Isipingo* was the first vessel to do so from either of the two big local shipyards since the *Highland Patriot* in May, 1932. The *Isipingo* and her sister *Inchanga* had been ordered in October, 1932 at a time when there was not a single ship on the ways at the Belfast yards. They were launched during the following year and, with only these two vessels to their credit, Workman, Clark (1928), Ltd. could still claim to have the second highest output of any British shipbuilder in 1933. Over 70 per cent of the shipyard workers in Belfast were unemployed.

Workman, Clark's historic yard had been closed for a time during the late 1920s but, following the reconstruction of the company in 1928, had resumed work. Under the enterprising leadership of Mr. William Strachan, it had hung on and by 1934 the outlook seemed to be slightly brighter, particularly as a third ship of the *Isipingo* type, to be called *Incomati*, was now under construction. Unfortunately, the company did not survive, closing down in 1935. Some of its facilities were taken over by the neighbouring Harland & Wolff yard.

The owners of the three sisters were Bank Line, Ltd., managed by Andrew Weir & Co., a family business. Andrew Weir himself, by then the first Lord Inverforth, received much praise for bringing employment to the stricken city of Belfast by ordering these ships. At the same time he sent his private steam yacht, *Venetia*, to Harland & Wolff to be refitted.

Weir's were in some ways a very conservative firm, having been one of the last British shipowners to operate windjammers. It was not until 1896 that they bought their first steamer but in the early 'Twenties they embraced the new technology of the diesel engine rather earlier than most British owners and were soon adding economical motor freighters to their fleet. So strong, indeed, was their commitment to the new mode of propulsion that in one year (1923) they ordered no less than 18 motorships. (Even in the mid-'Thirties, though, they were still advertising themselves as The Bank Line of Steamers!)

Calcutta figured largely in the network of cargo liner services which the company had built up. Their Indian-African Line ran from Rangoon and Calcutta to South Africa via the East African ports. For many years, it had been maintained by three very ordinary 4,000-ton single-screw vessels which plodded along at 12 knots or so and, in addition to cargo, carried quite large numbers of Indian deck passengers. Two factors now prompted the order for new ships to upgrade this service: on some parts of the route, it was meeting competition from more modern Dutch vessels; and by 1932, following the catastrophic collapse of the Kylsant group, Weir's were negotiating to take over a very similar service which had been operated by Bullard, King & Co., Ltd., a subsidiary of the Union-Castle Line and therefore part of the Kylsant empire. The transfer took place in January, 1933.

The new ships, though still of modest size, were a big improvement on their predecessors. The *Isipingo* could accommodate 50 first class (i.e.: white) passengers amidships and 20 second class (probably better-off Indians) at the after end of the ship, while up to 500 'native' passengers, as they were then called, could be carried in the 'tweendecks. Notably for those days, the first class cabins, including two de luxe suites on the boat deck, all had private facilities, in most cases with showers rather than bathtubs. First class passengers may have been limited in number but they enjoyed ample open deck-space and the public rooms, scattered over three decks, were said to be very comfortable. Designed and furnished by Hampton & Sons, Ltd., they were pleasantly fitted out in a conservative style, with no trace of the Art Deco modernity which made its belated appearance on British liners in the following year. The forward-facing dining room was panelled in light mahogany and there was a somewhat baronial smoking room, which was clad in oak and had a stone fireplace. Slightly more modern-looking, the sycamore-panelled lounge was flanked by two 'tea terraces', entered through French windows on their inboard side and enclosed on the outboard side by glazed screens which could be opened when the weather allowed. In sweltering East African heat, that must have been a very welcome relief. Floors were covered by a rubber-coated linoleum aptly called Ruboleum. A verandah café overlooked the swimming bath, which was let into No. 4 cargo hatch. There were five holds: two forward, two aft and one trunked through the superstructure and providing access to a deep tank for liquid cargoes. 17,000 cubic feet of the hold space was insulated. Cargo was loaded by ten derricks.

The *Isipingo* and the *Inchanga* were each driven by two 6-cylinder Sulzer-type diesel engines of a new design, which were built by Workman, Clark themselves and were rated at 1,165 ihp. The third sister, *Incomati*, however, was given two 8-cylinder Doxford engines which had come from the unfortunate *Bermuda* of the Furness Bermuda Line. That glamorous liner had burned while docked at Hamilton in June, 1931 after not much more than three years of service. She had been taken to the Workman, Clark yard to be repaired but in May, 1932, with restoration almost complete, she had burned again, this time terminally. Her four engines, however, could be salvaged and refurbished and Workman, Clark bought them as a speculation. Two of them were eventually used in the *Incomati*, which was thus somewhat faster than her sisters. She was also slightly larger. *Lloyd's List* hinted that a fourth ship might be built, using the remaining two engines, but this never happened. The *Isipingo* was laid down in March, 1933 and was launched on the 9th October. She and the *Inchanga* took their names from districts near Durban. She ran her trials on the 29th January, 1934, averaging 16.15 knots over the measured mile and 15.6 knots over a 7 mile course. She was hardly an express liner, therefore, but, with her white, cruiser-sterned hull and short buff funnel with a black top, she was a smart-looking ship, very much the typical motor-liner. After her trials, there was particular comment on the smooth-running of her engines – notable at a time when motor ships often suffered from excessive vibration.

In early February, she loaded cargo at Glasgow before sailing for Rangoon, where she arrived on the 15th March. She left there on the 22nd at the start of her maiden voyage on her intended route. Her first port of call was Calcutta, where she lay for some days loading cargo and embarking passengers before leaving on the 5th April. She then called at Colombo, Beira, Lorenço Marques, Durban, East London and Algoa Bay before finally arriving at Cape Town 34 days after leaving Calcutta. The *Isipingo*'s subsequent voyages varied slightly: Mombasa was a regular port of call and she sometimes put in at Zanzibar or Dar-es Salaam, while at the northern end of the route she might call at Vizagapatam. Apart from an engine problem in October, 1935, she seems to have been a reliable ship.

Despite the outbreak of the Second World War in September, 1939, she continued on her regular route for a time, although now under government control. Perhaps she was not considered big enough or fast enough to be useful as a troopship or an armed merchant cruiser. By 1942, with the Japanese threatening Rangoon, her northbound

voyages went no further than Calcutta. In any case, by late that year, she was ranging more freely, often sailing to Lagos and other West African ports, either from Durban or Cape Town or from Liverpool. In January, 1943, there was also a transatlantic crossing to Hampton Roads and New York. The *Isipingo* proved to be a lucky ship, emerging unscathed from the War. The *Incomati* was less fortunate, being sunk by *U-508* in July, 1943.

Government control of British shipping came to an end in 1946 and *Isipingo* and *Inchanga* were eventually able to resume their regular peacetime service. However, with Burma already heading for independence – which it gained in January, 1948 – the Rangoon calls became much less frequent and most voyages were now on a curtailed route between Calcutta, Madras, Colombo and Durban. Rangoon was not completely abandoned, however, and in the 1950s the sisters sometimes also called at Chittagong in what was then East Pakistan.

The passenger trade between Calcutta and East and South Africa was in decline, apparently more so than that out of Bombay, from where the British India company was able to continue its 'Durban Mail' service until as late as 1976. In the mid-'Fifties, the Bank Line decided to cease full passenger service on its India – Africa route and, in a three month refit at Calcutta, most of the *Isipingo*'s passenger accommodation was closed off and she was stripped of some of her lifeboats. She resumed service on the 25th March, 1956. The following year, Brian Gardner joined her as a young radio officer. He recollects that she still occasionally carried a few passengers from Mombasa to Colombo or *vice versa*. "They were accommodated in cabins below the bridge superstructure. The greatest number we carried at any one time was a party of two Irish nuns and six Singhalese novitiates. They were en route to a new home on the shore of Lake Tanganyika. We were led to believe that they would normally observe lengthy periods of silence in their day-to-day lives but were free to converse while travelling. True or not, I do recall that after a couple of days at sea, I, for one, was making every effort to avoid being 'buttonholed' by them."

Brian Gardner also remembers that the *Isipingo* carried "a fairly large crew – nearer 100 than the 30 or so normally found on a freighter of comparable size. Many were Indian stewards, or similar, and spent their time in maintenance and housekeeping. They were kept in employment because of the long periods they, or a family member, had previously served the company."

The *Isipingo*'s route remained more or less the same, with round trips taking up to 3 months. There were, though, occasional diversions, including visits to Madagascar and to Gan Island in the Maldives, where the RAF were building a staging post. Like many other vessels, she sometimes suffered inconvenient delays at East African ports. Occasionally, her voyage would be extended up the west coast of Africa to such ports as Lagos, Freetown and Dakar, which she had previously visited during her war service. (Andrew Bell explains that Elder Dempster had berthing rights for a route from Calcutta to West Africa but – in an arrangement similar to the 'slot-sharing' now common amongst airlines – would assign their cargo, such as gunny bags, to the Bank Line, which not only ran between Calcutta and South Africa but also had rights on the route from South to West Africa.)

Towards the end of her life, the *Isipingo* became rather incident-prone. In December, 1957 she damaged a propeller and shifted one of her shafts while manoeuvring at Calcutta. Then in June, 1958, with communal disturbances and labour troubles raging, she was one of a number of merchant ships requisitioned by the Sri Lankan government to evacuate Tamil refugees from Colombo. Seven vessels, including another Bank Line cargo ship, the *Crestbank*, carried 5,029 people to Point Pedro. On the 28th August, 1960, the *Isipingo* suffered what must have been a rather spectacular accident when her mainmast came down while she was using her derricks to load bagged asbestos at Lourenço Marques. And in March, 1964, she suffered an engine failure at Madras and, as a result, collided with the Vlasov-owned freighter *Gemstone*.

The end came in August, 1964 when the *Isipingo* left Calcutta for Hong Kong, where she arrived on the 24th. She had been sold to breakers, who took delivery of her two days later.

Her last years had been spent in rather humdrum service, but when she and her sisters were built in the troubled 'Thirties, they were significant and notable ships.

The majority of *Isipingo*'s passengers were Indians travelling to East and South Africa. *(Author's collection)*

The second Mauretania

Completed 1939.

35,739 gross tons.

Length overall: 771 ft. 10ins.

Breadth: 89 ft. 5ins.

Draught: 30 ft. 10½ ins.

Geared steam turbines.   Twin screw.

Service speed: 23 knots.

Scrapped, 1965.

The second *Mauretania* had more than a passing resemblance to the later *Queen Elizabeth*.
(Ambrose Greenway)

It is tempting to think of Cunard's second *Mauretania* as 'almost a great ship'. She was an extremely fine liner but, like the daughter of a famous mother, she never quite matched the achievements or the popular acclaim of the first *Mauretania*. That Edwardian masterpiece had been the *Concorde* of her day when she came out in 1907 – one of the most technically advanced liners of the time and also the fastest, the holder of the Blue Riband from 1909 to 1929. She had also been one of the most beloved ships ever to sail the seas – an impossible act for her successor to follow. To add to the handicaps with which the second *Mauretania* had to contend, she always had to bear comparison with her bigger and quicker contemporaries, the *Queen Mary* and *Queen Elizabeth*. In a way, the publicity said it all. She was hailed as the largest ship yet built in England – not in Britain, because much bigger ones had come from yards in Scotland and Northern Ireland. Nevertheless, by the standards of the time, she was a very large, luxurious and sophisticated liner.

She was never intended to be a giant record breaker. Sir Percy Bates, the Chairman of the Cunard Steam Ship Co., Ltd. and of Cunard-White Star, Ltd., made that very clear when in April, 1936 he announced their intention to strengthen their 'second line' services across the North Atlantic. When it became known in July that negotiations were underway with several British shipbuilders, it was rumoured that the order would be for two ships of a broadly similar type to the very successful 27,000-ton, 18-knot motorships *Britannic* and *Georgic* which the old White Star Line had bequeathed to the combined company. But in December it was announced that a single 33,000-ton (*sic*) turbine steamer would be built by Cammell Laird & Co., Ltd. of Birkenhead. She would be somewhat slower than the *Queen Mary* and the forthcoming *Queen Elizabeth* but, even so, just about quick enough to deputise for one or other of them in the express service when necessary. (She had a service speed of 23 knots compared to their 29 knots and her transatlantic voyages usually took six or even seven days against their five.) As to size, she was mainly intended for the London to New York service which was being maintained by the *Britannic* and *Georgic* and so her design was constrained by the dimensions of the lock at the entrance to the King George V Dock. It would be a tight squeeze and she would, in fact, be the largest ship yet to dock in the Port of London.

Winning such a major contract from Cunard was a great achievement for Cammell Laird. Although their yard was just within sight of the Cunard Building across the river in Liverpool, they and their predecessors had so far only built two liners for them, the *Cephalonia* of 1882 and the *Samaria* of 1920. When the new ship was launched, the Chairman of Cammell Laird said that building another Cunarder had been a 'long-standing ambition'. For Cunard too, the order was important. It was testimony to their recovery from the ruinous effects of the Great Depression.

The first keel plates were laid on the 24th May, 1937 on the Number 6 slipway recently vacated by the aircraft carrier *Ark Royal*. On the neighbouring slipway Number 5, the battleship *Prince of Wales* was taking shape. The political situation in Europe was becoming ominous and shipyards which had struggled to survive through the 'Twenties and early 'Thirties were benefitting from the rush to rearm. In retrospect, the proximity of these great warships can be seen as a portent of the events which would so affect the early career of the new liner.

Despite the requirements of her sophisticated design, construction of the *Mauretania* proceeded at a very rapid pace and by the end of July, 1938 she was ready to be launched. The publicity departments of Cunard and Cammell Laird went into action. Newspapers were primed to inform their readers that the local council in Birkenhead was marking the occasion by laying out a huge flower bed in which a large letter 'M' would be flanked by floral displays in the shape of the house-flags of Cunard and White Star. And it was said that no less than seven tons of fat and tallow, a quarter of an inch thick, would be used to grease the ways before the new ship was launched on the 28th July. The BBC National Service would broadcast the ceremony and the following day they would put out a programme about the two *Mauretania*s. It was indeed a significant time for British shipping, made more so by the fact that on the day before *Mauretania* was launched, *Dominion Monarch*, the new flagship of the Shaw, Savill & Albion Line and Britain's biggest motorship, would take to the water from one of the Swan, Hunter & Wigham Richardson yards on the Tyne.

Mauretania was named by Lady (Mary) Bates, the wife of Sir Percy and the grand-daughter of Charles McIver, one of the founders of the Cunard Line. As Lady Bates spoke the time-honoured words, four flags on each side of the bow, two Union Jacks and two Stars and Stripes, swung apart to reveal the revered name of *Mauretania* in letters 27-inches high, whereupon a band played *Rule Britannia*. (After the old *Mauretania* had gone for scrap, her name had been reserved for Cunard's future use by an agreement with the Red Funnel Line of Southampton that one of their Isle of Wight ferries would assume it until Cunard needed it again.)

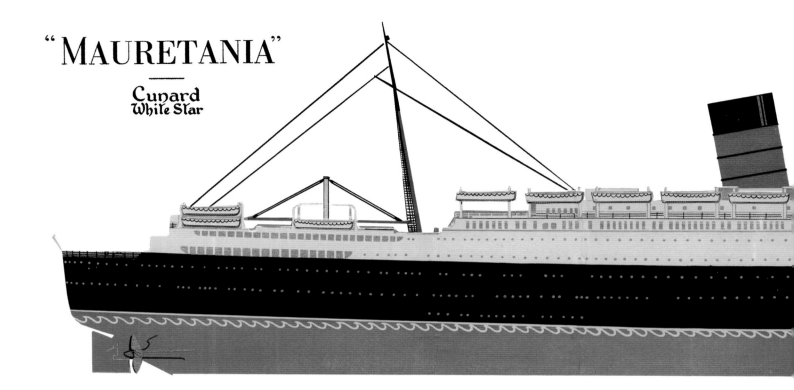

"MAURETANIA"

Cunard
White Star

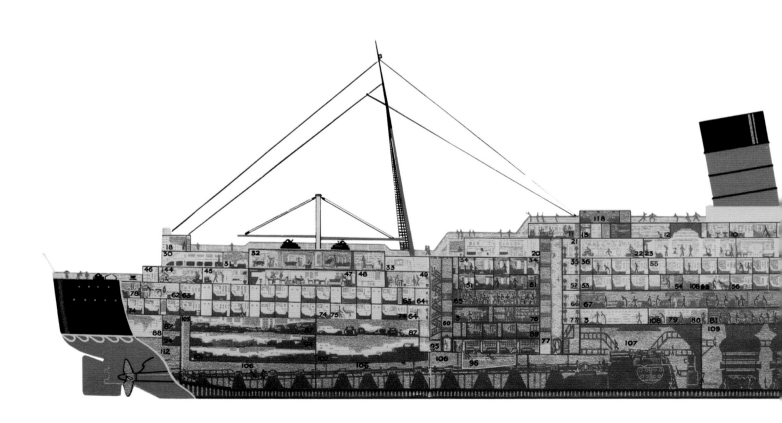

Before the *Mauretania* entered service her owners produced some spectacular publicity material, including a side elevation which opened out to reveal a cut-away drawing of her interiors. *(Clive Harvey collection)*

Because the River Mersey is about a mile wide at the point where the Cammell Laird yard is situated, it had not been necessary to fix drag chains to the new liner's hull in order to restrain her as she entered the water and so the launch was an unusually smooth, quiet affair without the customary clatter and clouds of rusty dust.

Once *Mauretania* was safely afloat, ten tugs towed her to the yard's wet basin where work continued. Again, the pace was rapid and by the 14th May, 1939 she was almost complete. In a manoeuvre described by *Lloyd's List* as 'the biggest and most intricate docking operation ever carried out on the Mersey', she was towed across to Liverpool and edged into the Gladstone Dry Dock where her rudder was to be fitted and she was to be readied for her trials. On the 31st May, she left for the Clyde where she ran her steaming trials, including sprints over the Skelmorlie mile. When she returned to Liverpool on the 3rd June, there was a certain coyness about the outcome, perhaps because neither the builders nor the owners wished too much publicity to be given to the fact that, as intended, *Mauretania* was slower than the *Queen Mary*. The official announcement merely stated that the trials had been 'highly satisfactory' and that vibration at full speed was negligible. Later, it leaked out that she had achieved 'a good 23 knots' over the measured mile and had touched 24.8 knots. Another source went so far as to quote an average speed of 25.14 knots,. Whatever, by most standards she was a fast ship.

As with her Dutch equivalent and near-contemporary, the *Nieuw Amsterdam,* it was notable that a ship of this size and type should be powered by only two sets of turbines and therefore had twin screws rather than the three or four which were still the usual thing on a big liner. As a consequence, the huge main gearwheels of her single-reduction system were the largest yet produced for a liner. Like the Yarrow water-tube boilers, the Parsons turbines were built by Cammell Laird themselves. Each set consisted of a high pressure, an intermediate pressure and a low pressure unit with the last two of these incorporating a reverse stage. They were rated at 42,000 shp.

The design of most of the interior spaces had been entrusted to the Glasgow firm of A. McInnes Gardner & Partners and much of the furnishing was the work of George Parnall & Co., Ltd. and Waring & Gillow, Ltd. The style was a judicious but rather grand compromise between the traditional and the modern – typically 1930s Cunard, with large expanses of highly polished veneer, including some cut from quite unusual woods such as primavera. Some of this panelling was fairly pale in colour and this, together with the artistic use of glass and metal, gave an air of lightness to some of the rooms. There was undoubtedly a feeling of expensive luxury. The two main cabin class public rooms and the three main tourist class rooms had 'the latest system of "air-conditioning"' – note the inverted commas: it was still something of a novelty on board ships. As for the third class spaces, it was said, perhaps a little hyperbolically, that they were 'in a style never previously attempted on an Atlantic liner'.

Following her launch on the 28th July, 1938, the *Mauretania*, the largest ship yet built in England, was towed to Cammell Laird's fitting out berth. *(Maurizio Eliseo collection)*

Above, the cabin class dining room and, below, the observation lounge whose curved shape resembled those of the equivalent rooms on the *Queen Mary* and the *Queen Elizabeth*. *(Clive Harvey collection)*

The passenger decks were divided between cabin class (i.e. first class in all but name) situated amidships; tourist class which was located aft; and third class forward. As on the two 'Queens', *Mauretania's* interiors were adorned by many specially-commissioned artworks. In the cabin class dining saloon, for instance, there was a massive carving depicting both the old and the new *Mauretania* and celebrating the link between Britain and America – with the former represented by St. Paul's Cathedral and the latter by a group of famous New York skyscrapers. That dining saloon was a very grand room indeed, two decks high and situated low down in the ship. The sides of the upper section were punctuated by several large, circular apertures, a feature which was repeated nearly seventy years later in the Queens Room on Cunard's *Queen Victoria*. *Mauretania's* other cabin class public rooms, almost entirely spread out along the Promenade Deck, consisted of a very smart observation lounge and cocktail bar, reminiscent of those on the 'Queens'; the Grand Hall (another imposing two deck high space, which also acted as a ballroom and was equipped to serve as a cinema – when not in use, the cinema screen was hidden by spectacular lacquered panels); a domed lounge; the smoking room; the writing room and library; and, one deck higher, a pair of linked verandahs which opened out to one of the two cabin class sun decks. Passengers in this class also had their own gymnasium and for much of the time had the exclusive use of the ship's

A comfortable cabin class stateroom. In those days portholes could be opened. *(Clive Harvey collection)*

indoor swimming pool, adjoining which were rooms for massage and for the then popular electric treatments. In addition, there was a children's playroom and a photographic dark room. Cabin class passengers also had their own enclosed promenade stretching along both the port and starboard sides and sweeping round the front of the superstructure (which must have meant that the occupants of the observation lounge were actually observing the passing promenaders as much as the sea beyond). From all this, it will be clear that *Mauretania* was indeed a luxury liner.

For tourist class passengers, there was a lounge, a smoking room, a dining saloon, a dedicated cinema, a children's playroom, and, notably in this class, a gymnasium, in addition to an open sun deck. Tourist class passengers also had the exclusive use of the swimming pool during certain periods. While by no means as imposing or as richly furnished as those in cabin class, the tourist class public rooms were spacious and comfortable and the lounge was very stylish. Nevertheless, I get the impression that the difference between the top two classes was much greater than it would have been had *Mauretania* been built after the War. As for the third class passengers, comment at the time was that on *Mauretania* the facilities they enjoyed were much better than usual in this class – they not only had a dining room, a lounge (even equipped with a grand piano and with a recess containing writing tables) and a smoking room but also a children's room, a combined cinema and games room and a dedicated sports deck.

As built, *Mauretania* could accommodate up to 486 passengers in cabin class, 396 in tourist class and 502 in third. In cabin class there were four special suites and almost all the other rooms, too, had full private facilities, which was notable for the time. In tourist class there were cabins ranging from 2- to 4-berth, some of which had private facilities. In this class, there were some intercommunicating cabins for use by families. Third class cabins had from 2 to 4 berths but none had facilities beyond the usual wash basin.

Not only was the second *Mauretania* a luxurious passenger ship but she also had a substantial general cargo capacity of 449,000 cubic feet plus a further 73,311 cubic feet of insulated space. There were five holds, three forward and two aft. The latter could accommodate about 70 cars in their upper 'tween decks.

To the Cunard-White Star management, it must have seemed that their expensive new liner was entering service at an inopportune time. The previous month, the chairman of another transatlantic passenger shipping company, the Anchor Line, had summed up the situation thus: "Last summer, the bottom dropped out of everything. Since then, conditions have not materially improved. People will not travel when there is a risk of war at any moment." No wonder Cunard-White Star were offering Atlantic Excursions from just £27 5s. 0d. in third class with the blandishment 'See America This Year'. (1939 was the year of New York's spectacular World's Fair, at which, incidentally, a model of the new *Mauretania* was being exhibited.)

As we have seen, the new ship was intended for the London to New York service, loading her cargo in the Port of London before calling briefly at Southampton to embark passengers. As a matter of convenience, however, her maiden voyage started from Liverpool, from where she sailed on the 17th June, 1939. Among her passengers were five people who had been on the maiden voyage of her famous namesake in 1907 and she was commanded by Captain A. T. Brown who had taken that old ship on her voyage to the shipbreakers' yard in 1935. Cunard-White Star advertisements had for some time been announcing that the new *Mauretania* would put in at Galway on this first crossing but a few weeks before she was due to sail it was decided that Cobh should be substituted as the Irish port of call. She arrived in New York on the 24th June, giving onlookers a foretaste of the massive two-funnelled profile of the forthcoming *Queen Elizabeth*, to which she bore some resemblance. The welcome she received left no doubt of *Mauretania*'s importance – hundreds of people watched as she

moved slowly up the North River and not only was there the usual greeting by spouting fireboats but several 'planes flew overhead and accounts of her arrival were broadcast by three radio stations, while *The New York Times* devoted a leader to her. She lay in New York for nearly a week, during which time, it was reported, Cunard entertained 6,800 guests at receptions on board and 12,400 members of the general public visited her.

Her first eastbound crossing terminated not in London Docks, as might have been expected, but at Southampton, from where, on the 19th July, she set off again for New York, helping out in the express service. After that, she at last crossed to London, entering the King George V Dock on the 6th August after disembarking her passengers at Southampton and at Tilbury. On the 11th August, having loaded cargo, she set off on the return voyage to New York. As it turned out, those two crossings were the only ones she would ever make on her intended route. A brief cruise from New York to Halifax and back followed before she made her next eastbound crossing – it was scheduled to take her to London but in the event was terminated at Southampton. She arrived there on the 1st September amid mounting tension.

The curved bridge front - as can be seen in this contemporary painting - and the general arrangement of the superstructure became signature features of a whole generation of Cunard liners. *(Clive Harvey collection)*

On that day, German forces invaded Poland and two days later Britain was once again at war. *Mauretania* made one more transatlantic round trip, carrying civilian passengers and returning to Liverpool, where she lay for two months. It was risky to leave her there, however, within reach of German bombers, and on the 9th December she sailed for the neutral safety of New York, having been given a token armament consisting mainly of two 6-inch guns. Once there, she rested at Cunard's Manhattan pier, on the other side of which lay the *Queen Mary*. Beyond the *Queen Mary*, the *Normandie* was tied up at the French Line pier, while across the slip from *Mauretania*, the great Italian liners continued to come and go for a few more months until Italy, too, entered the War. In March, 1940 the very new *Queen Elizabeth* arrived after her secret high-speed dash from the Clyde and *Mauretania* was shifted from her berth in order to make way for her. By now, the British government had decided that both *Mauretania* and the *Queen Mary* should be turned into giant troopships and on the 20th March *Mauretania* left for a long voyage via the Panama Canal and Honolulu to Sydney where the conversion would take place. She arrived there safely on the 14th April. (The *Queen Mary* left New York a day after her fleet-mate but, being too big to pass through the Panama Canal, she went via the Cape and Singapore.) At Sydney, many of *Mauretania*'s still new civilian fittings were removed and bunks and all the facilities necessary in a troopship intended to carry about 2,000 men were installed.

The early months of her career as a trooper were spent ferrying Australian and New Zealand servicemen. Her first voyage was as a member of Convoy US3, which also included the *Queen Mary*, *Aquitania*, the *Empress of Japan*, the *Empress of Britain* and *Andes* and was guarded by three warships. The convoy left Sydney on the 5th May and, after a long and dangerous voyage via the Cape, reached Greenock on the Clyde on the 16th June, where the 'passengers' were disembarked. Thereafter, *Mauretania* made several voyages from Australian ports (and one from Wellington) to Bombay, and once to Singapore. Most famously, however, she was a member of the convoy which was assembled in April, 1941 to take Australian and New Zealand troops to Suez. Her companions in that amazing cavalcade of great liners were *Queen Mary*, *Queen Elizabeth*, *Aquitania*, *Ile de France* and *Nieuw Amsterdam*. Between them, they were carrying something like 25,000 troops. Later, the capacity of these and the other big troopships was greatly increased and by the end of the War *Mauretania,* for instance, could accommodate as many as 6,000 men. As has often been pointed out, the ability of these ex-liners to move such huge numbers was an important factor in the Allies' ultimate victory. People who sailed on them, though, will testify that it was an extremely uncomfortable experience, particularly in the heat of the tropics.

In June, 1941, *Mauretania* began a long series of voyages which lasted until April, 1942, carrying South African servicemen from Durban to Suez. Another trip to Bombay followed, returning from which she came frighteningly close to colliding head-on with the *Ile de France*. Both ships were, of course, blacked out and made inconspicuous by their wartime grey livery and they were sailing at night through the murk of a dense monsoon. There was very nearly an appalling tragedy. By now, *Mauretania* was in sore need of overhaul and, on her return from another trip to Suez, she lay at Port Elizabeth for six weeks undergoing repairs to her engines and generators but there was no drydock in South Africa big enough to accommodate her and so her next voyage took her across the South Atlantic to Rio de Janeiro, where three years' accumulation of marine growth was removed from her hull, and then to Newport News for further work to be done.

Once back in Durban, she set off on another troop-laden voyage to Suez and then headed for Colombo, Fremantle, Sydney, Wellington, Pearl Harbor (where she arrived on New Year's Day, 1943) and San Francisco. By now – with India and Australia under threat of Japanese invasion; with fighting still raging in North Africa; with Empire forces having seized control of Madagascar from the pro-German Vichy French; and with huge numbers of American and Canadian servicemen being transported to Britain in readiness for the invasion of the Continent – troopships were crossing the oceans in many different directions. *Mauretania* became something of a wanderer, as can be seen from her movements during the first eight months of 1943 – San Francisco, Pearl Harbor, Wellington, Fremantle, Bombay, Diego Suarez (Madagascar), Cape Town, Freetown, Liverpool, New York, Trinidad, Rio de Janeiro, Cape Town, Diego Suarez, Colombo, Suez, Diego Suarez, Cape Town, Freetown, Liverpool.

Then, after drydocking, she joined the Atlantic Shuttle but, unlike the *Queen Mary*, *Queen Elizabeth*, *Aquitania* and several other major liners-turned-troopships, she was based in Liverpool rather than on the Clyde. Between August, 1943 and April, 1945 she made twenty-one voyages from either New York, Boston or Halifax to Liverpool, in the course of which she brought more than 100,000 American and Canadian troops to Britain. While in New York harbour on the 8th January, 1944, she had a slight collision with the tanker *Hat Creek* and required fairly minor repairs. Then, in June, 1944 she spent four weeks in Boston for drydocking and repairs to her turbines.

By the Spring of 1945, with the war in Europe obviously nearing its end, the eastward flow of American and Canadian troops subsided but it seemed that the conflict in the East could last for some time yet. *Mauretania*'s next voyage took her to Suez, Bombay, the Cape and back to Liverpool. By now, intense wartime service and intermittent maintenance had taken their toll of her boilers and she spent five weeks in Liverpool having them re-tubed. On the 3rd July, she sailed via the Panama Canal and Pearl Harbor to Wellington, Sydney and Fremantle, carrying New Zealand and Australian servicemen back to their own countries and then returning via the Cape. There followed another voyage to Bombay and then she reverted to the Atlantic Shuttle for six more round voyages to Halifax and back, but this time mainly taking Canadian troops homewards. It was now mid-1946, the World was at peace and no doubt Cunard-White Star were anxious to regain the use of their liner but, like many other troopships, she was still required for military service. She made a voyage to Bombay and then one to Port Said and Naples, followed by one to Singapore. On that long round trip she averaged 22.84 knots. Her last trooping voyage took her once more from Liverpool to Halifax. Among her passengers was Field Marshal Viscount Montgomery, the hero of the battle of El Alamein. *Mauretania* returned to Liverpool on the 2nd September and was then finally handed over to her owners by the Ministry of Transport. In all, she had steamed 540,000 miles in government service and had carried about 350,000 troops.

Arrangements had already been made for her restoration and only seven days after her arrival she was taken in hand by Cammell Laird as she lay in Gladstone Dock and the process of overhauling her and restoring her to her pre-War splendour began. It was an enormous job and at one stage it involved well over 1,000 workmen. To facilitate the much-needed complete overhaul of her engines, the giant floating crane *Mammoth* came alongside and lifted off the aft funnel (55 feet high and 35 feet across the top). During her war service, over half her cabin accommodation had been removed to make room for the huge number of bunks which had been required. Now it had to be built anew and the furniture which had been removed and placed in storage in Australia and the United States needed to be shipped back to Britain. And at the end of it all, *Mauretania* had to be dry-docked. The pre-War arrangement by which first class on the major Cunard-White Star liners had been called cabin class, so that under the rules of the North Atlantic Passenger Conference cheaper fares could be charged, had been abandoned. When she returned to service her accommodation was listed as 475 first, 390 cabin (ex-tourist) and a much reduced figure of 300 tourist (ex-third). The crew accommo-

After steaming over half a million miles in government service, the *Mauretania* was handed back to Cunard in September, 1946 and was then restored to her former splendour, as seen above. *(Maurizio Eliseo collection)*

Like several other Cunarders, the *Mauretania* had a large decorative map of the North Atlantic, in her case the work of William McDowell. Note the exaggerated size of the British Isles! *(Clive Harvey collection)*

dation had been improved and a number of former third class cabins were now occupied by crew members.

For a time, it was hoped that *Mauretania* would be available to return to civilian service by February, 1947 but there was the inevitable 'slippage' and it was not until a couple of months later that the restoration work was completed. It seems that as late as December, 1946 the intention may have been that she should resume her London – Southampton – New York service – certainly, *Lloyd's List* reported that the forthcoming *Caronia*, which was described as being 'of the *Mauretania* type', would probably join her on that run. In the event, however, the decision was taken that future sailings between London and New York would be made by cargo ships.

The good times were about to roll for Cunard. Although they had lost many ships during the War, their major units had survived. It took some time to bring them back into civilian service but with the German lines out of action, Cunard briefly enjoyed a dominant position in the transatlantic passenger trade such as they had only rarely had in the past. The 'Queens', *Mauretania* and *Britannic*, carrying dollar-spending Americans to a Britain which was virtually bankrupt, were recognised as vital elements in the country's quest for financial salvation. And indeed, the new *Caronia* was being specifically built to earn the all-important dollars. These were egalitarian times in Britain and, naturally, stories of rich passengers living it up in luxurious pleasure palaces aroused resentment

in a country where food was still rationed and taxes were high. But, just as the extravagances of the much-publicised socialite Lady Docker both repelled and fascinated a glamour-starved public, so the big Cunarders and their first class passengers were newsworthy and seemed to be symbols of hope for the return of better times. Britain was still a maritime nation and many people were proud of these ships.

On the 19th April, 1947, *Mauretania* left Liverpool for two days of speed trials in the Clyde. On her return, fierce gales in the Irish Sea prevented her from entering port for three uncomfortable days. Among the invited guests who were marooned on board were such dignitaries as the Mayor and Mayoress of Birkenhead. Finally, on the 26th April, after a very hurried turn-round, *Mauretania* sailed, on schedule and fully-booked, on her first post-War commercial voyage. It almost ended as soon as it had begun as she narrowly missed colliding in the Mersey with the Blue Funnel cargo ship *Memnon*. However, she arrived safely in New York on the 2nd May. She returned to Liverpool but after one more westbound crossing from that port she was based in Southampton for the regular six-day crossings to New York via Cherbourg and, usually, Cobh which were to be her main employment. (In 1949, Le Havre replaced Cherbourg as the French port of call.) One-way fares in 1947 ranged upwards from £81 in first class, from £52 10s. 0d in cabin class and from £40 in third.

It was in 1947 that the interests of the creditors of the old

White Star Line were bought out and Cunard-White Star once again became the Cunard Line. Throughout that year, *Mauretania* steamed back and forth across the Atlantic, at last enjoying the success of which the War had deprived her. Then, on the 10th January, 1948 she left New York on her first post-War cruise, a fortnight's jaunt to Nassau, La Guaira, Curaçao, Cristobal, Havana and back. She repeated it four times before resuming her Atlantic service at the beginning of April. From then onwards, Caribbean cruising out of New York became her regular winter occupation while most of the rest of each year was spent on the Atlantic run. Like the other Cunard passenger liners, she underwent a long overhaul in either Southampton or Liverpool every November or December; and by 1952, brochures for her cruises were indicating that *Mauretania* had been given an outdoor swimming pool, situated on the Sun Deck.

Her cruise itineraries varied quite considerably but for some years a one- or two-night call at Havana was almost always included. Famous for its nightlife, the capital of Cuba had long been a favourite port for fun-loving American passengers. (In the title song of the 1941 Hollywood musical *Weekend in Havana*, the gloriously flamboyant Carmen Miranda had opined that 'You'll hurry back to your office on Monday, but you won't be the same anymore'.) *Mauretania* gained the reputation of being a sea-kindly ship and over the years she proved to be very reliable. Inevitably, though, there were occasional incidents. In November, 1948, a strike of longshoremen brought the port of New York to a standstill and she was diverted to Halifax, from where her passengers were taken to their destination by train. In February, 1949, suffering from what was described as an 'engine irregularity', she limped back from the Caribbean to New York, where

problems with one of her low-pressure turbines were rectified. In August, 1950, during the McCarthy 'Red Scare', dockers in New York refused to unload a hugely valuable consignment of Russian furs which therefore remained on board when she sailed back to Southampton. It was in Southampton that, in April, 1954, she was slightly damaged by a floating crane and that, in September, 1954, she was briefly drydocked for propeller repairs. In June, 1955, she missed an Atlantic crossing because of a seamen's strike, mainly by catering staff, which was afflicting several Cunarders. Her passengers had already embarked at Southampton but now had to leave the ship.

The *Mauretania* made several Caribbean cruises each year from 1948 to 1964. *(Clive Harvey collection)*

With a helicopter hovering overhead, the *Mauretania* enters New York harbour, assisted by a Moran tug. *(Maurizio Eliseo collection)*

On the 22nd December, 1956, *Mauretania* left New York on her most ambitious cruise so far. Lasting 29 days, it took her as far south as Rio de Janeiro. Cruising was becoming more important to Cunard as passenger loads on the regular North Atlantic sailings began to diminish in the face of the growth of air travel. Even before the advent of the jet airliners in 1959, piston-engined 'planes were creaming off an increasing proportion of the business, particularly in the lucrative first class trade. For a decade, *Mauretania* had been very successful as a part-time cruise ship but she dated back to pre-War days and a new generation of modern ships was beginning to come into the New York market. In October, 1957, therefore, Cunard sent her to Liverpool for an unusually lengthy refit by the local branch of Harland & Wolff. Lasting over 100 days, it cost half a million pounds. The public rooms were thoroughly refreshed and, most importantly, air-conditioning was extended throughout both the passenger and crew spaces. During her long stay in the Gladstone Graving Dock, no less than four small fires occurred but fortunately none of them became serious.

On the 1st January, 1959, during a Caribbean cruise, *Mauretania* was forced to bid a final farewell to Havana. With the ship coming under small arms fire during clashes between government forces and supporters of the Castro uprising, passengers who had gone into the town had to be hastily rounded up in order that she could sail as soon as possible. The local dockworkers were on strike in support of the revolution and she was forced to leave without assistance. She was, in fact, the last cruise ship to sail out of the port.

On the 6th August, 1960, while she was leaving Cobh, a rope fouled one of her propellers, delaying her departure by a day since the local diver was on holiday. Details in the casualty report indicate just how important a port Cobh was for *Mauretania* – she had disembarked 153 passengers from Southampton and Le Havre and had embarked 343 for New York.

Brochures were calling *Mauretania* 'The ideal ship for your gay West Indies holiday' but in February, 1962 her cruising horizons widened when she set sail on a 38-day voyage from New York to Las Palmas, Madeira, Lisbon, Gibraltar, Tangiers, Messina, Piraeus, Larnaca, Port Said, Haifa, Naples, Villefranche, Barcelona, Gibraltar again and back to New York. It was later announced that 1962 would be her last full season on the Southampton – New York run and that in 1963 she would start a new service between New York and the Mediterranean. In a further change, Cunard was about to increase its presence in the cruise market. In late 1962, *Saxonia* and *Ivernia* of the Canadian route were converted to make them much more suitable for cruising and were renamed *Carmania* and *Franconia*. They were repainted in the Cunard cruising livery of several shades of green, hitherto worn only by *Caronia* — still, of course, with the company's traditional red and black funnel colours. *Mauretania*, too, was given a new identity – but not a new name. In her annual winter refit, this time at Southampton, her passenger accommodation was rearranged so that she could now carry up to 406 in first class, 364 in second and 357 in tourist and she too was painted in the green cruising livery.

On the 12th December, 1962, she left Southampton for New York, from where she made three Caribbean cruises before embarking on another long one to the Mediterranean. Then, on the 28th March, 1963, she began the new transatlantic service between New York, Naples Genoa and Cannes, calling at Gibraltar in both directions. This attempt to break into the Mediterranean trade was a daring move by Cunard since the stately and by now slightly dated *Mauretania* would be competing against ships which were more in tune with the times – American Export Line's sleek and stylish *Independence* and *Constitution* and the Italian Line's equally modern and glamorous *Cristoforo Colombo* and *Leonardo da Vinci*. The slight increase in *Mauretania*'s tourist class capacity during her latest refit had no doubt been made with an eye to the trade which was likely to be on offer but, in the event, Cunard found it difficult to cope with the inertia of Italian bureaucracy and there were delays in obtaining the necessary permission to carry migrants. The new service was not a success and as early as June the company announced that the season would be terminated prematurely in early October after just eight round voyages. A spokesman admitted that some westbound crossings had carried only about 200 passengers. (Many years later, it was revealed that it was on one of these crossings that Ted Arison and his family had moved to America – Mr. Arison, of course, went into the cruise business himself and now, in a reversal of rôles, his Carnival Corporation, presided over by his son Micky Arison, was taking over the Cunard Line.) Four Caribbean cruises ex-New York were substituted for the two cancelled Mediterranean round voyages and then *Mauretania* returned to Southampton.

It had been decided that she would now try her luck in the British cruise market. On the 14th January, 1964, she left Southampton on a 36-day cruise to the Caribbean followed by others to the Atlantic islands and the Mediterranean, for which she was marketed as a single-class ship. (It was during one of these cruises that it was discovered that several spare bearings, each weighing about a hundredweight, had mysteriously gone missing – presumably during her recent refit in Liverpool.) Then in June, at the beginning of the peak transatlantic season, *Mauretania* returned to her old Southampton – Le Havre – Cobh – New York run. On one of these voyages, she carried a television crew who filmed the voyage. She ended 1964 on a high note when, on the 27th October, she took important guests to Milford Haven for the opening of the Regent Oil Company's new refinery there and entertained the Queen Mother to lunch.

1965 was *Mauretania*'s final year in service. On the previous 23rd December, she had started her second season of cruises from Southampton, again carrying all her passengers in a single class. Her schedule included voyages to West Africa, the Caribbean, Norway and several to various parts of the Mediterranean. Then, in June, she crossed to New York, returning on a cruise-like route via Madeira, Lisbon, La Coruña, Le Havre, Rotterdam, Hamburg and Queensferry. There followed another crossing to New York, from where she made two cruises to Lisbon and back under charter to the Ford Motor Company, who seem to have used them as incentives for high-performing executives. Her final voyage was an amazing cruise whose itinerary is worth recording: she sailed from New York to

Mauretania was painted in the Cunard cruising livery of several shades of green in 1962 but her years of success were over. *(Hugh Lalor collection)*

In 1965, *Mauretania* met her end at Iverkeithing. Above, we see her shortly after her arrival. Below, the ship has already lost half of one of her funnels *(Maurizio Eliseo collection)*

Madeira, Casablanca, Gibraltar, Tangiers, Cagliari, Palermo, Valletta, Alexandria, Beirut, Haifa, Rhodes, Istanbul, Piraeus, Heraklion, Dubrovnik, Trieste, Venice, Messina, Naples, Ajaccio, Villefranche, Barcelona, Palma, Motril, Malaga, Lisbon, Cherbourg and Southampton. The cruise lasted 56 days but, alas, was not heavily patronised – on arrival at Southampton, she was said to be carrying 354 passengers.

On the 20th November, 1965, only ten days after arriving home from that final cruise, she sailed from Southampton for the last time, heading for Inverkeithing where she was to be scrapped by Thos. W. Ward who were reported to have paid £360,000 for her.

Although *Mauretania*'s last few years had been unsuccessful, her disappearance was regretted by many, including the very young Hugh Lalor who, in his childish handwriting, wrote a letter to Cunard pleading for a reprieve for the ship and asking if he could please have one of the models which he had seen in travel agents' windows. It is pleasing to report that, although he did not get his model, he did receive a pile of brochures and several letters addressed to 'Dear Master Hugh'.

Southern Cross

Completed 1955. 20,204 gross tons.

Length overall: 603 ft. 10ins. Breadth: 78 ft. 6ins.

Draught: 25 ft. 10ins.

Geared steam turbines. Twin screw.

Service speed: 20 knots.

Became *Calypso* (19,313 gross tons), 1973;

Calypso 1, 1980; *Azure Seas* (14,673 gross tons),

1980; *OceanBreeze* (21,667 gross tons), 1992.

Scrapped, 2003.

Shaw, Savill's *Southern Cross* was an entirely one-class ship. *(Ambrose Greenway collection)*

The 5th November, 1952 was a big day for Shaw, Savill & Albion Co., Ltd. and for the Harland & Wolff shipyards at Belfast. While the refrigerated cargo ship *Cymric* was being launched, the similar *Cedric* was being prepared to leave for her speed trials. But perhaps most importantly, Shaw, Savill chose the occasion to confirm their long-awaited order for a new passenger liner. She would be the twenty-seventh ship Harlands had built for the line and they had been holding a vacant slipway for her beneath the famous gantries of their Queen's Yard for some months.

In 1952, Shaw, Savill & Albion, part of the Furness Withy group, had a large fleet of both passenger and cargo liners. The passenger ships fell into four very distinct categories. Most prominently, there was the massive-looking 27,000-ton quadruple-screw motor ship *Dominion Monarch* of 1939, which sailed in solitary splendour on what was sometimes very aptly called the 'Clipper Route', the old sailing ship track between Britain, Australia and New Zealand via The Cape. A giant combination liner which could carry huge amounts of cargo, especially frozen meat on her return voyages, *Dominion Monarch* had fine accommodation for over 500 first class-only passengers but tended to be unpopular with her crew.

Then there was a quartet of sturdy post-War 15,000-tonners, again with a large cargo capacity, which could accommodate just 85 first class passengers each. These ships operated on the route to New Zealand via the Panama Canal. One of them, *Gothic*, served as a temporary Royal Yacht during the Queen and Prince Philip's Commonwealth Tour in 1953-4.

The third group consisted of four much older and less prestigious liners which also sailed on the route to New Zealand via Panama (except for the *Arawa* which ran to Australia and New Zealand via The Cape but offered her passengers a cheaper, slower, less grand service than that of *Dominion Monarch*). These ships, too, were quite large cargo-carriers. Shaw, Savill & Albion had inherited three of them from the famous old Aberdeen Line of Geo. Thompson & Co., once a fellow member of the Kylsant group before the collapse of that mighty empire.

Finally, there were the three *Bay* liners which operated on the U.K. – Australia route via Suez under the separate name of Aberdeen & Commonwealth Line. They were members of a group of five emigrant- and cargo-carriers which had been built for the Australian government's troubled Commonwealth Government Line soon after the First World War. When that line's losses became too heavy for the Australian taxpayer to bear, they had been sold to the Kylsant group who placed them under the management of Geo.

Thompson & Co. The *Bay* ships' hulls were henceforth painted in the traditional Aberdeen Line green. By the early 'Fifties the *Bays*, like the vessels in the third group, were ageing and would have to be withdrawn within the next few years.

Decisions clearly had to be made about the future of the company's passenger services. In addition to the looming competition from the airliners, the post-War flow of migrants from Britain was abating and foreign lines operating under flags of convenience were eager to win the official migrant contracts – and, indeed, they did eventually succeed in wresting them from the hands of the British companies. Furthermore, constant labour disputes in the docks and other delays were making it increasingly difficult and costly to maintain a regular schedule with liners which carried both passengers and large amounts of cargo. Shaw, Savill's chairman and managing director was Basil Sanderson, the son of a former White Star Line chairman, and he it apparently was who came up with the idea of replacing some of the older Shaw, Savill & Albion and Aberdeen & Commonwealth ships with a bigger, faster liner devoted entirely to carrying large numbers of so-called tourist class passengers (i.e.: migrants and other travellers in lower fare accommodation) – no first class passengers and no cargo. Without cargo, she would spend less time in port and, using her extra speed, she would be able to make four voyages per year rather than the three which was all that most of the existing ships could manage. Later, in August, 1954, the headline to an article in *Lloyd's List* proclaimed, perhaps with a little hyperbole, 'A Revolutionary Ship. No Cargo Delays for the *Southern Cross*.'

It is said that Sanderson's contention that the most efficient design for such a liner would have the engines and boilers placed as near as possible to the stern was at first met with scepticism but was eventually accepted by his colleagues. In this respect, *Southern Cross* has sometimes been credited with being a great technical innovation but, as I point out in the later chapter on *Canberra*, this was far from the truth. She was, though, the largest passenger ship of this type so far built. To me, it seemed that the funnel was placed so disconcertingly far back that it almost looked as if it might topple off the stern; and despite having a streamlined superstructure and mast, with the bridge placed well towards midships, she looked rather ungainly – certainly less graceful than her later (and much less successful) running-mate *Northern Star*. However, her engines-aft layout, long superstructure and lack of class division did mean that her tourist class passengers enjoyed the full, uninterrupted run of a succession of public rooms and of the huge outdoor decks.

Furthermore, without the intrusion of engine room casings and funnel uptakes the midships area, which is the most stable and comfortable part of most ships, could be more fully utilised. It was, though, admitted that the cost of building the new liner was slightly higher than that of an equivalent ship of more orthodox design.

The keel of the new ship was laid in February, 1953 on the slipway next to the one on which the *Reina del Mar* was also

BETTER TRAVEL...

Shaw Savill

★
★ ★
★

SOUTHERN CROSS
✦
NORTHERN STAR

A typical passenger line brochure of the 1960s.
(Clive Harvey collection)

about to be built and she was launched by the Queen on the 17th August, 1954, a day which was unfortunately marred by high winds and driving rain. This was the first time a reigning British monarch had launched a merchant ship and was a huge honour for Shaw, Savill. Perhaps the *Gothic*'s recent stint as Royal Yacht had influenced the decision and maybe the fact that the new liner would be linking several Commonwealth countries also weighed in her favour. The Queen had, it seems, also agreed to choose which of a list of possible names the new ship should be given and the Royal pin had descended on *Southern Cross*, very suitably for a liner trading with the Antipodes.

Harland & Wolff themselves built the two sets of Pametrada steam turbines (each consisting of a high pressure and a low pressure unit and a reverse turbine) which produced a total of 20,000 shp and were double reduction geared to twin screws. Denny-Brown fin stabilisers were installed; and especially capable evaporators were fitted, not only to supply feed water for the boilers and to satisfy the needs of the passengers and crew but also to provide the ballast needed to maintain the trim of an engines-aft vessel carrying no cargo. (Salt-free water would have to be pumped into the fuel tanks as, one by one, they became empty.) The ship's unusual design was the result of co-operation between C. J. Dixon, Shaw, Savill's naval architect, and R. R. Cameron, his opposite number at Harland & Wolff.

Southern Cross had accommodation for up to 1,160 passengers in 405 cabins. There were 49 single-berth rooms and 194 doubles, a few of which had an additional pullman berth. The majority of the passengers, however, slept in either 4- or 6-berth cabins. The engines-aft layout meant that the designers had been able to include more inside cabins than usual and it was said that it was partly for this reason that the entire passenger accommodation was air-conditioned – as, notably, were some of the crew spaces. One unusual feature was that the inside cabins were fitted with what were called 'sunrise lights' – these came on automatically at 7 am, at first very faintly but gradually getting brighter until 8 o'clock when, having presumably woken up the passengers, they were switched off. The walls in the cabins and passenger alleyways were all covered with either light blue or cream Formica giving 'an airy and attractive appearance' while at the same time reducing cleaning and maintenance costs. In one respect, though, the *Southern* Cross's forward-looking designers failed to anticipate the future – only 32 cabins were given their own showers and lavatories.

Lloyd's List described the ship as 'comfortable but not ornate' – she was, after all, a tourist class liner. The long Lounge Deck housed six public areas, starting with the Forward Lounge, a large room spreading across the full width of the ship and with views through rows of large windows on three sides. Then, separated from the Forward Lounge by curved screens, came the Library and the Writing Room. There followed the Smoke Room, clad in grey veneers made from the long-submerged elm piles of the original Waterloo Bridge in London, dating back to the early nineteenth century. (These had also provided the veneers which furnished the walls of the captain's cabin on the *Queen Elizabeth*.) Next, the two deck high Cinema Lounge, decorated with cherry wood and green leather, was a dual purpose room which not only had a stage and screen but also a dance floor. It had raised side sections and there was a balcony at the far end. Finally came The Tavern, an airy space leading onto the outside deck through large sliding doors. Lower down in the ship were the two restaurants, each with marble pillars and light metal screens with etched glass panels, but one furnished with veneers of figured aspen and the other with figured white ash. There was also a hospital with an operating theatre; and passengers had the use of a shop, two hairdressing salons, a laundry and an ironing room. The décor was light and modern and had a certain unity, most of the rooms having been designed and furnished by Heaton, Tabb & Co., although Hamptons and Maples had also contributed one room each.

Suitably, *Southern Cross* was a very open-air ship with 42,000-square feet of outside deck space. In addition, there were no less than three broad open promenades fringeing each side of the ship and there were two swimming pools, one indoors and one outdoors on the top deck. Separate playrooms were provided for infants and small children while older children had their own recreation room.

Southern Cross's funnel was painted in Shaw, Savill's own dis-

tinctive shade of buff with a black top; and at first her superstructure was pale green, perhaps inspired by the livery of Cunard's *Caronia*. Her hull was grey. Although hardly a luxury liner, she became extremely popular and proved to be very reliable, suffering remarkably few accidents or mechanical problems during her time with Shaw, Savill.

She left the yard for her sea trials on the 22nd February, 1955, returning on the 24th. Finally, on the 3rd March, she sailed for her future home port of Southampton, calling en route at the Clyde, where she ran her speed trials on which she recorded 21.35 knots, and at Liverpool, where she disembarked one party of invited guests and took on another for the rest of this

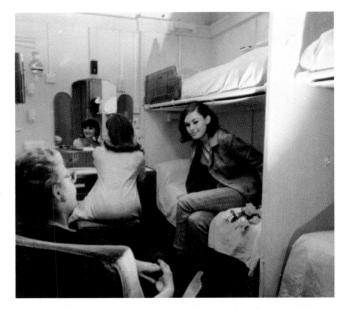

Most of the passenger accommodation on the *Southern Cross* was far from luxurious. Note the exposed beams, pipes and ducts in the picture on the right. *(Clive Harvey collection)*

pre-maiden voyage. Then, on the 11th March, she left Southampton on a brief 3-night shake-down cruise. It was not until the 29th March, that she set off on her official maiden voyage inaugurating Shaw, Savill's new round-the-World service which took her in a westerly direction to Trinidad, then through the Panama Canal and across to Papeete, Suva, Wellington, Sydney, Melbourne, Fremantle, Durban, Cape Town, Las Palmas and finally back to Southampton. The voyage took 74 days and was accounted a great success. Fares for the entire voyage ranged between £226 and £326 (with a supplement for the cabins with private facilities), while passengers travelling only as far as Sydney paid between £116 and £166. Even before her maiden voyage she was fully booked for the whole of 1955.

It was stressed that she was entirely intended to be a liner on a regular service. Nevertheless, after her first voyage she did make three cruises to the Mediterranean. On one of these, she also visited Funchal in Madeira and Oran. For many years after that, however, she made no cruises whatsoever,

concentrating entirely on four circumnavigations per annum – two of these were westabout and two were eastabout. Each year, one voyage would end at Liverpool from where she would slip across the Irish Sea to her Belfast birthplace for an overhaul.

This routine continued uninterruptedly for several years during which the main incident was a brush against a lock gate in the Panama Canal in November, 1957. On a few occasions, the itinerary was varied with a call at Barbados or at Port Everglades and Bermuda; and over the years Lisbon, Auckland, Brisbane, Miami, Caracas and Willemstad also received at least one visit. In June, 1966 *Southern Cross* was delayed by the Seamen's Strike which kept her tied up in Southampton Docks for five weeks longer than usual, inflicting a costly loss of revenue on her owners.

Perhaps the most spectacular event in her career with Shaw, Savill was her proud first meeting with her new running-mate, *Northern Star*, as they swept past each other in mid-ocean during *Northern Star*'s maiden voyage in September,

One of the advantages of *Southern Cross*'s engines aft design was that she had a huge expanse of uninterrupted sun and sports deck space. *(Ambrose Greenway collection)*

1962. *Southern Cross*'s success and the faltering viability of *Dominion Monarch* had prompted the ordering of the new liner, similar in conception to *Southern Cross* but slightly larger and improved where this seemed desirable. *Southern Cross*'s schedule henceforth became three westbound and just one eastbound voyage per annum.

By 1969, Shaw, Savill had changed tack and had decided to make a determined entry into the growing cruise market, both from Britain and from Australia. In February and March, 1970 *Southern Cross* made three trips from Sydney which took her to New Zealand and the South Seas. Then on the 6th June, having returned to Britain, she started a series of five cruises from Southampton to the Mediterranean and the Atlantic islands. Meanwhile, in January, the company had bought a further passenger ship. She had been Canadian Pacific's much-admired transatlantic liner *Empress of England* but for Shaw, Savill she became the tourist class-only *Ocean Monarch* and was eventually sent to the Cammell Laird yard at Birkenhead for a far-reaching reconstruction to make her more suitable for hot weather liner voyages and for cruising. Alas, the project proved to be a disaster both for the shipping company and for the shipyard. The work took five months longer than expected, causing the cancellation of almost an entire programme of cruises and costing much more than the originally estimated amount. (Thirty years later, history repeated itself when the later owners of the Cammell Laird yard were ruined by a contract to reconstruct a passenger ship, this time the *Costa Classica*.)

Through the rest of 1970 and the early months of 1971 *Southern Cross* made a few more round-the-World voyages, twice pausing for a few cruises out of Sydney. Then, with *Ocean Monarch* scheduled to take over the Summer, 1971 cruise programme from Southampton, she was shifted northward to Liverpool from where she ran four cruises, again to Mediterranean and Atlantic island destinations.

But she was living on borrowed time. The British merchant navy was shrinking inexorably – month after month the shipping papers were recording the withdrawal of yet more once-profitable ships. In November, 1970 the Furness Withy group announced that, because of rising costs, there would be a cull of no less than 23 of its ships – including the famous Royal Mail Lines passenger vessel *Andes*. *Southern Cross* was not included in the list of victims but within a few months it was announced that she, too, was to go. There had been an abrupt change in the group's attitude to the passenger business. Little more than a year earlier, not only had the Shaw, Savill & Albion subsidiary announced the purchase of the future *Ocean Monarch* but Furness Withy themselves were making it known that they were looking for a ship which would be suitable for an innovative 'bed and breakfast' cruise service. Now, suddenly, the passenger fleet was being cut back.

AN ITALIAN VIEW OF SOUTHERN CROSS

Like most major shipping companies, the Italian Line kept a watchful eye on what rival lines were doing and they maintained a file of reports on interesting ships belonging to other companies. Among the documents in this file, there is an account by Fiorello Farolfi, the Chief Purser of the *Vulcania*, of a visit he paid to the innovative new *Southern Cross* when she was moored near to the *Vulcania* in Naples on the 19th August, 1955.

Things did not begin well when Farolfi asked to see *Southern Cross*'s Chief Purser but was instead confronted by 'una specie di gigante in uniforme' (a kind of giant in uniform) who turned out to be the Master at Arms. However, he did eventually meet an Assistant Purser, with whom he got on well, and he was allowed to inspect the ship despite this being against the company's rules. With the help of a gift of a bottle of spumante, Farolfi also managed to obtain various items of publicity material.

He must have had a culture shock. The *Vulcania* of 1928 was one of the last survivors of an age when ocean liners, particularly Italians, were sumptuously and ornately decorated, at any rate in first class. Some of *Vulcania*'s first class cabins even had verandahs. The austerity of Southern Cross's cabins did not impress him - he notes, with an emphatic exclamation mark, that only 32 out of her 405 cabins had private facilities. The food appalled him. Where were the antipasti? There was only one kind of soup on offer, and plenty of potatoes. The sweets were 'terribili'. The scanty wine list was merely an appendix to the menu.

There was an almost military discipline about the ship. The restaurant was open for breakfast for only 45 minutes. What shocked him more was that payment for any purchase of wines, tobaccos, etc. had to be made in advance at the Purser's office. And, according to the Passenger Information booklet, "the Commander inspects the steamer every day, circumstances permitting, at 11 am and passengers are requested to vacate their cabins between 9.30 and 11.30 am to enable them to be cleaned and made ready for inspection." Furthermore, "children are not allowed in the Public Rooms, nor are they allowed on the Sun Deck or the Sports Deck, except on the portion reserved for them." Here Farolfi has inserted another enormous exclamation mark. It was also necessary to pay a deposit when withdrawing books from the library. And he wondered why the Purser's office was such an unsafe place that "Passengers may deposit valuables but these lie at passenger's risk and are not insured."

He was completely underwhelmed.

Northern Star was still a relatively young ship and Shaw, Savill were spending large sums of money on the transformation of *Ocean Monarch*, so *Southern Cross* was obviously the one to go. With hindsight, it was an unfortunate decision – over the next few years both *Northern Star* and *Ocean Monarch* suffered persistent and expensive mechanical problems and the *Ocean Monarch*'s crew was prone to bouts of disruptive – and sometimes violent – behaviour. As a result, Shaw, Savill's reputation suffered and in the end they gave up and withdrew from the passenger business.

Meanwhile, having concluded her Liverpool cruise season, *Southern Cross* made one final eastbound circumnavigation, returning to Southampton on the 18th November, 1971. She was offered for sale and for a while lay idly in Southampton docks, latterly at Berth 46 next to the Cunard liners *Carmania* and *Franconia* which had also recently been withdrawn. Then, on the 25th April, 1972 she steamed off to cheaper moorings in the King Harry Reach on the River Fal in Cornwall, where she was joined by the two Cunarders three weeks later. At one time, entrepreneurs hatched a tentative scheme to use her as a floating hotel and leisure centre as she lay in the River Fal but there were local objections and the project was dropped.

Although some adventurous shipowners – for instance Norwegians speculating with profits made in the tanker market – were bringing new cruise ships into service, few of them were interested in taking over a middle-aged ex-liner, particularly when, with oil prices quadrupling between 1972 and 1974, she was powered by fuel-thirsty steam turbines. A further problem was that most of her cabins lacked the private facilities which passengers now expected.

However, *Southern Cross* did eventually find a buyer but the price, approximately £500,000, was little more than her value as scrap. N. & J. Vlassopoulos, Ltd., then a prominent London-Greek family-controlled shipping firm, bought her in January, 1973 and registered her under the Greek flag but in the ownership of a Panamanian one-ship concern, Compañìa de Vapores Cerulea. On the 5th March, 1973, now called *Calypso* and under her own power, she left the Fal for Piraeus, where she arrived on the 13th. The Vlassopoulos family already had one passenger vessel, the former Israeli combi-liner *Zion*, which was being reconstructed as a cruise ship especially for charter to the Thomson travel group. They had called her *Ithaca* since they came from that Ionian island, said to be the home of Ulysses. The choice of the name *Calypso* for their second passenger ship commemorated the

The *Southern Cross* was converted into the *Calypso* by the Ulysses Line at great expense partly because of the need to completely rebuild the cabin accommodation. *(Bruce Peter collection)*

As the *Calypso* she was frequently chartered or block-booked to other companies. *(Author's collection)*

sea nymph with whom Ulysses had a seven year-long fling. Both ships were to run under the family's trade name, Ulysses Line, and the stylised image of a classical Greek sailing ship was painted on their funnels.

The conversion of *Calypso* was a lengthy and costly business. The old cabins were stripped out and completely new ones were installed – importantly, all with private facilities. They ranged from doubles to 4-berths. The ship could now accommodate up to 950 passengers – all, of course, in one class. Most of the public rooms were given a more modern, 1970s-fashionable décor with much less wood. The internal layout was largely unchanged, except that the Library and the Writing Room were re-positioned and the former indoor swimming pool deep down near the bow became a disco. In compensation for that, a second outdoor pool was erected on the open air sun deck above the former Forward Lounge (now called the Ithaca Lounge). The whole of this deck was now sheltered by a substantial windscreen – the only major change to the ship's external shape. She was painted white with thin blue and orange stripes along the sides of her hull. The whole conversion was designed by Technical Marine Planning, London.

It was over two years before *Calypso* was ready for service. Then, on the 25th April, 1975, she left Piraeus on the first of several Mediterranean cruises under charter to the tourist off-shoot of Hapag Lloyd. There followed a round voyage from Dublin to Civitavecchia, presumably carrying Irish Catholics going to Rome to celebrate Holy Year. Thereafter, she mainly operated under the auspices of the Ulysses Line itself, but only very rarely did they handle the actual marketing of her cruises – usually, her accommodation was block-booked by such companies as Thomson Cruises, who offered her voyages in the British market; SÜR in Germany; Zeetours in The Netherlands; TFC in South Africa; and Extra Value Travel in the United States. Often, therefore, she had a very cosmopolitan passenger list. In this she differed from her fleet-mate *Ithaca* which was chartered directly by Thomsons and carried mainly British passengers. *Calypso*'s first cruise block-booked in this way was to Norway, starting from London, Tilbury on the 20th June, 1975 and included a call at Rotterdam to embark Continental passengers. Either this or a call at Zeebrugge became part of her regular routine.

Her first really long-distance cruise as *Calypso* left Rotterdam on the 10th January, 1976 and Tilbury on the 11th, going round Africa, outward via the west coast, then visiting the Seychelles and Mauritius and coming back via the east coast and Suez. On her return, she set off for New York where she arrived on the 28th March and then made eleven cruises to Bermuda, one of which went further to Nassau. Allan Jordan comments 'It was very odd. An advertisement appeared in the paper and she arrived, ran a few cruises and then vanished.' By mid-June, she was back in London and Rotterdam and starting another summer season – at first to Norway and the Baltic and then to the Atlantic islands and to the Mediterranean.

There was then a slightly obscure episode in which *Calypso* is recorded as passing through the Suez Canal on the 18th October and as lying at Jeddah on some unspecified dates. In those days, Mohammedans making the Hajj pilgrimage would often sail to Jeddah in specially chartered ships before starting the long overland journey from there to Mecca. In many cases, the ships would remain at Jeddah for several weeks awaiting the return of their passengers. The Hajj in 1976 fell in November and December and it therefore seems probable that *Calypso* had been taken up for a Hajj voyage. The as yet unanswered question is: where did she go to pick up her white-clad pilgrims embarking on this most important spiritual journey of their lifetime; and then again to return them – was it Pakistan, India, Bangladesh, Malaysia, Indonesia? One of the last three seems most likely.

In her early days with the Ulysses Line, she had several mishaps – she brushed up against the *Høegh Dene*; and on another occasion one of her reverse turbines was disabled; then, twice in 1976, her propellers were fouled by towing wires.

The mid-'Seventies were not a good time to have entered the cruise business. The World fell into recession but costs were still rising. Ulysses Line admitted that they had lost money on their passenger operations in 1976. Negotiations to renew the arrangements under which Thomson Cruises used the two Ulysses ships ended in disagreement over price and Thomsons turned instead to Epirotiki Lines but soon withdrew from the cruise market altogether. It was not until the mid-1990s that they returned.

However, having lain at Piraeus since she had made that Hajj voyage, *Calypso* re-entered service in March, 1977, running a programme of cruises out of Rotterdam and London (later Zeebrugge and Southampton), more or less as before. Ulysses Line had now taken over the British marketing themselves. During the late months of that year, *Calypso* was operating out of Piraeus and Genoa and made a long trip down to South Africa. 1978 saw some springtime Mediterranean cruises, followed by the usual Rotterdam and London programme, then back to the Mediterranean before embarking on another visit to South Africa, which included a couple of cruises from Durban to Mauritius. Throughout 1979, *Calypso* operated

out of either Genoa or London, but with Amsterdam replacing Rotterdam.

That proved to be the end of her European career. Ulysses Line had entered into an agreement with the Paquet Line, a famous old French shipping company who had been operating in the American cruise market for some years. The two Ulysses ships were now to be based in Miami and their cruises would be sold by the French company under the label Paquet Ulysses Cruises. *Ithaca* would be called *Dolphin IV* but *Calypso* would retain her name. Whereas *Dolphin IV* was to run 3- and 4-day 'fun cruises' from Miami to the Bahamas (which she did very successfully for many years), *Calypso* was to be employed on longer voyages. As I write this, I have in front of me a brochure which says: 'Welcome to cruising à la *Calypso*. It's the style of French chefs. The taste of free dinner wines. And the excitement of a unique experience.' By now, her original Cinema Lounge had become a cabaret theatre and a conference lounge had been added to the facilities. A block of new cabins had been built out forward on Atlantis Deck and two of the other cabins had been combined to form a suite.

On the 6th January, 1980 *Calypso* left Miami on the first of a series of 7-day cruises to Nassau, San Juan, St. Thomas and Puerto Plata (Dominican Republic). May saw her making a positioning voyage through the Panama Canal to Acapulco, Los Angeles and San Francisco and by the 6th June she was in Vancouver starting a season of sixteen 7-day cruises up the Inside Passage to Alaska.

Then, quite suddenly, she changed hands. During her season sailing out of Vancouver, she was bought by Western Cruise Lines, a new offshoot of the Eastern Steamship Lines, which was itself owned by the Norwegian shipping company Gotaas-Larsen. Eastern had for some years been successfully operating *Emerald Seas*, a much-converted American P2 troopship, on 3- and 4-day cruises from Miami to the Bahamas. This was the same route on which Paquet Ulysses Cruises were running *Dolphin IV* and it was profitable – a few hours of very slow and economical overnight steaming combined with either two or three days when the ship served as a static floating hotel. Eastern now wished to replicate this formula on the West Coast with cruises out of Los Angeles (San Pedro) to Ensenada in Mexico. (From 1988 onwards a call at Catalina Island was also included.)

It was reported that the new owners paid $23 million for *Calypso* (which had recently been re-named *Calypso 1*) and that they spent a further $4 or $5 million on refitting her. In particular, the forward sun deck had its swimming pool removed and was enclosed to accommodate a large casino. On the 14th November, 1980, the much-travelled ship started her new service, flying the Panamanian flag and now called *Azure Seas*. Her funnel had been re-painted blue and bore a reproduction of her new owners' flag. Brochures described her as a 'Big Do-As-You-Please Party Boat' and 'The Spacious Party Boat for Frolicking and Feasting', leaving little doubt as to the kind of cruising experience she offered. In this new career, she proved to be highly successful.

In October, 1986, the Eastern and Western companies merged with Sundance Cruises of Seattle to form a new line called Admiral Cruises. Sundance, the recent brainchild of Stanley McDonald who had previously founded Princess Cruises, was running *Stardancer*, a 40,000-ton ex-ferry, on cruises to Alaska and to Mexico. The newly combined Admiral Cruises may be said to have lacked cohesion, with its somewhat rag-bag fleet (a former troopship dating back to 1944, an ageing ex-liner and a converted ferry, admittedly very modern) operating on a variety of geograficially diverse routes. However, it had ambitions and was soon ordering a new 48,000-tonner. Except that she now wore a ring of five white stars on her blue funnel, the merger did not greatly affect *Azure Seas*.

Gotaas-Larsen were not only part-owners of Admiral Cruises but also had a major interest in the much larger Royal Caribbean Cruise Line, which was one of the most important players in the growing Miami-based cruise market. In 1988, Royal Caribbean took over Admiral Cruises, which did, however, continue to operate as a separate entity within what was now called the Royal Admiral group. Quite large amounts of money were spent on *Azure Seas*, particularly during a refit in 1989 from which she emerged with a larger casino, a smaller theatre and an additional twelve suites – indications, perhaps, of the preferences of her passengers.

On the 21st December, 1990, while lying at her Los Angeles berth, she was scraped by the Israeli container ship *Zim Iberia*. Luckily, although damage was extensive it was superficial and after temporary repairs she was able to make a delayed start to her next cruise. Then in May, 1991, after almost eleven successful years and more than one thousand 3- and 4-day cruises out of Los Angeles, she was replaced by the bigger and better *Viking Serenade*, the former *Stardancer*, which had been transferred to the Royal Caribbean fleet and extensively rebuilt and upgraded. *Azure Seas* was shifted to Port Everglades from where she began making 7-day circuits round the eastern Caribbean to Coco Cay, San Juan, St. John and St. Thomas.

But inevitably there were doubts about her future. Only a few months later, it was announced that the Admiral Cruises operation was to be closed down and that its two elderly and relatively down-market steamers had been offered for sale. There was no place for them in the Royal Caribbean fleet of huge new ships offering passengers a range of facilities which boggled the mind. Quickly, *Azure Seas* was bought by Dolphin Cruise Line, successors (under different ownership)

to the Ulysses Line. She would once again be a fleetmate of her old friend *Dolphin IV*.

The former *Southern Cross* thus started yet another new career in May, 1992 when, as *OceanBreeze* and now registered in Liberia, she began sailing on 7-day cruises from Aruba which included calls in Martinique, Barbados, St. Lucia, Bonaire and Curaçao. On some cruises, she would

In 1980 the former *Calypso* became the West Coast fun ship *Azure Seas*. *(Author's collection)*

make a 'partial transit' of the Panama Canal. (This was really a 'taster' to give her passengers the experience of travelling along the canal – she would enter the flight of the Gatun Locks, be raised to the level of Gatun Lake, where she would sail for a while, and then return again to sea level.) *OceanBreeze* now wore Dolphin's white livery with three blue and green bands sweeping upwards at the bow and then continuing along the hull. Her funnel bore the stylised outline of a leaping dolphin. To use a piscatorial analogy common in the cruise business, Dolphin were 'bottom feeders' (i.e.: they operated at the cheapest level of the market). They were often acknowledged, though, to offer their passengers rather good value for their money.

Further change came in May 1996 when, following the sale of *Dolphin IV*, *OceanBreeze* took that ship's place in the 3- and 4-day market out of Miami to Nassau and sometimes to Cozumel. Six months later, her base for these cruises was moved to Port Everglades. Although she was now over forty years old, it was considered worthwhile to give her a refit to bring her into compliance with the new 1997 SOLAS safety regulations, including the removal of considerable amounts of woodwork. This was a restless period in the ship's long career and in June, 1997 she moved to New York to take over a short programme of cruises to Halifax, Portland and Newport originally scheduled for her fleetmate *IslandBreeze*, the former *Transvaal Castle* (see a later chapter). After that, she was posted to Montego Bay in Jamaica for a new series of Caribbean cruises including calls at Cartagena and San Blas and, again, a visit to the Panama Canal.

Dolphin Cruise Line had been purchased by a company called Cruise Holdings which also owned Seawind Cruises. Cruise Holdings also acquired Premier Cruise Line whose sole remaining vessel was the former Home Lines' *Oceanic,* which was by now called *Starship Oceanic*. They also bought Holland America's famous *Rotterdam*, which they renamed *Rembrandt*. They thus had a fleet of six classic veteran steamers – in addition to the former *Southern Cross, Transaavaal Castle, Oceanic* and *Rotterdam,* there were also the ships which had once been the *Federico C.* and the *Infante dom Henrique.* The entire fleet was now operated under the name Premier Cruises and most of the ships had dark blue hulls with the line's name painted in large letters along their sides. Their funnels bore a new logo of a ship's prow. Unfortunately, Premier's business model proved to be flawed. With competition increasing from the spectacular, ever-bigger vessels of the major groups, it became more and more difficult to

As Premier Cruises' *OceanBreeze,* the now almost 40 years old ship was part of a fleet of vintage ex-liners. *(Bruce Peter collection)*

extract a profit from these old and expensive-to-run ex-liners. In January, 1999 *OceanBreeze*'s career veered off in yet another direction. Premier Cruise Line chartered her to a new company called Imperial Majesty Cruises, which had been set up by Floridan hotel interests to run two-night cruises from Port Everglades to Nassau. Still named *OceanBreeze*, she retained her blue hull but now bearing her charterers' name near the stern and with a golden crown on her funnel. Then, in May, 2000 Imperial Majesty Cruises bought her outright for $16 million. It seemed ironic that, having in her youth enjoyed great success on the longest sea route in the World, she was now apparently doing well in a service which involved very little sailing at all. Once again, luck had been with her – she had escaped Premier's undignified re-branding of its fleet as Big Red Boats and then its bankruptcy which, after ignominious and lengthy detentions, ended the active careers of most of her fleetmates. In the end, *OceanBreeze* did not outlive some of them but her last years were very much happier than theirs.

During her time with Imperial Majesty, I saw her in Nassau. She was still looking smart and was emitting satisfying steamship sizzling sounds. Bruce Peter sailed in her during this period and remarks: "For a liner designed in the early-1950s, she looked remarkably modern – futuristic even. Some forty-plus years later, she still retained something of that 'things to come' quality in her highly curvaceous silhouette. But viewed close up, the detailed design of the outdoor spaces could have been found on a British liner of the inter-War era

She was very well-maintained (except for the forward sun deck which was covered in soggy blue woollen carpeting which stank of fungal growth) [...]. The pièce de résistance of her interior décor was the flamingo feather chandeliers in the casino – definitely not from the Shaw, Savill era!' His favourite haunt was the outdoor café at the stern 'where they provided tea and delicious cakes under a wavy awning. There one could best enjoy the quiet of being on a steam turbine liner, with only the sound of the ship's wake and steam hissing from the safety valves on the funnel way above.' On one occasion, he chatted with a Ukrainian seaman who was enjoying a cigarette break on deck. 'He gestured towards the *Island Escape*, a former Soviet ferry, which was tied up at the next berth. "Ferry stronk sheep,' he opined, 'But these one is eefen stronker."'

Time finally caught up with her in 2003, when Imperial Majesty seized the opportunity to buy the slightly older but dieselised, and therefore more economical, *Regent Empress* whose owners had just gone bankrupt. In July, *OceanBreeze* was sold to Indian shipbreakers who then re-sold her to Bangladeshi breakers. She arrived at Chittagong under her own power in October but before she could be beached she was battered by a storm. Suffering hull cracks, she began to list but was eventually rescued by tugs. She was finally dragged up onto the beach on the 8th November. Demolition was briefly delayed by the appearance of possible buyers but nothing came of their intervention and in the end the forty-eight year old *OceanBreeze* was dismantled.

The final phase of the career of this much-travelled ship was in short trips out of Port Everglades for Imperial Majesty Cruises. *(Bruce Peter collection)*

Reina del Mar

Completed 1956.

20,234 gross tons.

Length overall: 600 ft. 9ins.

Breadth: 78 ft. 4ins.

Draught: 30 ft. 1in.

Geared steam turbines. Twin screw.

Service speed: 18 knots.

Re-built as cruise ship, 1964 (21,501 grt).

Scrapped: 1975.

Much reconstructed, *Reina del Mar* became a successful cruise ship. *(Ambrose Greenway collection)*

Britain and the British played a huge part in the development of South America in the nineteenth and early twentieth centuries. Of all the commercial enterprises involved, one of the most influential was the Pacific Steam Navigation Co. This venerable concern dated back to 1838 and had been established with a Royal Charter. Its main route was from Liverpool to the west coast of South America, making the long trek round the toe of the continent until, in 1914, the opening of the Panama Canal considerably shortened the voyage and transformed the trade. For many years, the Pacific Steam Navigation Co. was an extremely important concern, not least because between 1877 and 1905 it also participated in the Orient Line service to Australia. In 1910, it was bought by the Royal Mail Steam Packet Co. It survived its parent company's collapse in the early 'Thirties but in 1938, after a few years of semi-independence, it once more became a subsidiary, now owned by the re-formed Royal Mail Lines, Ltd. (part of the Furness Withy group).

By that time, many of the South American countries had become much less lucrative markets for British companies. Nevertheless, the ships of the Pacific Line (as the Pacific Steam Navigation Co. was sometimes known) still ran a frequent service to a whole succession of often quite small ports strung out along the coasts of Colombia, Ecuador, Peru and Chile. Mostly, they were cargo vessels but there were also a few sizeable passenger liners which, en route, also tapped into the trade to and from Bermuda and the Caribbean.

In 1931, the company had introduced the splendid new 20,000-ton *Reina del Pacifico* (Queen of the Pacific), a very typical Harland & Wolff motorliner. A contemporary shipping journalist commented enthusiastically on the 'ornate Spanish Moroccan décor' of her first class accommodation. For some years after the Second World War, the *Reina del Pacifico* was left to maintain the company's passenger service on her own. However, in 1953 it was decided that she should have a running-mate although there was some doubt over whether there would be sufficient trade to keep two ships profitably employed throughout the year. Accordingly, the *Reina del Mar* – for such the new liner was to be called – was designed to be suitable for part-time cruising although, in the event, she only made one specifically cruising voyage for the Pacific Steam Navigation Co.

Like the *Reina del Pacifico*, the *Reina del Mar* (Queen of the Sea) was built by Harland & Wolff at Belfast but, unlike the older vessel, she was a steamship. Modern development of the marine steam turbine had made it in some respects more competitive with the diesel engine and the new ship was pow-

ered by Parsons turbines, built by Harland & Wolff themselves, which gave a total output of 18,700 shp and were double reduction geared to twin screws. The hull was partly riveted and partly welded, prompting the comment in one of the shipping journals that she might well be one of the last liners to be built in this way since recent research had confirmed that the relatively smooth surface of completely welded hulls gave a more efficient passage through the water.

Like most passenger liners of the time, she also carried cargo, for which she had five holds, three forward and two aft of the machinery spaces. In the contemporary manner, she was a single-masted ship with most of her 17 cargo-handling derricks attached to king-posts. She was, in fact, rather stylish-looking with a raked and slightly rounded bow, a curved bridge front and a streamlined funnel.

She was launched on the 7th June, 1955 by the wife of Mr. H. Leslie Bowes, the company's managing director, in the presence of the ambassadors of Colombia, Ecuador and Peru and the Prime Minister of Northern Ireland. Much later, after *Reina del Mar* was completed, Mr. Bowes revealed that she had cost about £5 million, 12½% above the original estimate, which was considered to be a fairly good outcome in the conditions prevailing at the time. Interestingly, fitting her with the stabilisers and air-conditioning which passengers were now coming to consider essential had cost roughly £500,000 – half the £1 million which had been the price of the entire *Reina del Pacifico* in the early 'Thirties. Understandably, fares on the new ship were slightly higher than those on the old one.

The company had not ordered a new passenger liner for a quarter of a century and, although presumably the more experienced Royal Mail Lines parent may have had an input, the passenger quarters of the new vessel shewed evidence that the designers had been instructed to start with a completely blank sheet of paper. The list of designer/contractors for the passenger spaces reads like a roll call of some of the most prominent British furnishers of the day: Hampton & Sons; Maple & Co.; Waring & Gillow; Heaton Tabb; and White Allom. Despite this, there was clearly a unity of style throughout most of the ship. It was a modern style, but restrained and tasteful. As the correspondent of *Lloyd's List* wrote, 'Milk bar chromium is conspicuous by its absence'.

Reina del Mar was a three-class vessel, carrying up to 201 passengers in first class, 218 in cabin class and 343 in tourist class, a total of 762. Perhaps because she was intended for possible use as a nominally single-class cruise ship, there was said to be less difference than usual in the standards of the first and second class passenger quarters. In first class there was a choice of either single- or two berth-cabins, including seven designated as special and four as de luxe (two of which could be converted into sitting rooms linked with the adjacent cabins). Each special or de luxe cabin had decorations suggestive of one of the countries which were to be served by the ship. All cabins in first class had private facilities with either a bathtub, a hip bath or a shower. The single fare from Liverpool to Valparaiso in one of the de luxe cabins was £490 per person. The first class areas contained much light-toned wood veneer and, when she was introduced to the press, there was comment on the quality of the woodwork throughout the ship – said to be a feature of a number of recent Harland & Wolff-built liners. There was also much use of Formica and other plastics, including several sculptures made of Perspex. The extensive range of first class public rooms included, low down in the most stable part of the ship, a domed restaurant overlooked by a musicians' gallery. Mainly clustered on the promenade deck, there were a pleasant forward-facing enclosed verandah; a domed lounge decorated in green and gold; the library; a writing room; a card room which was more traditionally styled than the other rooms; a cocktail bar; a colourfully decorated smokeroom; an outdoor lido café surrounding the swimming pool on the after deck; two rooms for children (a dining saloon and a playroom); and a children's paddling pool (prudently fenced in on the seaward side). First class passengers enjoyed an ample amount of outside deck space, including open promenades along part of the length of the superstructure and an observation platform on top of the monkey island. All classes could enjoy film shows in the new-fangled Cinemascope system, either in their lounges or outdoors.

Cabin class passengers slept in one-, two-, three- or four-berth cabins, naturally somewhat smaller than those in first class. They did not have private lavatories, baths or showers. A few of them on C Deck were interchangeable between first and cabin class. Situated towards the after end of the ship, the cabin class public rooms were, some commentators felt, quite as attractive as those in first class, although slightly more simply furnished. Tourist class passengers were consigned to one-, two-, three-, four- and six-berth cabins in the bow of the ship. Their public rooms were said to be far superior to those on the *Reina del Pacifico*, as indeed were the crew quarters. The tourist class fares from Liverpool to Valparaiso started at £125.

Reina del Mar's introduction into service was perhaps rather overshadowed by that of Canadian Pacific's new *Empress of Britain*, which came out at about the same time, but she was a fine ship nonetheless and was said to be 'the largest and fastest liner in the west coast trade'. Someone described as 'Our Special Correspondent' wrote in *Shipbuilding and Shipping Record* 'Would I like to travel to South America on the *Reina del Mar* in preference to other ships? Definitely.' It may not have been utterly coincidental that the Italian

As built, with her streamlined bridge front and aerodynamic funnel, the *Reina del Mar* was a smart and modern-looking ship. (*Clive Harvey collection*)

Line chose that moment to announce that next year they would be transferring the magnificent *Conte Grande* to their Genoa – Valparaiso service.

Reina del Mar was completed in March, 1956 and ran her speed trials between the 20th and the 22nd. She arrived in her home port of Liverpool on the 9th April, where she was handed over to her owners. On the 20th, she left on a three-day 'shake-down cruise' to the Western Isles. Then on the 3rd May, she set out on her maiden voyage. Before heading out across the Atlantic, she put in at La Pallice on the Biscayan coast of France (an unusual port of call for a passenger liner) and at Santander and La Coruña in Spain. Ships on the South American routes usually carried considerable numbers of Spanish passengers, particularly emigrants and seasonal workers who travelled in what was often euphemistically called tourist class. For this reason, the *Reina del Mar* carried a Spanish doctor in addition to the English-speaking medical staff. Her next call, after a 7-day transatlantic passage, was at Bermuda where she anchored in Grassy Bay since she had too deep a draught to be able to get into Hamilton harbour. Then she made a round of Caribbean ports – Nassau, Havana, Kingston and the Ecuadoran port of Cartagena. (On many later voyages, with the company anxious to pick up as much extra trade as possible, she also called at Trinidad, Curaçao, La Libertad and at La Guaira in Venezuela.) After transiting the Panama Canal, she sailed down the Pacific coast, calling at Callao (Peru) and Arica, Antofagasta, Valparaiso and San Antonio (all in Chile). Jim Nurse, who in his youth was a junior officer on two of the company's freighters, tells me that at some of these west coast ports Pacific swells could make docking and mooring difficult. The *Reina del Mar*'s first outward voyage had taken 34 days. On the return leg she made additional calls at Mejillones, Pisco and Vigo and at Plymouth to disembark London-bound passengers. This was certainly a very port-intensive service. Subsequent voyages followed more or less the same pattern until the changes in Cuba following Fidel Castro's 1959 revolution caused *Reina del Mar* to cease her calls at Havana a year later.

Apart from three small and quickly extinguished fires, one of which delayed her departure from Liverpool by a day, *Reina del Mar* led an unexciting life for several years until she was held in Liverpool for two weeks in July, 1960 by a seamen's strike which had started on the Cunarder *Carinthia*. Then in 1963 she suffered a bout of turbine trouble and also had a few fairly minor bangs and scrapes.

Although she had been designed with the possibility of cruising in mind, it was not until the 29th December, 1961 that she sailed on a slightly more cruise-like trip – one of her regular South American voyages, but with additional calls at Las Palmas in the Canary Islands, Fort de France and at Bridgetown (Barbados). Thereafter, her line voyages over each

New Year holiday period took in some extra, tourist-attractive ports such as Madeira and Port Everglades. But even then she remained emphatically a liner on a regular route – except in August, 1963 when she made her one and only dedicated cruise for the Pacific Steam Navigation Co., a 16 day round trip from Liverpool to La Coruña, Naples and Lisbon. For

The service to the west coast of South America carried both English- and Spanish-speaking passengers.
(Clive Harvey collection)

this voyage she ran as a two-class ship, her cheapest berths being offered for as little as £50.

The days of the old-fashioned liner services were numbered. With trade withering, *Reina del Pacifico* was sent to the breakers in 1958, leaving *Reina del Mar* to carry on alone until the company abandoned its passenger service altogether in 1964. The final sailing left Liverpool on the 2nd January, returning on the 5th March.

It was a desperate time for passenger shipping and many fine liners were being sent prematurely to the scrapyards. However, *Reina del Mar* escaped that sad fate. A South African entrepreneur, Max Wilson, had persuaded the Canadian Pacific, Royal Mail and Union-Castle lines to invest in an ingenious scheme to popularise cruising in the British and South African markets. Members of the public were invited to make regular deposits of cash with an organisation called the Travel Savings Association, which would pay them interest. When subscribers had accumulated sufficient money in their account, they could use it to buy one of the cruises to be run by the operating company, Travel Savings, Ltd. These commenced in 1963 and at first used Canadian Pacific's *Empress of Britain* together with *Empress of England* and the ageing *Stratheden* (chartered from P&O). It was decided,

however, that the Travel Savings Association, often known simply as TSA, should have a dedicated ship specially converted to suit its requirements. *Reina del Mar* was about to become available and she was sent to her builders in Belfast for a far-reaching refit. She lay at Musgrave Wharf from the 10th March to the 30th May, 1964, undergoing a major operation which at one time involved 1,200 workmen. It was estimated that the work would cost nearly £600,000 but some reports said that eventually the figure was more like £750,000. But all was not well with TSA. Costs, particularly those involved in running the savings scheme, were proving to be too high. For this reason, the charter of *Empress of Britain* was terminated prematurely and negotiations were started with Anthony Chandris with a view to his taking a 20% stake in the venture and purchasing *Reina del Mar*, which the Chandris Line would operate with a cheaper Greek crew. This naturally caused an outcry but, in the event, the negotiations collapsed. Then, shortly before *Reina del Mar* was due to start her first cruise, Max Wilson resigned as Managing Director and it was agreed that the ship should be managed by the British & Commonwealth Shipping Co., Ltd., the parent of the Union-Castle Line. This was perhaps thought to be a convenient arrangement since their South African organisa-

The dining room, with its domed roof and musicians' gallery, contrasted sharply with the Spanish style of the equivalent room on the *Reina del Pacifico*, the running mate of the *Reina del Mar*. *(Clive Harvey collection)*

tion would be well-placed to oversee those cruises which were to be based in Cape Town.

The conversion had wrought considerable changes in *Reina del Mar*. The lowest passenger decks now extended into what had been the cargo spaces in the bow, with the very deepest being below the waterline; and the space once occupied by the tourist class dining room was given over to more new cabins. A two-deck high block of new superstructure, topped by an open sports deck, was thrust out over the former forward cargo holds. It contained yet more cabins and a huge lounge able to seat no less than 650 people and with what was claimed to be the largest bar afloat. Higher up the ship, a 321 seat cinema was built onto what had been the first class sun deck and above that was a balcony overlooking the sports deck. These substantial alterations at the forward end of the ship drastically altered her appearance – not for the better, it

On this page, a first class cabin, the lido and the snug cocktail bar. *(Clive Harvey collection)*

has to be said. Less obtrusively, the superstructure at Boat Deck level was extended aft to accommodate an enlarged lido area. Aesthetically, the re-shaped *Reina del Mar* certainly did not compare favourably with some of the handsome conversions made in Italian yards about this time. However, the addition of 135 new cabins and of extra berths in some of the existing ones increased her passenger capacity to 1,047. Many cabins still lacked private facilities and it was announced that on some cruises she would sail as a two-class ship while being designated a single-class vessel on others. To cater for the larger number of passengers, the first class dining room had been extended into what had originally been the cabin class lounge and smoke room.

On the 10th June, 1964, *Reina del Mar* left Liverpool wearing black TSA logos on her yellow funnel. She was carrying 746 passengers to New York and back but there was still uncertainty about her future. A journalist who enquired whether the scheduled season operating out of South Africa and the cruise to Japan for the Olympics would actually take place was told 'That is the plan at the moment' but, in fact, the Japanese cruise never happened. The ship made two more New York trips that summer and a single 14 day cruise from Liverpool to the Canaries and Madeira. On her third voyage to New York, instead of returning to Liverpool she

made for Southampton, which henceforth became her base – partly, perhaps, so that she could be integrated into Union-Castle's operations from that port. Over the next few years, her cruises from Southampton were almost entirely 14-day jaunts to the Canaries or, more frequently, to various Mediterranean destinations.

In October, Union-Castle bought out the other partners in the TSA operation. The savings scheme had been closed down in July and from now on *Reina del Mar* would sail as an orthodox cruise ship under the Union-Castle name. Within a month, she was repainted in the Union-Castle colours of red and black funnel and the famous lavender hull. Henceforth, she always sailed as a single-class ship with her capacity slightly reduced to 1,026 passengers. Despite these changes, she remained in the ownership of the Pacific Steam Navigation Co. until, in 1969, she was transferred within the Furness Withy group to Royal Mail Lines. She remained, under charter to Union-Castle, however.

Meanwhile, on the 1st December, 1964, she sailed for Cape Town to begin her first season of cruising from that port. It consisted of three round voyages to Buenos Aires, Montevideo, Santos and Rio de Janeiro, although not always in that order. She arrived back in Southampton on the 21st March, 1965 and quickly

Much reconstructed, the *Reina del Mar* became a popular Union-Castle cruise ship, a frequent caller at ports in the Canary Islands. Unusually, her name appeared on the stern three times *(Bruce Peter collection)*

resumed her cruises to the Mediterranean. Over the next decade, as Union-Castle's only dedicated cruise ship, she continued to divide her time between the British and South African markets. As David Hutchings noted in his book *Southampton Shipping*, 'She was very popular and could often be seen well down on her marks as she sailed through The Solent, heavily laden with passengers'. In her book *Union-Castle Line Purserette*, Ann Haynes quotes from letters she wrote to her parents while she was working on *Reina del Mar* in April, 1966: "The passengers are mostly middle-aged with some very young teenagers and a few in between. Most of the older people seem to come from 'up North' [...]. 971 passengers on board, one death so far [...]. (At) the Masked Ball I wore a black mask, with white lace doilies round the edge, and a red rose. Helped judge the passenger masks [...]. We always seem to have something to do and we always seem to be in port or getting ready for the next one [...]. Oh well, it's great fun [...]. It's quite a ship!'

1966 was an eventful year for *Reina del Mar*. In June she lay, three abreast between *Edinburgh Castle* and the cargo mailship *Good Hope Castle*, in the Western Docks, Southampton during the disastrous 45 days-long Seamen's Strike. Then, in October, she had to be docked at Southampton without the aid of tugs during another strike. December was a particularly troublesome month, with the failure of a boiler draught fan causing her to put back into Cape Town shortly after leaving; and then a bent blade making it necessary to take one of the turbines out of action.

In those days, still in the aftermath of the Cold War, cruises to countries of the Soviet Block were something of a rarity but in 1967 *Reina del Mar* varied her Mediterranean programme with a single Baltic voyage which included a call at Leningrad. In each of the next three years, and again in 1973, she made a similar cruise with visits either to Leningrad or Helsinki. The only other deviation from her regular pattern came in March, 1973 when she made a longer than usual cruise which took her to the Caribbean once again – four weeks from Southampton to Tenerife, Port of Spain, Trinidad, Antigua, Point à Pitre, Fort de France, Barbados, Madeira and back to Southampton.

Over the years, Union-Castle ships were the setting for some notable crimes, such as the murder of Gay Gibson, a young actress, by a steward on *Durban Castle* in 1947 and the theft of a substantial amount of bullion from the strong room of *Capetown Castle* in 1965. The loss of £29,000 – worth well over a quarter of a million in 2009 money – from the Purser's safe on *Reina del Mar* in July, 1971 was not as tragic or as sensational but it was still a serious crime and attracted attention in the Press, not least because it followed recent thefts on the *QE2* and *Australis*. Police boarded the ship on her return to Southampton and interviewed all the passengers and members of the crew. As far as I have been able to ascertain, the thief, or thieves, were never apprehended.

In October, 1973, the Union-Castle Mail Steamship Co., Ltd. finally bought *Reina del Mar* from Royal Mail Lines, Ltd. However, the rocketing price of oil and the rise in other costs soon claimed her as a victim. Although she was still extremely popular, she could no longer generate sufficient revenue to be profitable. Hindered by a damaged propeller, she returned to Southampton at the end of her 1974-75 South African season and lay idle for nearly two months during which time she was sold to Japanese metal merchants who passed her on to shipbreakers in Taiwan. On the 28th May, she sailed for Kaoshiung where demolition commenced in December.

She lost some of her good looks when she was converted for cruising with the addition of extra forward upperworks and the lumpy structure of the cinema behind the bridge. *(Clive Harvey collection)*

Oriana

Completed 1960.

41,923 gross tons.

Length overall: 804 ft. 0ins.

Breadth: 97 ft. 2ins.

Draught: 32 ft. 0ins.

Geared steam turbines. Twin screw.

Service speed: 27½ knots.

Scrapped 2005.

The Orient Line was never afraid of giving its ships an unorthodox apperance. *(Bruce Peter collection)*

When she was launched in November, 1959, several notable claims were made for the Orient Steam Navigation Company's *Oriana*. She was briefly – until the launch of *Canberra* four months later – the largest passenger ship built in Britain since the *Queen Elizabeth* had taken to the water in 1938. A more permanent distinction was that she was the biggest liner ever to come from an English yard. She was also said to be the first British liner with a bulbous bow – a sorry commentary on the conservatism of our naval architects and shipbuilders in the years before and after the War. More creditably, it was also stated that 'by means of a system of transverse propulsion, she will be the first liner able to move sideways under her own power' (in more modern parlance, she was to be fitted with side thrusters). Later, it was claimed that she had more electronic navigational and other devices than any other merchant ship.

The P&O company had for many years had a major financial stake in the Orient Steam Navigation Co., Ltd. There had, though, always been cultural differences between the two, such as P&O's employment of large numbers of crew members from the Subcontinent whereas the Orient liners usually had all-white crews. Also, since the mid-'Thirties, décor on the Orient ships had been lighter and less conservative than that favoured by P&O. But increasingly the Australian passenger services of the two companies were being co-ordinated.

For many years, in fact, *Oriana* ran in double harness with P&O's new *Canberra* (see a later chapter). Roy Turner, who was Naval Architect Director at Vickers-Armstrongs' Barrow-in-Furness shipyard, tells me that the plan had been to have four new ships, two for each company, but in the event the third and fourth were never ordered. Both *Oriana* and *Canberra* were much larger than earlier ships in their owners' fleets and they were both ultra-modern. However, they differed sharply in several ways. Most obviously, *Canberra* was sleek and streamlined whereas *Oriana* was massive and chunky. Orient Line's naval architects, led by Charles F. Morris (who later wrote a fascinating book setting out the very practical considerations which often led them to prefer function over conventional fashion) and those of Vickers-Armstrongs, were never afraid to be unorthodox when there seemed good reason. As far as propulsion machinery was concerned, though, *Oriana* was the more conventional of the two liners, having her engines and boilers in a roughly midships position while on *Canberra* they were placed further aft. And *Oriana* had geared turbines whereas *Canberra* was powered by a turbo-electric system. What both ships had in common was that they were very speedy and reduced the passage time between Britain and Australia by about a week, with *Oriana* being the quicker of the two. Some people preferred one, some the other; and there was always a frisson of rivalry between the two ships and between their fans.

As I explain in the later chapter on *Canberra*, the 'Fifties and the 'Sixties were a time when the lines vying for the passenger traffic on the routes from Britain and Europe to Australia were raising their game, introducing a string of bigger, better and faster liners. *Oriana* and *Canberra* were the Orient and P&O companies' quite sensational responses to the challenge. Furthermore, they were designed with an eye to developing a greater presence on the trans-Pacific routes onto which the Orient Line had begun venturing in 1954.

Detailed discussions with Vickers-Armstrongs (Shipbuilders), Ltd. had been going on for some considerable time when, in late August, 1956, it was confirmed that the order for *Oriana* had been placed. Vickers-Armstrongs and their predecessors had already been responsible for ten Orient ships, including every one commissioned since the *Otranto* of 1926. Furthermore, nine of them had come from Vickers' Barrow-in-Furness yard rather than the former Armstrongs' yard on the Tyne. (In remaining faithful to this one builder, the Orient management differed from the P&O people who tended to 'shop around' and who, it was said, had been miffed when, in the early post-War years, Vickers had yielded to government pressure to give priority to three ships for the Dodero Line of the Argentine rather than to the new liners which P&O needed so urgently. It seems that the Peron government in Buenos Aires was threatening to suspend desperately needed shipments of meat to Britain, where tight food-rationing was still in force, unless the Argentine order was given precedence. According to Roy Turner, completion of P&O's *Chusan* was delayed by three months and about 300 already recruited Indian seamen had to be accommodated on board the unfinished ship throughout that time.)

The willingness of the Orient Line's naval architects and management to approach the design of new ships without too many ingrained preconceptions is particularly evident in the exterior shape of *Oriana*. As on her predecessors *Orcades*, *Oronsay* and *Orsova*, her bridge was placed almost amidships. This, it was claimed, gave its occupants a better view aft when she was manoeuvring in confined spaces. Although she was not a large cargo-carrier, she did have five holds with a capacity of approximately 200,000 cubic feet (50,000 cubic feet of which was refrigerated) yet there was relatively little conspicuous clutter of gear on her decks – just eight discreetly placed

As can be seen from these renderings taken from an introductory brochure, *Oriana* had an unusually angular appearance both internally and externally. *(Paolo Piccione collection)*

electric cranes. The two cranes on the foredeck were mounted on rails which ran transversely across the deck, enabling them to load and unload on either side of the ship. Stores and baggage were loaded through side ports. Except for a short signal post, *Oriana* was devoid of either kingposts or masts. The design of the hull, with a prominent knuckle at the bow, had been fixed after tank tests of no less than sixteen differently-shaped models.

To save weight, aluminium alloy was used for the pre-fabricated and welded superstructure with the result that it was possible to add an extra deck and to increase the passenger capacity by about 150. Critics would say that this, and the ship's much derided 'boxy' design, gave her a rather 'built-up' appearance. The highest placed 'box' was surmounted by a relatively modest funnel which was sometimes described as looking like an inverted plant pot. This shape was echoed further back and lower down by a similar structure which provided ventilation for the engine room.

Several generations of Orient Line ships had been given galleried sterns. On *Oriana* this was carried to an extreme with no less than three levels of open stern deck. Most strikingly, though, her twenty lifeboats (made from the relatively new glass-reinforced plastic material) were stowed in specially designed gravity davits suspended along high, open promenades within the ship's sides. They were thus 30 feet nearer the waterline than would have been the case had they been sited on the top deck. (Placing the lifeboats within the ship's sides was not a new idea – the Californian pleasure steamer *Catalina* had a similar arrangement as early as 1924 as, more significantly, did Royal Rotterdam Lloyd's *Willem Ruys*, laid down before the War but not completed until 1947 – nevertheless, its adoption for *Oriana* and *Canberra* was notable.) *Oriana* was given Denny-Brown fin stabilisers and, as already mentioned, had a bulbous bow and two sets of side thrusters, one fore and one aft. Roy Turner makes the point that fuel capacity on *Oriana* was carefully planned so that on the Australian run she needed only to refuel at Aden or Colombo where prices tended to be cheaper, whereas *Canberra* might find it necessary to top up elsewhere. So proud of *Oriana* are Barrow men that such facts are still cherished. However, Mr. Turner does concede that the decision to fit the ship with DC electrics rather than AC, as on *Canberra*, seems in retrospect to have been unduly conservative.

Oriana was driven by two sets of Pametrada steam turbines, forward power in each case coming from a high pressure, an intermediate pressure and a low pressure unit. These had been built by Vickers-Armstrongs themselves and were double reduction geared to two propellers. Together they could achieve a maximum output of 80,000 shp, which enabled *Oriana* to record the very fast mean speed of 30.64 knots on her trials. To put that into context, it was a full half knot faster than the figure achieved much later by *Queen Mary 2* which is probably the speediest large passenger ship sailing to-day.

At first, *Oriana* had a passenger capacity of 688 in first class and 1,496 in tourist class. The first class cabins housed either one or two passengers and all had private facilities with, as on *Canberra*, special taps dispensing iced drinking water. The most expensive accommodation was in a special suite on Stadium Deck with its own sitting room, dining room, pantry and verandah. Like a few of the other first class cabins, it had a television set – then a cause for comment. There were six other suites, less extensive but still with verandahs. Some of the other first class cabins were, again as on *Canberra*, arranged on either side of 'courts' – short passages leading to the sides of the ship – so that even inside cabins could have windows which gave natural light, albeit indirectly. The tourist class cabins were all either 2- or 4-berth but some of them were criticised for being rather cramped. Indeed, it was accepted that cabin accommodation on the

Orient Line ships was generally somewhat inferior to that on their P&O rivals. However, on *Oriana* all passenger accommodation in both classes was air-conditioned, as – laudably – were the crew's quarters.

Ever since the ground-breaking *Orion* of 1935, the interior design of the Orient ships had been entrusted to the architect Brian O'Rorke. Supported by Sir Colin Anderson, who was a member of one of the line's founding families and a director of the company, he had given the fleet a distinctively light and modern style. *Oriana*'s interiors, however, were the work of quite a large team, led by Mischa Black although Brian O'Rorke was still very much involved. Among the other contributors were the well-known firm of Ward & Austin. There was, nevertheless, a unity of style – very angular and very nineteen-fifties, with a quite daring choice of colours. Like the present day Fred. Olsen, snr., Sir Colin was personally responsible for the selection of the often very modern artworks which adorned his company's ships.

First class passengers had a whole range of public spaces including the small Red Carpet Room, which was used for lectures, concerts and other special events; and The Look Out, a forward-facing observation lounge which, at its other end, faced the Stadium. (The Stadium was an open but sheltered area which was one of two outdoor spaces reserved for first class passengers, who, of course, had their own swimming pool.) The Plough Tavern was named after a recently demolished Victorian pub in London, some of whose elegantly etched windows had been rescued so that they could be installed on *Oriana*; while the spacious Princess Room had a large mural by John Piper. In addition, first class passengers were provided with their own ballroom; a Junior Club room for their children; the curiously named Monkey Bar; Port and Starboard Galleries; a library; a shop; a restaurant; and the Silver Grill - an extra tariff dining room with its own kitchen, bar and lounge. (Superior alternative restaurants of this kind were a feature on Orient Line ships but disappeared some time after the fleet was merged into that of the parent P&O company.) There was a two-level cinema where first class passengers occupied the balcony, leaving the body of the hall to tourist class.

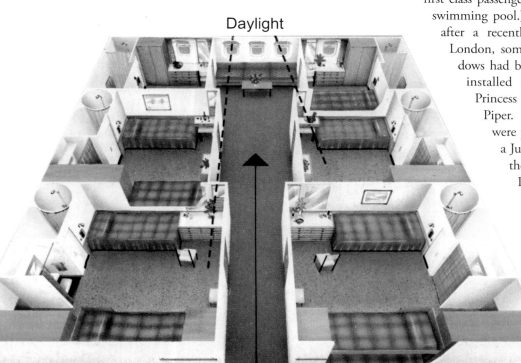

Daylight

Court

As on the *Canberra* (seen here), some groups of cabins were laid out to form "courts" which allowed even inside rooms to receive some natural light. *(Author's collection)*

Most of the tourist class public rooms were lower down in the ship and situated towards the after end. However, the airy Ocean Bar was high up on Verandah Deck and led out to one of the two tourist class swimming pools. In addition to further deck space, tourist passengers also had all the usual public rooms, perhaps the most notable of which were the Midships Bar, the Ballroom and, especially, the Stern Gallery with its 100 feet long crescent of full-height windows. The tourist class restaurant was also on a large scale, occupying the full width of the ship and able to seat no less than 784 diners.

Oriana's keel was laid on the 18th September, 1957. The occasion was marked on all the existing ships in the Orient Line fleet, scattered around the globe, when, at the exact moment, passengers and crew members drank a toast to the new liner. She was launched on the 3rd November, 1959 to the sound of a specially-commissioned fanfare written by Benjamin Britten. The ceremony was performed by Princess Alexandra, whose portrait was later to be hung on board. An engine room telegraph had been specially set up on the launch platform and the Princess started the liner moving down the slipway by shifting the lever from 'Stop' to 'Slow Ahead'. As Arthur Crook explains in the following chapter, it had been necessary to dredge the area at the end of the slipway so that the launch could be safely accomplished. (In fact, such a big ship was altogether a tight fit at Barrow. Later, as she was towed through the entrance to the dock system where the fitting out berth was situated, there was only about a foot of clearance on either side. Then, there were difficulties in mounting the funnel because the crane was hardly tall enough. And, according to *Lloyd's List*, the ship had to be tilted slightly so as not to foul the underside of a bridge when she left the docks.) She was called *Oriana*, thus following Orient's tradition of giving their liners names beginning with 'Or'. The name *Oriana*, in fact, harked back to the pseudonym for Queen Elizabeth I sometimes used by sixteenth century poets but in this case it was also intended as a compliment to the present day Queen Elizabeth II.

On the 4th November, 1960, the new liner left Barrow for drydocking at Falmouth and then for her trials. The weather was particularly stormy and for a time, off the Cornish coast, she got into quite serious difficulties. There are various accounts of exactly what happened. According to one source, the Suez Canal light door (the opening in the bow behind which was installed the lamp required on all vessels passing through the canal) was stove in. To enable repairs to be made, the ship was turned so that she had her stern to the waves – but then the quartering sea caused such a roll that the generators failed due to the lubricating pumps to the gearboxes losing suction. For an hour the ship was deprived of power. Other sources allege that severity of the situation was increased by the fact that the non-return flaps (i.e. flaps in the sloping ducts which connect tanks on one side of a ship with those on the other and which are forced shut when liquid begins flowing in the wrong direction) had for some reason not been fitted. As a result, the ship's list was accentuated but was eventually suppressed by cross-ballasting (i.e. liquids were transferred from one side to the other). At the height of the crisis, the ship was listing so severely that a piano broke spectacularly loose and crashed down a stairwell. Presumably the speed trials took place in rather kinder circumstances but, even so, it was thought that *Oriana* would have achieved an even higher speed had the weather been more benign. She was formally handed over to her owners on the 13th November, when it was revealed that she had cost something between £14 and £15 million. On the 15th, she arrived at Southampton which was to be her homeport – she was considered too big to use Tilbury which had been the base for several generations of Orient liners. To accommodate her and the forthcoming *Canberra*, the Southampton port authorities had built a new terminal at Berths 105 and 106.

On the 22nd November, *Oriana* set off on a 5-day shakedown cruise to Lisbon and back; and then at 2 pm on the 2nd December she began her first commercial voyage on her intended route. Like so many previous Orient liners, she called at Naples, passed through the Suez Canal and then continued to Aden and Colombo before striking out across the Indian Ocean to Fremantle and then to Melbourne and Sydney, which she reached on the 30th December. Her arrival marked the opening of a new passenger terminal at Circular Quay which had been specially built for her and for *Canberra*.

The *Oriana* was specifically designed to be able to pass through the Panama Canal. *(Maurizio Eliseo collection)*

P&O Cruises 1978

Fly/Cruises, Tours and Island Holidays

To the Aegean, Black Sea, Egypt,
Mediterranean, Canaries, Caribbean, The Fjords, Baltic and USA

ORIANA

P&O Cruises

From there she sailed on a brief cruise to Hobart, Wellington, Auckland and back to Sydney.

Then she began her first trans-Pacific crossing. In recent years, the Orient Line ships had been making occasional sailings from Sydney to Honolulu, Vancouver, San Francisco and Los Angeles. Sometimes they came back to Britain eastwards through the Panama Canal; sometimes they returned westwards by way of the Australian ports and Suez. By now, with P&O having bought out the remaining independent equity shareholders in the Orient company and with the passenger operations of both concerns being jointly marketed as P&O-Orient Lines, a more concerted attack was being made on the Canadian and West Coast American markets.

Oriana left Sydney on the 18th January, 1961, eventually reaching Vancouver on the 2nd February, San Francisco on the 5th and Los Angeles on the 8th. She was back in Sydney on the 28th and then set off for home via the Suez route, reaching Southampton on the 24th March, 1961. It had been a very successful maiden voyage although *Oriana's* unusual looks had no doubt aroused mixed reactions among her beholders, as indeed they continued to do for the rest of her career.

During the next few years, her schedule was quite varied. Occasionally, her outward voyage by way of Suez took her no further than Sydney and she would then return the way she had come. More often, she would head on to Auckland, Suva, Honolulu, Vancouver, San Francisco and Los Angeles and then either complete an entire eastward circumnavigation or turn back to Sydney before sailing home in a westerly direction. Sometimes, she would interrupt her voyage in Sydney in order to make one or two cruises to New Zealand ports and to the South Seas. Further variations occurred after 1963 when, having reached Los Angeles, she sometimes proceeded home via Yokohama, Kobe, Hong Kong, Singapore and Colombo; and, on other occasions, she now went out in a westerly direction, calling at Bermuda, Port Everglades and elsewhere before passing through the Panama Canal on her way to Los Angeles. And in 1964, she began making a 10- or 14-day cruise from Southampton every year in July and August.

Opposite page. In addition to making long liner voyages, *Oriana* was also a very succesful cruise ship. *(Author's collection)*
Above. She was a familiar sight in Sydney harbour for a quarter of a century. *(Ambrose Greenway collection)*

In 1964, the gradual integration of the Orient Line into P&O was taken a step further when the pale yellow hulls of the Orient ships, usually described as corn coloured, were repainted in P&O white and their funnels became a deeper yellow. The disappearance of the very distinctive Orient livery was greatly regretted in many quarters. However, for *Oriana* there was the consolation that she now carried a model cockerel above her bridge, signifying that she was the fastest ship in the P&O fleet. Two years later, the Orient Line name and flag finally disappeared from the passenger trades but, in *Oriana*, Orient had bequeathed to P&O a hugely successful ship which is said to have paid for herself within her first five years of service.

In 1966, the P&O group lost their contract from the Australian government to carry subsidised migrants. This was no doubt a considerable blow. It was not regretted, though, by many of the tourist class stewards who had found the migrant passengers demanding and disinclined to give tips, while their children could be very troublesome. 1966 was also the year of the great Seamen's Strike but *Oriana* was not affected as she was well away from British ports throughout that period. However, the 1967 Arab-Israeli War and its lengthy aftermath did take its toll on her operations as the Suez Canal was closed until 1975, forcing shipping to take the much longer route round the Cape of Good Hope.

Inevitably, there were several quite serious incidents during the ship's career. On the 3rd December, 1962, she collided with the American aircraft carrier U.S.S. *Kearsarge* while approaching Los Angeles in a dense fog. The two ships met each other almost head-on and the liner's bow was seriously gashed but fortunately it was possible to make temporary repairs before she resumed her voyage four days later. There followed an acrimonious dispute between the U.S. Navy and the Orient Line.

In February, 1966, one of *Oriana*'s holds was flooded when huge waves broached the hatch. Then, in April, 1968 she made violent contact with a rock in the Panama Canal while avoiding a tanker which had lost steerage control. *Oriana* not only damaged her starboard propeller but also jolted the shaft out of kilter. Both were replaced but it has been alleged that she was never again quite able to achieve the very high top speed which had once been within her reach. She completed her voyage to Southampton on one propeller and, of course, arrived several days late. This and the time she then spent in the King George V dry dock meant that her next voyage was delayed and a subsequent cruise from Sydney had to be cancelled.

In June, 1970, fire broke out in the engine room but it was extinguished before too much damage had been done. More serious was another fire which erupted in the boiler room two months later, fortunately without loss of life. *Oriana* had only just left Southampton and, once the blaze had been extinguished, she was towed back to port. Damage was considerable. Ted Scull was on board at the time and he and other passengers had the unusual experience of remaining on the ship for three days while she was in the King George V dry dock. Repairs took six days in all. In May, 1978, while on a cruise from Southampton to the Caribbean, *Oriana* was the object of a bomb scare. However, a bomb disposal squad which was flown out to her could find nothing and it was concluded that it was all a cruel – and expensive – hoax.

Earlier, from 1969 onwards, with passenger bookings for her liner voyages being eroded by the growth of air travel, *Oriana* had begun to make many more cruises, not only from Southampton and from Sydney but also from her regular ports along the Canadian and American west coasts. These latter excursions sometimes involved two transits of the Panama Canal, interspersed by a visit to the Caribbean. By 1973, she was making just two liner voyages each year – outward to Sydney in November-December and then, at the end of the Southern Hemisphere summer, home to Southampton in March-April. It was on one of these homeward voyages that, during her call at Nassau, she embarked numbers of officials and other British residents who were returning home after the Bahamas gained their independence. In later years, one of her more notable cruises was in August – September, 1980 when she sailed from Southampton for Quebec, Montreal, Corner Brook, Boston, New York and back to Southampton. According to Kevin Griffin, she had to dock downstream of the Jacques Cartier Bridge at Montreal as she was too big to pass under it.

One consequence of cruising becoming her predominant purpose was that her class divisions were abolished. Changes made in the mid-1970s included, as already mentioned, the replacement of the elite Silver Grill restaurant by additional cabins. Nevertheless, her regular passenger capacity was reduced to 1,677, with some of the less desirable accommodation being improved. She continued to have a following of extremely loyal regular passengers but there were beginning to be comments that some of her once smart furnishing was becoming a little shabby.

Her career changed forever when P&O recognised that their luxurious *Sea Princess*, the former Swedish liner *Kungsholm* which had been running year round out of Sydney, was not entirely suitable for their Australian market which included a large proportion of young passengers and which, in any case, required a bigger ship. Accordingly, *Sea Princess* was brought home to serve the British market – where she became very successful – and *Oriana* was permanently stationed in Sydney to take her place from early 1982. *Oriana* left Southampton on her final liner voyage on the 12th November, 1981. As so often before, she went westward via the Panama Canal, Vancouver, San Francisco and Los Angeles. P&O proudly pointed out that, with *Canberra* joining her each year during the Southern Hemisphere summer season, Sydney would be playing host to the World's third and fourth largest passenger ships, with a combined capacity of well over 3,200 berths. In fact, this decision by P&O may be said to have changed history – if *Oriana* had been in British waters in April, 1982, she too might have been requisitioned as a troopship during the Falklands War, perhaps taking the place of the *QE2* whose turbines had the reputation of being unreliable. And *Oriana*, too, might have become a national heroine.

However, she had already arrived in Sydney on the 21st December, 1981. Some changes had been made to render her more suitable for the younger Australian market – a gymnasium had been installed, the Midships Bar had become more like a pub and a hamburger bar had been built. Some would say that a great ship was being 'dumbed down' but there is no denying that she was hugely popular during her time in Australia. Her new schedule took her to the various New Zealand and South Pacific ports she had visited so many times before but every year there was at least one longer

cruise which included a stay in either Hong Kong or Singapore during which she was drydocked.

Popular though she was, *Oriana* was struggling with mechanical problems and was becoming expensive to operate. After only four years as P&O's permanent Australian cruise ship, it was announced that she would be withdrawn on the 27th March, 1986. Bruce Miller, *Steamboat Bill's* Sydney correspondent, reported that her last few cruises were emotional affairs, with crowds gathering to see her final departures from the main Australian ports and with the other ships in the harbours sounding their sirens in farewell.

On the 28th May, after a short lay-up, *Oriana* made her 482nd and last departure from Sydney Harbour. She was on her way to Osaka, having been sold the previous month to a Japanese construction and development group, Daiwa House, who intended to use her as a static hotel, conference centre and museum in Beppu Bay, in an area famous for its hot springs. After a refit at an Osaka shipyard, during which her funnel and ventilator were painted pink, she opened for business in August. But making a success of running an old liner in this way is extremely difficult, as successive operators of *Queen Mary* would attest.

The last nineteen years of *Oriana*'s life were spent as a floating hotel and leisure centre in various ports in the Far East. *(Peter Knego)*

Oriana remained at Beppu until the 17th July, 1995 when she left under tow for Qinhuangdao on the Chinese coast. She had been sold to an organisation called the Hangzhou Jiebal Group to become a floating hotel and an accommodation centre for government use.

This employment lasted until late 1998 when she was towed away to become a tourist attraction at Pudong, a newly developing riverside area of Shanghai. It would seem that Hangzhou Jiebal had an interest in the company which now owned her. After an expensive refit, she began this latest phase in her long career on the 18th February, 1999 but, despite featuring in the city's Millennium celebrations, she was unsuccessful in her new rôle and was closed and put up for sale in 2000.

Jonathan Boonzaier visited her shortly before this happened and was bitterly disappointed by what he found. "She looked a magnificent sight tied up on the Huangpu River but the story on board was the complete opposite. The interiors of the ship were completely gutted leaving only the bridge, a handful of first class cabins and part of the engine room as token displays of the original ship. Every other exhibit on board was a fake mock-up in 'Hello Kitty Cutesy style' and all public rooms had been removed and replaced by large banqueting halls and restaurants. Even the original dining rooms had gone. I can only describe her as a tatty tourist trap."

Perhaps surprisingly, she eventually attracted a buyer, this time from the city of Dalian in eastern China. Her new owners transformed her interiors – it would seem in a spectacular, very Chinese way. They described her as an Emperor's Palace, more prosaically as a museum, banqueting hall and part of a theme park. She was opened to the public in 2002 but we shall never know whether she would have been a success in the long run because on the 17th June, 2004 the area was hit by a ferocious storm. *Oriana* was ripped from her moorings and, with a huge gash in her bow, she ended up listing heavily and partially flooded. Her owners did not immediately give up, however. They patched her up, stabilised her and sent her to a shipyard. Mercifully, perhaps, it was decided that it was not worthwhile to attempt to repair and restore the old liner and, in August, 2005, demolition began at a scrapyard at Wayou.

Jonathan Boonzaier comments, "In my opinion, she'd purposely put herself out of her misery." Peter Knego had also visited her in Shanghai and he too hated what had been done to her but "I was thrilled to see her one last time and loved her strange architecture. I wish ships could be even a fraction as interesting as *Oriana* and *Canberra* and their quirky legion now."

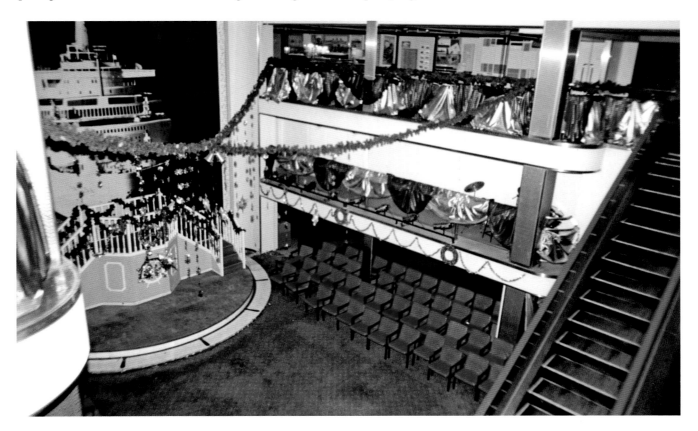

During her time at Shanghai, *Oriana*'s interiors were greatly reconstructed; one of the main rooms was the Great Hall. *(Peter Knego)*

Above, the ship's very characteristic Orient Line stern now bore the names of both Shanghai and London. Below, the glorious name of the once proud flagship of the Orient Line is about to disappear for ever at the scrayard at Wayou.
(Peter Knego; and Julian Nicholas at www.oceanlinermuseum.co.uk)

BUILDING THE ORIANA
By Arthur W. Crook

I was employed by Vickers-Armstrongs at Barrow-in-Furness from 1944 to 1959 (when I was approached by Lloyd's Register to join them as a Passenger Ship Safety Surveyor). During my last seven years with Vickers I was a member of the Naval Architects' Department (the design office). There, I was involved in many of the design calculations for the *Oriana*, including the preparation of hydrostatic and other stability curves and the subdivision curves, plus the launching calculations which, I remember, resulted in a considerable amount of dredging at the way ends in Walney Channel in order to allow *Oriana*'s bulbous bow to drop safely from the slipway when she entered the water. In fact, she was sucessfully launched on the 3rd November 1959 and was towed round to her fitting-out berth.

She was specified by her owners to have a cruising speed of 27½ knots, as distinct from the 20-22½ knots of her

The intricate body plan of a large passenger ship is drawn on the floor of the mould loft in a shipyard in the early 'Sixties. *(Maurizio Eliseo collection)*

Orient Line and P&O predecessors. She also had to be able to pass through the Panama Canal as the Pacific Ocean was becoming a popular cruising area. In order that, after being launched, she could enter the Barrow dock system and then, when she was completed, be able to exit it, her beam was restricted to just over 97 feet. (The dock entrance was 100 feet wide).

So as to save weight and improve stability, it was decided to use aluminium alloy in the structure for the higher decks. This allowed a complete extra deck to be added without adversely affecting her stability. However, because of the chemical effects of sea water upon bi-metallic joints, considerable thought had to be given to the method of attaching the aluminium alloy structure to the steel hull. Also, due to the Board of Trade's requirements for double fire insulation on load-bearing aluminium structures (because of the low melting temperature of aluminium) a great deal of research had to be undertaken to ascertain which of these structures were load-bearing. I was assisting a colleague in the Naval Architects' Department in this exercise until I left Vickers in 1959.

It may be of interest to readers to learn how ships of this type were built in those days before computers, huge building deck blocks and outside elevators became the norm. In fact, nowadays naval and interior architects, equipment suppliers, classification societies, ship-operating personnel, etc. could not function without computers and thus many individual skills of the 'Fifties, 'Sixties and 'Seventies have been lost. I hope that the following account will give the general reader some idea of the sheer complexity of the shipbuilding process, the enormous resources needed to construct a ship of the *Oriana*'s type and the talent and skill of the people involved.

Owners would approach one or more shipyards with their requirements for a new vessel, based upon experience with previous ships of their own (or belonging to rivals) and would indicate various parameters – size; speed; range; passenger numbers; standard cargo capacity; ports of call (with any beam or draught or height limitations which applied there); delivery date; and price range. The shipyard would then develop a design and specification (if not already produced by the owners) based upon previous successful vessels and the owners' requirements. After the ship's basic dimensions had been fixed, a small scale plan of the body lines would be produced in order to enable the hydrostatic properties to be calculated and the ship's form to be established. (This was known as a design body plan).

Scale models would then be built and would be tested while being propelled at varying speeds and drafts in a large tank. (Vickers had their own testing tank at St. Albans). The object was to check the theoretical calculations which had already been made of power/speed values, based on extrapolation from previous ships and other published data. The new vessel's lines could then be further refined by ship designers in the Naval Architects' Department and passed on to the Mould Loft. This loft was a huge room with a flat floor on which kneeling men drew an exact, full-sized body plan of the ship, showing every single side frame section. The distance between the frames would already have been agreed by the classification society (Lloyd's Register or one of several other bodies, such as the Bureau Veritas) who established the scantlings (i.e. the size and thickness of the steel of these frames and of the plating, the keel size, the deck details, etc.). A midship section would be produced on this basis, including any extra stipulations the owners might have made regarding, for instance, the thickness of the keel or other plating.

From the enormous body plan on the floor of the Mould Loft, wooden templates were made to the shape of each frame and shell plate so that the Plating and Frame Bending Shops could produce each one exactly to the necessary shape and size, ready for erection on the launching ways where the keel and the double bottom structure would already have been laid. As part of my training during my apprenticeship, I worked in the Platers' Shed for a few weeks – I particularly remember how very hot it became as great plates of steel were heated and bent into shape.

While all this physical work was happening, the naval architects would carry out further stability calculations based on the results of the hydrostatic calculations and curves. These curves were produced from the original design body plan and involved what are known as Simpson's Rules which establish mathematical formulae for areas under curves. In those days, calculations were made entirely by hand, using slide rules (both flat and circular – the circular barrel type (Fuller's Patent) was the equivalent of a flat side rule many metres long and thus gave accuracy up to 5 or 6 decimal places I still retain mine for old time's sake). Devices called planometers were used to calculate area, while integrators were used for some other figures. Mathematical calculations were made by the naval architects without the aid of electrical calculators – it was all a world away from the age of computers, although sometimes crude adding machines were used to check long columns of figures. An attempt would also be made to calculate the eventual lightweight, vertical and longitudinal centre of gravity of the vessel when empty (i.e. without liquids, stores or personnel). The results could only be verified much later, at the time of the inclining experiments after the ship had been completed.

The next stage was to decide on the spacing and height of the watertight bulkheads within the hull in relation to the ship's anticipated draught and the resulting freeboard. This was done after it had been decided which SOLAS (Safety of Life at Sea) Convention, and any subsequent national rules, would be applicable to the ship. The *Oriana* was built to comply with the regulations stipulated in the 1948 SOLAS Convention (which had become applicable by international law in 1952). The calculations regarding the bulkhead spacing ('subdivision calculations' as they were known) depended upon passenger numbers and their disposition relative to the waterline and the bulkhead deck (i.e. the deck up to which the bulkheads extend).

When it had been decided how high the bulkheads would extend and how they would be spaced, more calculations were required to arrive at the flooding and damage stability results. (Laid down by SOLAS, these rules are governed by certain assumptions regarding the nature of the possible collision damage. On what is known as a one-compartment ship the aim is to ensure that she will stay afloat if the hull has been breached in the area between a pair of watertight bulkheads. On a two-compartment ship such as the *Oriana* it is assumed that there has been an impact destroying a watertight bulkhead which has caused the flooding of two compartments. Other assumptions are made regarding whether the flooding takes place only above the double bottom (i.e. the space between the lowest deck tank top and the outer bottom shell) or whether the double bottom is also flooded. Which assumptions are made depends upon which SOLAS convention is being applied. These flooding calculations govern the decision regarding the ship's operating maximum draught. By contrast, the draught on cargo vessels (i.e. those which carry 12 or fewer passengers) is allocated by the Load Line (Freeboard) Convention.

Once the position and the height of the bulkheads had been determined, the question of the disposition of the machinery spaces had to be considered and agreed with the yard's Engineering Department, who would already have been made aware of the shipowners' requirements regarding speed, fuel consumption, range, auxiliary electrical loads, etc. and would have prepared machinery designs for the engines, boilers and auxiliary equipment based upon the required horsepower, the propellers and shafts and the electrical load, etc. Needless to say, there was always a dispute between the engineers and the naval architects regarding the allocation of space for the machinery.

Then the size and position of all the tanks for the liquids on board would have to be decided, bearing in mind the space available, the vessel's range and the ports at which she would be fuelled; and the capacities of these tanks would be calculated, together with their centres of gravity.

Tables would have to be produced giving values at different depths, capacities and weights (i.e. calibration). It should be remembered that under the 1948 SOLAS Convention dirty ballasting (i.e. filling empty fuel tanks with sea water) was acceptable; but under the 1960 SOLAS rules (after the *Andrea Doria* disaster) it no longer was.

Once the naval architects had completed the incredibly complicated work of establishing all these basics, the whole procedure of producing detailed working plans for the actual construction of the vessel and its machinery would be entrusted to the ship and engine Drawing Offices. Here hundreds of draughtsmen were employed in producing the thousands of plans involved (usually in pencil upon paper and not always neatly). These would then be tidied up and neatly and accurately reproduced on sheets of blue tracing cloth by female workers in the Tracing Office. (At Barrow, there must have been upwards of a hundred tracers at work in the ship and engine departments.) These tracings were then used to reproduce many copies for distribution to the classification and government bodies, the owners and, of course, the various shipyard departments.

I won't go into the actual construction of the hull beyond saying that it really was 'heavy engineering' with huge pieces of metal being lowered into place by tall cranes and connected by automatic welding procedures, and that, by the time *Oriana* was being built, the hulls of most ships were no longer riveted but were entirely of welded construction.

When a ship was structurally complete up to its main/upper strength deck, with some machinery already fitted, it would be ready for launching. (To-day, most large vessels are no longer launched but are built in huge docks which are then flooded so that the ship can be floated out.) The old launching procedure involved considerable thought and calculation. Ships were constructed on sliding wooden ways which sat upon longer, fixed and inclined ways which were lubricated with tons of thick grease so that, when the time came, the

The hull of the new *Oriana*, sheathed in scaffolding, nears completion. *(Dock Museum, Barrow-in-Furness, 3312)*

Above. *Oriana* is ready for the launch. Note the fore poppets and the brackets, temporarily welded to the hull in order to attach the drag chains. Below. At the fitting-out berth. *(Dock Museum Barrow-in-Furness, 1324 and 3316)*

sliding ways could move along them easily. While the ship was being built, the sliding ways were secured by means of fixed blocks, wedges, etc. but these would be removed prior to launching so that the vessel would be held in position only by means of a trigger arrangement, controlled from the launching platform. As is well-known, the launching process would be activated by the ship's godmother, who had usually been chosen by the directors of the owning company.

The launch of a big ship was a very tense and emotional event during which she would be subjected to some of the greatest stresses of her life. Vessels of *Oriana*'s size would never be launched sideways (this was only the case with smaller vessels and submarines built in certain yards) but would enter the water stern first so as to avoid damage to the propellers and rudders (which could occur as they dropped off the way ends if they were to enter the water last). Incidentally, the propellers were sometimes secured in place in order to act as water brakes to slow down the ship's speed into the water.

Oriana creates a spectacular wake, while at full speed during her sea trials. *(Dock Museum, Barrow-in-Furness, 3356)*

Passenger liners usually have fine underwater lines (shape) and therefore the calculations involved prior to the launch were considerable, involving the estimation of the hydrostatic and other particulars of the ship at intervals during her brief progress down the slipway. These included way end and fore poppet pressures, the time taken for the stern to lift, centres of buoyancy, etc. plus the speed of launch (depending on temperature and the amount of friction between the fixed and moving ways). If the ship was to be launched into a narrow seaway (as was the case with *Oriana*), then heavy drag chains would have to be attached to the hull and would be activated at intervals so that they arrested the ship's movement once she was afloat. The bow, which was the last part of the ship to enter the water, was supported by fore poppets (i.e. wooden structures shaped like a cradle and attached to the bow - see page 135). When the stern suddenly lifted as the vessel entered the water, there was a sharp crushing effect on these poppets at the other end of the ship and they therefore contained soft packing to absorb the stress.

When the *Oriana*'s launch was successfully completed, she was towed by tugs to the fitting out berth for completion. Both external and internal work was now carried out simultaneously. While the minor deckhouse structures were being constructed, attention would be given to the interior design of public rooms and cabins. Interior décor architects, as distinct from naval architects, would produce detailed plans with furnishings, colours, etc. and several different sample cabins would be built in the shipyard, reproducing the owner's requirements and would be discussed and eventually agreed upon.

Upon completion of the vessel's structure, machinery and outfitting prior to her departure, an inclining experiment would be carried out to ascertain the ship's final displacement and her vertical and longitudinal centres of gravity, thus determining the deadweight available (i.e. the amount of liquids, stores and personnel she could carry). She would then be provided with final Trim and Safety Books for all conditions of loading and all the other relevant operating instruction books which had been compiled for the use of her operating staff.

The new ship would then leave the yard for comprehensive trials. These involved speed and power trials, some of them over a measured distance, in *Oriana*'s case on the Clyde. Other tests would take place in the open sea. There would also be detailed tests of all the equipment on board, supervised by the yard but witnessed by representatives of the owners and of the classification body. At this stage, the ship would still be under the control of her builders but on the satisfactory completion of the trials she would be handed over to the owners.

The relevant assigning authority (in the case of a British flag ship, the Board of Trade, later the Department of Trade and Industry) would, on completion of construction, trials and surveys, issue the full term Safety, Load Line and Tonnage Certificates, whilst the relevant classification society would issue its certificates for hull and machinery.

It was the usual practice for personnel from the shipyard and from the classification body to sail with the ship for a few weeks after she had entered service in order to advise and instruct the officers and the crew in her operation. I myself have done this on many occasions.

Usually, there would be a period of guarantee (twelve months) when any faults or discrepancies found during service would be corrected by the yard and any changes now required by the owners would be carried out at the same time.

In my opinion, *Oriana* was not as attractive a ship externally as the *Canberra*, having some of the jail-like characteristics at the stern handed down from previous Orient liners. She had a much shorter active life than *Canberra* – remaining in service for less than twenty-six years, although she then went on to survive for almost another twenty years in various static roles. There is no doubt, however, that technically and operationally she was in many ways superior to her much-vaunted running-mate.

Oriana's distinctive funnel and, below, the ship, seen in her prime, *at Wooloomooloo (Bruce Peter collection and Ambrose Greenway)*

Canberra

Completed 1961.

45,270 gross tons.

Length overall: 818 ft. 6ins.

Breadth: 102 ft. 6ins.

Draught: 32 ft. 8¼ins.

Turbo-electric. Twin screw.

Service speed: 27½ knots.

1994: 49,073 gross tons.

Scrapped, 1997.

The daringly streamlined *Canberra*. *(Ambrose Greenway collection)*

To misquote Dickens, 'She was the best of ships, she was the worst of ships'. At first, some cynics in P&O nick-named her *Westphalia* because she had been designed by John West and was considered to be a failure. Yet, by the end of her life *Canberra* had become a great British heroine and was adored by many of her passengers.

In the late 'Fifties and early 'Sixties, some passenger shipowners had to make difficult decisions. The new commercial jet 'planes, introduced on the North Atlantic run in 1958 and then gradually taking over on other routes, represented even more lethal competition for the ocean liners than the previous generation of piston-engined aircraft. True, the figures for the number of people travelling by ship did not immediately plummet – the demand for travel on some routes was expanding so rapidly that there was enough traffic for both modes of transport. But before too long, the passenger lists of the liners were shrinking. One of the last routes on which the ships could still hold their own was that between Europe and Australia – partly because of the distance involved and partly because there were still large numbers of migrants for whom the cost of air travel made that alternative impossible. But few people in the shipping industry doubted that eventually the aeroplanes would prevail.

For owners who intended to stay in the passenger business and needed to introduce new ships to replace ageing tonnage, this represented a difficult problem. Some opted to commission super-modern, dual purpose vessels which could maintain a liner service but had also been specifically designed with cruising in mind. Thus, the 'Sixties saw the introduction of three outstandingly modern British ships, Cunard's *Queen Elizabeth 2* on the North Atlantic and the Orient Line's *Oriana* and P&O's *Canberra* on the route 'down under'. (Interestingly, P&O had previously revived an idea they had put to Cunard and to Canadian Pacific soon after the end of the War: that of jointly ordering a ship which could operate on the Atlantic during the northern hemisphere summer and on the Australian run during the southern summer. The answer in both cases had been 'no'. Now, a decade later, they tried once more to interest Cunard in the proposition but again they demurred, ostensibly on the grounds that one ship could not satisfy the differing needs of the two routes.)

As the late 'Fifties and the 'Sixties progressed, other operators on the Australian route also commissioned notable liners. Shaw, Savill & Albion, for instance, introduced their very advanced *Southern Cross* and *Northern Star* in a round-the-World service which included calls at Australian ports. Lloyd Triestino brought out their new Monfalcone-built *Galileo Galilei* and *Guglielmo Marconi*, which some would say were the finest liners on the Australian run. Achille Lauro converted two substantial Dutch liners and another Italian operator, Cogedar, transformed the former Cunard passenger-cargo liner *Media* into the sleek *Flavia* while Chandris very successfully updated a large pair of former American vessels as the *Ellinis* and *Australis*. (Also, the Sitmar Line acquired the Cunarders *Carinthia* and *Sylvania* with the intention that they, too, should be converted for the Australian service. However, the loss to Chandris of the Australian government's official migrant contract caused Sitmar to abandon the project and, when the pair finally emerged, they had been remodelled to become high class cruise ships.)

Competition was intense but P&O had the advantage of being by far the longest-established and best-known of these lines, having run a service between Britain and Australia since 1852. The initials P&O stand for The Peninsular & Oriental Steam Navigation Co. (Note that in this case Peninsular ends with the letter 'r' – it is an adjective rather than a noun. The peninsula concerned is the Iberian and, indeed, P&O and its predecessor businesses had already been running to Spain and Portugal since the 1820s, and later to Egypt, India and the Far East.) Over the years, P&O became the parent of a huge group of shipping companies, including the British India Steam Navigation Co., the New Zealand Shipping Co., the Union Steamship Co. of New Zealand and many more. It had also acquired a large stake in the Orient Line which it finally took over in 1965.

In December, 1956, a few weeks after the Orient Line confirmed that they had ordered *Oriana* from Vickers-Armstrongs, P&O signed the contract for Harland & Wolff of Belfast to build a running-mate, the ship which was eventually called *Canberra*. Her keel was laid at Harland's Musgrave yard on the 23rd September, 1957. By the standards of the time, she would be large – in fact, the biggest passenger ship to emerge from a British yard since the *Queen Elizabeth* of 1940. *Lloyd's List* opined that 'she is without doubt the most costly merchant vessel to be built in the United Kingdom'. She was originally estimated to cost £12½ million but by the end the figure had risen to about £16 million. Even so, Harland & Wolff lost money on the contract.

Sometimes described by over-enthusiastic publicists as 'The ship that shaped the future', *Canberra* was indeed a very modern vessel – even though not quite as innovative as they would have had us believe. She was certainly powerful and speedy, driven by turbo-electric machinery built at the British Thomson Houston works at Rugby (two sets of steam turbo-alternators which together developed up to 85,000 shp and which powered electric motors connected to the twin propellers). Among the advantages of this system were its quietness and smooth running and the ease with which it could be driven in reverse. P&O had been early exponents of turbo-electric drive in the 'Twenties and 'Thirties with their *Viceroy of India* and the first two 'Strath' sisters.

On *Canberra*, the boilers and machinery were placed aft of midships. There was nothing new in that. The Matson Line had introduced several engines-aft cargo/passenger liners half a century earlier and the numerous C4-S-A1-type American troopships of the Second World War also had this arrangement. Afterwards, there were a few smallish liners with a similar configuration, including the French *El Djezair* and several streamlined motorships built for the Norwegian coastal service. Then, in 1955, Shaw, Savill & Albion brought out the much bigger *Southern Cross*, to be

followed in 1962 by the *Northern Star*. And, of course, the engines of several generations of oil tankers had also been placed aft. The arrangement could lead to difficulties with a ship's trim, however – as was demonstrated when *Canberra* ran her builders' trials. When she was at speed, the concentration of weight towards the rear of the hull (exacerbated, no doubt, by the fact that she was carrying neither passengers nor cargo) caused her bow to lift almost clear of the water. In order to correct this, huge amounts of ballast had to be placed in the forward end of the ship. This added weight caused an expensive increase in her fuel consumption and also deepened her draught, making her unable to enter some of the shallower ports which she might have visited when in cruising mode.

She had two slender, streamlined, side-by-side funnels towards the after end of the superstructure. (At one time, it had been proposed that these funnels should be canted outward but the upright shape eventually chosen was found to be more efficient.) Another feature of the design was the positioning of the lifeboats, mounted inboard above open promenades let into the ship's sides at main deck level

In the 1960s, the combined passenger services of the P&O and Orient lines spanned the globe. *(Paolo Piccione collection)*

John Brown, one of the yards competing for the order to build the *Canberra*, submitted this version of John West's design. In the end the order went to Harland & Wolff. *(Bruce Peter collection)*

(although it was not called that). Again, as explained in the chapter on *Oriana*, this was not a completely new idea. Nevertheless, it was still very unusual when *Canberra* and *Oriana* were introduced. *Canberra* may, or may not, have been 'The ship that shaped the future' but there can be no denying that she was very modern, with an extravagantly curved style which was almost American. Most of her superstructure was built of aluminium alloy, which is said to have saved 1,500 tons of weight and made it possible to include an extra deck.

A great deal of original thought had gone into many details of her design, ranging from the mixer taps in the bathrooms to the highly mechanised system of cargo stowage – in the case of two of her three holds, through side ports. In total, there were about 150,000 cubic feet of cargo space. She was given not one but two sets of Denny-Brown stabilisers and, like the slightly earlier *Oriana*, she had one of the new thwart thrusters at her forward end. Mr. West's design may have had its shortcomings but it was certainly up-to-date. He had to work within certain constraints. For instance, the ship must be of a size which would enable her to pass through the Panama Canal. On the other hand, she must be considerably larger than the liners of 28,000 and 29,000 tons commissioned by P&O in the immediate post-War years since the company felt that it would no longer be economic to build a ship of that size. And the planned reorganisation and integration of the P&O and Orient Line services to Australia and to the Far East, including their extension across the Pacific to the West Coast of America, dictated that the new ship must be a true express liner, faster than the existing vessels.

As built, *Canberra* could accommodate up to 548 first class passengers and 1,690 in tourist class. Her passenger quarters were air-conditioned throughout. The design of her interiors was entrusted to an exceedingly bright team headed by Sir Hugh Casson. Although he was derided by the radical progressives of the post-War era, Casson could, as Bruce Peter points out, 'do modernist when called upon. He surrounded himself with talent. The *Canberra* was a magnificent example of that. Was ever an ocean liner so finely detailed? I doubt it!'

Below the open Games Deck and the rounded bridge housing and the streamlined mast, there were eight decks of passenger space, with first class occupying the forward half of the ship and the after half allotted to tourist class. The first class accommodation included cabins which could sleep one, two or three passengers. The most expensive were four verandah suites and eight de luxe rooms. Particularly notable were the Court Cabins, groups of six or eight so arranged on either side of lateral alleyways as to form enclosed 'courts'. Each of these cabins had a window which admitted natural light, either directly from outside or indirectly through the court. As we have seen in the previous chapter, *Oriana* was also given Court Cabins; and it is interesting to compare this arrangement with a not dissimilar one favoured by the great American naval architect George G. Sharp in such ships as the American Export Lines' 'Four Aces'. On *Canberra*, each first class cabin had private facilities and, notably for the time, a television set. All cabins in both classes had taps serving iced water, presumably in deference to the tastes of the hoped-for

American passengers. The tourist class cabins made provision for two or four passengers and although some had full facilities, many others were merely given wash basins. (Chris Mason, who in his youth took a holiday job in P&O's booking department, remembers that some cabins were so ingeniously designed that they could be either twin-berth with facilities or four-berth without.) A few of the best tourist cabins could be used for first class passengers if necessary.

Many of the public rooms matched the modernity of the ship's exterior. Extensive use was made of plastic materials, partly for aesthetic reasons but also because maintenance costs were minimal compared with those for painted or varnished surfaces. As a result, the outfitters found it necessary to develop new techniques, particularly in bonding over a million square feet of plastic sheeting onto wood – notably to form the gold and silver panels which were part of the decoration of the tourist class dining room and lounge. The overall décor was clean, modern and bright.

One of the most popular first class public rooms was the Crow's Nest, a forward facing observation lounge and bar, high up on the Games Deck and very contemporary

in style. A fine spiral staircase linked it with the Meridian Room lounge, some decks lower, which was divided up into several distinct zones. Lower still in the ship was the dining room with its sunken centre section. Other first class rooms were the Lido café which led out to the first class swimming pool; the Bonito Club with its dance floor; the Menzies Room library and writing room; a nursery and playground; and the Stadium, an almost circular sun deck which could be enclosed to become the site of evening entertainments. It proved not to be entirely satisfactory and, some years later, was converted into a theatre. There was also a two-deck high 332-seater cinema which could shew Cinemascope films and was intended for the use of both classes – separately, of course.

Tourist class passengers had the use of two swimming pools, one of them with an adjoining café called Alice Springs. Again, their dining room was situated low in the ship. Seating up to 704 passengers, it was said to be the largest restaurant afloat. Another notable room was the Cricketer's Tavern (facing page, Bruce Peter collection), decorated with pictures of famous cricketers including Sir Donald Bradman and with suitable memorabilia.

A contemporary artist's rendering emphasises *Canberra*'s curvaceous shape and her enormous open decks. *(Paolo Piccione collection)*

Above, the Pop Inn, with its short-lived David Hockney pokerwork panels, was the province of teenaged passengers. Below, the decorative ceiling panel of the Peacock Lounge was quickly removed, one of the victims of the need to reduce weight at the stern. *(Bruce Peter collection)*

The first class dining room eschewed the formality of such rooms on earlier ships. *(Bruce Peter collection)*

This was very apt since Australian passengers might well be aficionados of their national game and many English and Australian test teams had travelled in P&O ships over the years. The captain of the current English team, Colin Cowdrey, had acted as a consultant in the decoration of this room. Also striking was the Pop Inn, intended for teenagers and complete with a juke box. This room had decorations by very young artists, including wooden panels with poker-work motifs by the emerging David Hockney. (They did not last long as they proved to be an irresistible attraction for youthful passengers with ballpoint pens and pen-knives.) There were also lounges including the William Fawcett Room and the Island Room which contained the dance floor. Inevitably, there were smoking, writing, reading and card rooms and a nursery and playground. The usual facilities such as medical centre, hospital, shops and launderette were available to both classes.

Building a liner of this type was a huge job and as many as 4,000 or 5,000 men could be working on her at any one time. The launch had to be postponed by a fortnight owing to delays caused by industrial disputes but it eventually took place on the 16th March, 1960 with the deed being performed by Dame Pattie Menzies, the wife of the Australian Prime Minister, using a bottle of Australian wine. Unfortunately, the weather was so cloudy that plans to have an RAF *Canberra* bomber fly overhead at the crucial moment were cancelled.

Canberra enters the water on the 16th March, 1960. *(Bruce Peter collection)*

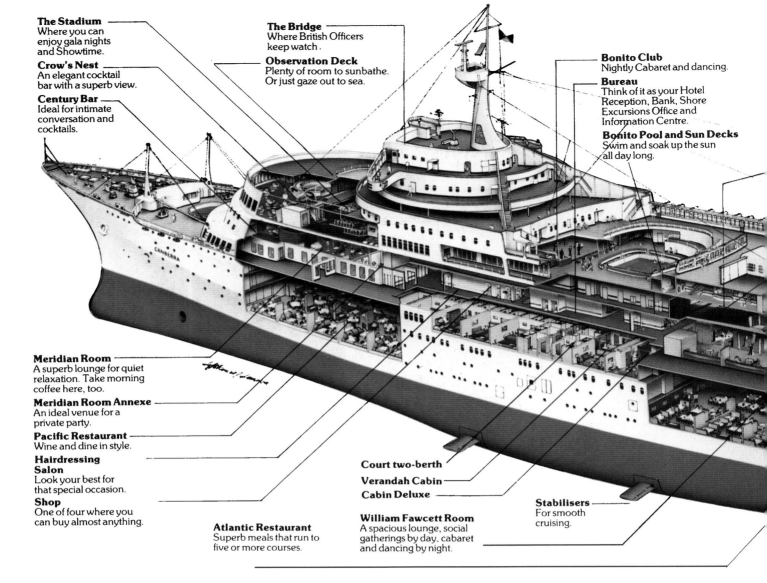

The Stadium
Where you can enjoy gala nights and Showtime.

Crow's Nest
An elegant cocktail bar with a superb view.

Century Bar
Ideal for intimate conversation and cocktails.

The Bridge
Where British Officers keep watch.

Observation Deck
Plenty of room to sunbathe. Or just gaze out to sea.

Bonito Club
Nightly Cabaret and dancing.

Bureau
Think of it as your Hotel Reception, Bank, Shore Excursions Office and Information Centre.

Bonito Pool and Sun Decks
Swim and soak up the sun all day long.

Meridian Room
A superb lounge for quiet relaxation. Take morning coffee here, too.

Meridian Room Annexe
An ideal venue for a private party.

Pacific Restaurant
Wine and dine in style.

Hairdressing Salon
Look your best for that special occasion.

Shop
One of four where you can buy almost anything.

Atlantic Restaurant
Superb meals that run to five or more courses.

Court two-berth

Verandah Cabin

Cabin Deluxe

William Fawcett Room
A spacious lounge, social gatherings by day, cabaret and dancing by night.

Stabilisers
For smooth cruising.

Even the starting platform in the engine room on *Canberra* had a sleek modern appearance. *(Maurizio Eliseo collection)*

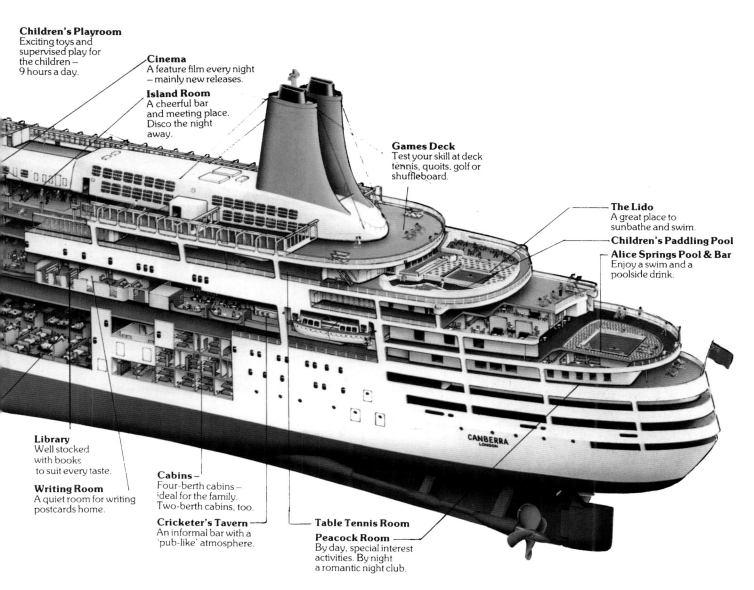

Children's Playroom
Exciting toys and supervised play for the children – 9 hours a day.

Cinema
A feature film every night – mainly new releases.

Island Room
A cheerful bar and meeting place. Disco the night away.

Games Deck
Test your skill at deck tennis, quoits, golf or shuffleboard.

The Lido
A great place to sunbathe and swim.

Children's Paddling Pool

Alice Springs Pool & Bar
Enjoy a swim and a poolside drink.

Library
Well stocked with books to suit every taste.

Writing Room
A quiet room for writing postcards home.

Cabins
Four-berth cabins – ideal for the family. Two-berth cabins, too.

Cricketer's Tavern
An informal bar with a 'pub-like' atmosphere.

Table Tennis Room

Peacock Room
By day, special interest activities. By night a romantic night club.

CANBERRA
LONDON

By April 1961, the ship was ready. The years 1960 and 1961 saw a late boom in building large passenger ships in Britain, with the completion not only of *Canberra* but also of *Oriana, Windsor Castle, Transvaal Castle, Empress of Canada, Aragon, Arlanza* and *Principe Perfeito*. But of them all, it was *Canberra* which most caught the public's attention. As David Hutchings remembers, there was even a special series of programmes on BBC children's television, called *Crow's Nest* and featuring John West himself. It included instructions on how to build a model of the ship. After her builders' trials, *Canberra* left Belfast for Southampton on the 29th April. This was necessary because the dry dock at Belfast, although large enough to

have housed *Titanic* and her sisters, was marginally too narrow to accommodate *Canberra*. So, she had to be sent to the King George V dock at Southampton and it was there that the extra ballast which had unfortunately been proved necessary was installed. On the 16th May, she sailed for the Clyde, where she was to run her acceptance trials. In a portent of troubles to come, her departure was slightly delayed by a small fire and by engine trouble. During her trials, she achieved a mean speed of 29.27 knots over the measured mile, more than a knot slower than *Oriana* but nevertheless confirming her as a true express liner.

In his book *Southampton Shipping*, David Hutchings remembered, 'Her maiden voyage left Southampton on a very hot 2nd June, 1961 and was a gala occasion (in spite of an unsightly slick along her starboard waterline) that assured her of a place in the affections of the city.' After calls at Gibraltar and Naples, she passed through the Suez Canal, and then continued to Aden and Colombo. She made her first Australian landfall – arrival in Fremantle – 31 hours late, having been delayed by persistent condenser trouble. En route for Melbourne, the same problem continued to slow her. However, she proceeded to Sydney, spending four days there and then departed for Auckland, Honolulu and Vancouver where she ended her maiden voyage on the 17th July. She returned via San Francisco, Los Angeles, Honolulu, Wellington, Sydney and then the same ports as on her outward voyage. Southampton to Southampton had taken 94 days. Inevitably on a new ship, there had been problems – including not only the condenser trouble but also a breakdown in the electrical system which temporarily plunged her into darkness and caused a highly uncomfortable loss of air-conditioning in the heat of Aden – but the new P&O flagship had created a fine impression and had received a tremendous reception at many of her ports of call.

However, her second outward voyage was even more troubled than her first. Her departure from Southampton on the 22nd September was delayed for a few hours by another small fire, in the engine room. Then, between Aden and Colombo, she began to experience problems due to the breakage of a small blade in one of her turbines, which slowed her from 27 to 22 knots and again she was late arriving in Australia. It was not until Honolulu that it was possible to complete running repairs. The third round voyage seems to have gone reasonably well except that towards the end she began to be slowed by a boiler malaise and was 12 hours late arriving back in Southampton. The start of the fourth round voyage was therefore delayed by five days while the boiler tubes were given a thorough cleaning, but otherwise it seems to have been blessedly free of major problems. This time, she went no further than Honolulu and Los Angeles and returned via the Panama Canal, Curaçao and Trinidad. She then spent a month at Southampton receiving repairs under the one year builder's warranty and also various modifications.

On the 20th July, 1962, she started her first season of summer cruises from Southampton – a week-long jaunt to Madeira and Gibraltar; a Mediterranean cruise calling at Naples and Piraeus; and two trips to New York and back. According to a piece in *The Daily Telegraph* headed 'New York Hails "Cut Price" Liner', the two transatlantic cruises

Sydney was *Canberra*'s second home. Here she is seen manoeuvring near the famous Harbour Bridge, with which, on another occasion, she collided. *(Ambrose Greenway collection)*

had been arranged in conjunction with the U.S. government to encourage Britons to visit America and the fares for the 14-day round trips ranged from £70 to £357.

On the 19th September, *Canberra* began her 1962-63 season on her regular route and all went well except that, in dense fog, she collided with a barge while leaving Vancouver. The barge sank, fortunately without loss of life, but damage to *Canberra* was confined to a slightly bumped hull.

If P&O and Harland & Wolff dared to hope that at last the technical problems plaguing the troublesome new liner were over, they were brutally disillusioned on the next voyage. On the 4th January, 1963, after she had made her usual call at Naples, a serious electrical fault occurred in the main engine room switchboard. In an urgent attempt to rectify the problem, one of the engine room staff took extreme measures which were contrary to 'recognised practice'. The result was an 'arc of great severity' and fire broke out. The unhappy man was lucky to escape terrible injury. The ship was left without power and the nearby *Stratheden* rushed to stand by her stricken fleetmate, for instance providing the bread which *Canberra*'s disabled bakery could no longer produce. Eventually, *Canberra* managed to get moving under her own steam and struggled into Malta. An airlift had been organised to take her 2,200 passengers to their destinations – she often seems to have been carrying nearly full loads in these early years – and the ship was taken in hand by the Malta dockyard for temporary repairs. She then made her way back to Belfast for more permanent rectification. At the same time, her boilers were re-tubed and some hull repairs were also made. The next scheduled sailing had to be cancelled and it was not until the 11th May that she set off for Southampton and a quick visit to the drydock. Finally, she sailed on the 24th but it had to be a shortened voyage – no further than Sydney.

At last, *Canberra* began to hit her stride. Built for tropical conditions, she was more suitable for cruising than those North Atlantic liners which were also trying their luck in the cruise market and she became very popular with passengers. But she still spent most of the year on those long voyages to Australia and sometimes across the Pacific. On the 1st March, 1965, she had a minor but very newsworthy accident. While she was being backed away from her Sydney berth in a stiff breeze, a tow-line to one of the tugs parted and the top part of *Canberra*'s mast hit the underside of Sydney Harbour Bridge and was bent forward at right angles. She also touched bottom, but without apparent damage. She was able to proceed with her voyage.

Hitherto, many of the tourist class passengers on *Canberra*'s outbound voyages were migrants travelling under the government-subsidised Assisted Passage scheme. In 1966, however, P&O lost their contract to carry these passengers and

there was a change of emphasis: *Canberra* was still sailing two or three times a year to Australia but between voyages she spent more time in the South Seas and the Pacific, making what were effectively cruises from Sydney, Vancouver, San Francisco and Los Angeles – although these were also popular with point-to-point travellers. That year, she was tied up in Southampton during the long Seamen's Strike which immobilised large parts of the British merchant marine and caused the cancellation of three of *Canberra*'s cruises. On her line voyages, she was now sailing more frequently one way or the other through the Panama Canal and the closure of the Suez Canal as a result of the Arab-Israeli War of 1967 meant that she also began taking the long route via Cape Town.

Canberra did not appear again in the casualty reports until July, 1971 when, while she was manoeuvring at Funchal, a tug got out of position and was capsized by the tow rope. No lives were lost and damage to the liner was slight. Then in February, 1972, being a conspicuously British ship, *Canberra* was boycotted by tugmen in Melbourne who were angered by 'Bloody Sunday', the incident during the Northern Irish 'Troubles' in which demonstrators in Londonderry were shot by British troops. *Canberra* was forced to anchor in Melbourne Bay and her passengers had to be ferried ashore in the ship's lifeboats. She was also involved in another labour dispute in December that year. Companies in the P&O group traditionally employed many Asian seamen and stewards and, indeed, the Goanese stewards were famous for their excellent service to passengers. However, when there was an outbreak of dysentery on the *Orsova*, some of her Asian crew members refused to take the necessary medical tests and were dismissed. 150 men walked off the *Canberra* in sympathy but were eventually persuaded to return by an official of the Indian seamen's union who had been specially flown to Southampton to address them.

By now, things were becoming difficult. A new generation of jet airliners was able to compete more effectively on the long haul to Australia and New Zealand and it was decided that in future *Canberra* would be used mainly for cruising, for much of the year based in New York, where she would be marketed by Cunard. This was a bold move since, although she had called there occasionally during cruises from Southampton, she was still little known to the local public and P&O had no established reputation there. To prepare her for the American market, she was converted into a single-class ship, albeit with a wide variety of cabins; many of her linoleum-clad floors were carpeted; and she was given a casino, the first on a P&O ship.

Her first cruise from New York started on the 31st January, 1973 and took her to Grenada, Barbados and St. Thomas.

But passenger bookings were alarmingly low (she was only about 30% full) and after one more cruise *Canberra* was laid up off the coast of North Carolina. Eventually, she was returned to service and made fifteen more cruises out of New York but the whole experiment was a disaster. At one time, it seemed that P&O might lose half a million pounds on the New York season, although, in the event, passenger numbers improved on some of the later cruises. Nevertheless, so serious did the situation become that in early June it was announced that at the end of her New York stint this hugely expensive ship, still only 12 years old, was to be sold for scrap. (It was admitted that she had been losing money for the last two years.) However, there was a change of heart in the P&O boardroom and on the 14th August it was made known that she had been reprieved. On that very day, *Canberra*, which earlier in the year had been stranded off Grenada for three days, ran aground near St. Thomas. On this occasion she managed to get off under her own power two days later.

Soon after *Canberra* returned to Southampton on the 5th October, 1973, P&O may have been regretting their decision to spare her. The fraught political situation in the Middle East caused the price of oil to rocket upwards, making a fuel-thirsty ship such as *Canberra* particularly vulner-

able. Nevertheless, P&O pressed ahead with the planned revamping of her passenger spaces. Some of the former tourist class four berth cabins now accommodated just two passengers in rather more comfort, reducing total passenger capacity to 1,737. *Canberra* left Southampton for a Caribbean cruise on the 15th December. She was, in fact, taking the place of *Orsova* – by deciding to spare *Canberra* from the scrapper's torches, P&O had condemned the less modern *Orsova* to that fate.

1974 set the pattern for subsequent years, with *Canberra* leaving Southampton in January for a long round-the-World voyage (on this occasion via Madeira, Fort Lauderdale – where she was delayed by a bomb hoax – St. Thomas, Caracas, the Panama Canal, Acapulco, Los Angeles, San Francisco, Honolulu, Suva, Auckland, Sydney, Hong Kong, Singapore, Mauritius, Durban, Cape Town, Tenerife and Lisbon) and then spending the rest of the year sailing out of Southampton on a variety of two- to four-week cruises. She soon established herself as one of the most popular cruise ships in the British market and – now often steaming more slowly – found it easier to turn a profit.

In May, 1981, she was caught in the backwash of a long-running labour dispute in Southampton where, on her arrival, dockers prevented her from mooring. Eventually,

Like several ships on the Australian run, *Canberra* was designed to provide facilities for sun-worshipers and sports enthusiasts. *(Peter Knego)*

When she returned from her exploits in the Falklands War of 1982, *Canberra* was in sore need of renovation. Here she rests at her berth in Southampton, while work begins on her hull. *(R. Bruce Grice)*

she put out into The Solent and passengers leaving the ship, and those arriving for the next cruise, were ferried by tender to and from Portsmouth.

The following year, *Canberra* achieved huge national fame. The Argentine invasion of the Falkland Islands and South Georgia prompted the British government to mobilise a task force to liberate them. Since they are more than 8,000 miles away this required a huge number not only of warships but also of many different types of civilian vessels. The Britsh merchant marine was no longer rich in passenger ships but it was just about possible to requisition sufficient to fulfil the various requirements. The majority came from the P&O group, thus underlining the fact that they were one of only two British concerns still retaining a major presence in the passenger trades. The P&O contribution included *Canberra*; *Uganda*, which became a temporary hospital ship; the North Sea ferry *Norland*; and several other ferries which were mainly used to carry equipment rather than troops. The other passenger ships requisitioned for Falklands service were *Queen Elizabeth 2*; the ferry *St. Edmund*; the little *St.Helena*; and, later, the ferry and accommodation ship *Rangatira*. In Admiralty jargon, they were STUFT (Ships Taken Up From Trade). The *QE2* and *Canberra* temporarily became the World's biggest troopships.

The process of converting a whole platoon of merchant ships for war service was completed in an amazingly short time. *Canberra* was finishing her latest world cruise and she was joined at Gibraltar by a survey team who made a hasty assessment of the conversion which would be necessary. On arrival in Southampton on the 7th April, she was taken in hand by Vosper Thornycroft and by the evening of the 9th she was able to sail. While lying at the quayside, she had been given two previously fabricated helicopter landing decks, equipment for refuelling at sea, extra communications gear, some light armament and numerous other modifications. The Bonito Club had become a hospital and an operating theatre had been set up in the Stadium Lounge. She had also embarked stores and a full complement of nearly 2,000 Royal Marines and paratroopers, all in just three days. Patriotic feelings were running high and crowds gathered to see her go.

After the long trek south – towards the end of which she zig-zagged to make her a more difficult target for Argentine submarines – she arrived off the Falklands on the 17th May and on the 20th entered the enclosed San Carlos Water where, over the next 17 hours, she disembarked her 'passengers' in tenders and lifeboats while undergoing persistent air attacks which sank the nearby H.M.S. *Ardent*. Somehow, *Canberra*'s luck held and she was not damaged. Having left San Carlos Water, she eventually began the long haul to Grytviken in South Georgia where she met the *QE2* and took onboard the troops she too had brought to the south. By the 1st June, *Canberra* was back in San Carlos Water and disembarking the *QE2*'s troops and stores. Her assignment was not yet over and, after a few days lying low some hundreds of miles away, she was back in San Carlos Water to embark well over 3,000 Argentine prisoners of war following the end of hostilities. She repatriated them to Puerto Madryn. Her final duty was to take home to Britain a shipload of troops, including the survivors of some of the Royal Marine units she had brought to the Falklands two and a half months earlier.

Her arrival back in her home port of Southampton on the 11th July was a hugely emotional occasion with a Royal Marine band playing on board and with the ship surrounded by a flock of welcoming boats while crowds cheered and waved flags onshore as she made her way up Southampton Water. She had sailed over 25,000 miles with hardly a hint of mechanical trouble – what a contrast to those early problematic years. From now on, while *Canberra*'s career was not without blemishes, she was a British icon and there was a persistent demand for her cruises.

Restoring her to cruise ship form took considerably longer than had the conversion into a troopship but on the 11th September, 1982 she set sail on her first post-Falklands cruise, accompanied overhead by the RAF's famous Red Arrows team who staged one of their spectacular aerial displays. Thereafter, she continued to divide her time between home-based cruises and, in most years, a single round-the-World voyage. Her Falklands exploits had also caught the attention of many Australians and on her first return to Sydney she was given a noisy, emotional greeting including a fly-past by Royal Australian Air Force jets. Such was her prestige that in Britain she was separately marketed under the name Canberra Cruises for a while after 1986. Over the next few years, P&O spent large sums of money on her during a series of sometimes quite far-reaching refits, including the installation of new propellers of a modified design. Nevertheless, to the end of her career some of her former tourist class cabins still lacked private facilities. Chris Mason complains that much of her original stylish décor was now compromised by fussy drapes and cheap-looking standard furniture but others felt that the softening of her 'Sixties modernity actually improved her.

Luis Miguel Correia points out that in the late 'Eighties and early 'Nineties, *Canberra*'s cruise schedule often included a visit to Funchal in Madeira to witness the spectacular New Year fireworks display. P&O still persists with this custom, with at least one of their ships joining the throng in Funchal harbour every year. In 1987, *Canberra* hit the headlines again when, in heavy seas some way off the Pacific coast of Mexico, she went to the rescue of a family in a small dinghy. They had been attempting a round-the-World voyage but their yacht had sunk the previous day. In a fine piece of seamanship, Captain Hannah manoeuvred *Canberra* so as to shelter them from the wind and gradually edged up to them so that they were able to climb a ladder suspended down the ship's side and reach safety.

As *Canberra* aged, she began again to experience occasional mechanical problems. In June, 1989, one turbine was out of action for several days, leaving the ship to limp on, driven by just a single screw. In January, 1993, her World cruise was interrupted for ten days at Fort Lauderdale while problems with her port propeller shaft and bearings were rectified. Most spectacularly, in December, 1994, a faulty fuel pump caused her to lose all power while off the Isle of Wight in a Force 8 gale. The situation was serious and she drifted to within three miles of shore before being able to anchor. Tugs came to her rescue and lifeboats and other craft stood ready. Eventually, some power was restored but her anchor chains had become entangled. In the end, she was able to get moving and made it to safety in Southampton, escorted by the tugs.

She was affected by politics when the Gulf War made it advisable for her to complete her 1990-91 World cruise via The Cape rather than through the Suez Canal. Also in 1991, in a purely financial transaction, P&O sold her to Abbey National March Leasing but chartered her back for further service. In June, 1994, *Canberra* took part in the celebrations to commemorate the 50th Anniversary of D Day, the landings by Allied troops in Normandy which began the liberation of continental Europe – she was present at the Naval Review at Spithead and was one of a number of passenger ships which carried contingents of war veterans to participate in the celebrations on the French side of the Channel.

Inevitably, the order for a new *Oriana* in 1992 raised questions about *Canberra*'s future. It would be difficult to bring her into compliance with forthcoming SOLAS safety regulations. And by now her aluminium alloy superstructure was badly cracked in places and she continued to experience mechanical problems. Nevertheless, she sailed on for five more years. Towards the end, in February 1997, Clive Harvey was a passenger on the final section of her last World cruise. Although she looked splendid from the outside, 'once on board it was a different story. She had long ago lost her original furnishings and her public rooms were shabby and tired. A curious smell pervaded the Stadium Theatre so that we called it 'the hamster's cage.' There were several occasions during that voyage when the engines would just stop and the ship would be dead in the water for a little while and the air-conditioning barely worked so that we had to sleep with the cabin door open' Despite it all, she kept the loyalty of her devoted fans to the last.

It had been announced in 1996 that she would be withdrawn towards the end of the following year and she was offered for sale with the stipulation that she should not be used for passenger service in European waters. Premier Cruises were said to be interested in her but in the end there were no takers. On the 30th September, 1997, she came into Southampton to a huge welcome at the conclusion of her final cruise. P&O made the old ship's last arrival at her home port a very sentimental occasion, with a 'Canberra' bomber flying overhead, but, looking forward rather than backwards, they decided against allowing her a similarly sentimental final departure. She slipped away in the late evening of the 10th October, not quite un-noticed but without the kind of farewell she deserved. She had been sold to shipbreakers at Gadani Beach in Pakistan. Scrapping proved to be difficult because her deep draught presented problems when they tried to drag her up onto the beach but eventually the doughty old ship succumbed.

Canberra displays her distinctive stern and her low-slung lifeboats. *(Ambrose Greenway collection)*

Transvaal Castle

Completed 1961. 32,697 gross tons.

Length overall: 760 ft. 2ins. Breadth: 90 ft. 2ins.

Draught: 32 ft 0ins. Geared steam turbines.

Twin screw. Service speed: 23½ knots.

Renamed *S.A. Vaal*, 1966.

Renamed *Festivale*, 1977. Now 26,632 gross tons.

Renamed *IslandBreeze*, 1996.

Renamed *The Big Red Boat III*, 2000.

Scrapped, 2003.

Unlike other British liners of the 1960s *Transvaal Castle* had a traditional profile. *(Ian Shiffman, Table Bay Underway)*

The Union-Castle Mail Steamship Co., Ltd. was one of the really great shipping lines and *Transvaal Castle* was the last passenger-mailship it commissioned for its historic service between Southampton and South Africa. It was in 1857 that the Union Steamship Co., Ltd. (later merged with the rival Castle Packets Co., Ltd.) gained its first contract to carry the mails between the two countries. Over the next 120 years, the line went through periods of stagnation but there were others of great energy. At different times, three forceful men drove it ahead – Sir Donald Currie (the founder of the Castle Line), the Hon. Owen Philipps (who later became Lord Kylsant) and Sir Vernon Thomson. Union-Castle survived the collapse of Lord Kylsant's far-flung shipping empire in the early 1930s, although it took some years to unravel the situation and float it off as a separate, quoted public company. In 1956, control was gained by the Cayzer family, whose Clan Line ran a large fleet of cargo ships on the routes to South and East Africa and to Indian and Pakistan. The two companies and their various subsidiaries were combined to form a powerful new group called the British & Commonwealth Shipping Co., Ltd., although each continued to operate under its separate name.

Union-Castle had some lesser passenger vessels which served both South and East Africa, plus a fleet of cargo liners. But it was the mailships which gave it its prestige. The almost exact regularity of their weekly sailings from the Western Docks in Southampton – 'Every Thursday at Four O'Clock', later changed to 'Every Friday at One O'Clock' – and the conservatively styled comfort in which they carried their first class passengers, gave them an immensely solid reputation. And the distinctive Union-Castle livery of lavender-coloured hulls and red funnels with black tops made them instantly recognisable. The ships of the pre-War period had a racy, low-funnelled motor ship look while the post-War vessels had a more stately appearance. The company had by now reverted to steam turbine propulsion for its express liners which accordingly had huge steamship funnels. Their bows had a graceful flare and the front of the superstructure was pleasingly rounded. That superstructure was, though, relatively short since these ships carried rather fewer passengers than many equivalent liners on other routes, and considerably more cargo. The development of the mailship fleet had tended to go in waves, as the service was periodically speeded up, usually when the terms of a newly renewed mail contract demanded it. In the 1960s, eight ships were needed to maintain the schedule.

The takeover by the Cayzer interests led to changes. It was stated that the eventual aim was to make a further reduction from 13½ days to 11½ days in the time the mailships took between Southampton and Cape Town. *Pendennis Castle*, already under construction, was modified with this in mind; and *Windsor Castle*, introduced in 1960, and *Transvaal Castle* of 1961 were designed so as to be suitable for this accelerated service. But it was not until 1965 that the upgrading of some of the other members of the fleet and the replacement of two of the older passenger liners by a pair of high-speed mail-carrying freighters made it possible to introduce the new schedule. And the long, exclusive association with the shipbuilders Harland & Wolff, a legacy from the Kylsant days, now ceased: *Windsor Castle* was built by Cammell Laird at Birkenhead and *Transvaal Castle* came from the John Brown yard at Clydebank.

The 1960s were a worrying time for passenger shipowners – the travel market was growing but the new jet airliners were taking a rapidly increasing share of it. In Union-Castle's case, political developments in South Africa were also affecting passenger carryings. Furthermore, a change was taking place in the composition of the passenger lists. At the press conference to mark the delivery of *Transvaal Castle* in December, 1961, Sir Nicholas Cayzer revealed that so far that year the company's ships had carried between 15% and 20% fewer first class passengers from Britain to South Africa, while the figures for tourist class were more or less unchanged. In the opposite direction, first class numbers were down by 20% whereas tourist class carryings had fallen somewhat less, by 10%.

The big British lines reacted to the changed climate by introducing new ships which were very different from their predecessors. P&O and its associated Orient Line brought out the technically advanced, faster and more egalitarian *Canberra* and *Oriana*. Shaw, Savill & Albion had already introduced the *Southern Cross* into a round-the-World service – an engines-aft, tourist class-only liner which carried no cargo – and now followed her up with the similar *Northern Star*. And Cunard's sleek *Queen Elizabeth 2*, was much less rigidly class-divided than the old 'Queens' and, unlike them, was designed for a dual career as transatlantic liner and cruise ship. All these ships were, in varying degrees, styled in a modernistic way. Union-Castle, although regarded as a rather conservative company, also tried to move into the new world with their *Transvaal Castle*. Although her outward appearance was less extreme than those of the other lines' ships, a social revolution had

R.M.S. TRANSVAAL CASTLE

R.M.S. Transvaal Castle
The new Hotel Ship

the going's good by UNION-CASTLE
THE BIG SHIP WAY TO AFRICA

'The new Hotel Ship' *Transvaal Castle* was a one-class vessel. *(Clive Harvey collection)*

taken place within her.

Transvaal Castle was described as a 'hotel ship' (sometimes as 'The Grand Hotel of the South Atlantic'). She was a one-class liner with air-conditioning in all cabins and public rooms. True, she still offered a wide range of accommodation – everything from a huge suite, complete with two bathrooms and a faux fireplace, at the forward end of the Observation deck where there were also four large de luxe cabins, to a number of four-berth cabins low down in the hull, each with facilities limited to just one wash basin – but every public room was open to all passengers, regardless of their grade of accommodation. Sir Nicholas Cayzer claimed that they had aimed for 'segregation by style'. It was hoped that people would find their own level – some rooms were designed to appeal to those with formal tastes; and others, more lightly and brightly decorated, were aimed at – shall we say? – passengers with less grand preferences. One has the impression that there had always been a certain grandeur about many of the first class passengers on the Union-Castle mailships – how, one wonders, did they now react to the new social mix? I asked Ann Haynes, who served as a 'purserette' (i.e. – lady purser) on *Transvaal Castle*. She said that the arrangement seemed to work well. There was another change: the restaurant was largely staffed by female stewards who wore 'attractive pale mauve straight dress uniforms'. Union-Castle now not only had 'purserettes' but also 'stewardettes'. When the company advertised for 40 of them, they received over 1,000 applications. The passenger spaces were the work of several designers,

With its entire central portion blocked off to accommodate a cargo hatchway, the dining room lacked cohesion. Note the presence of female 'stewardettes'. *(Clive Harvey collection)*

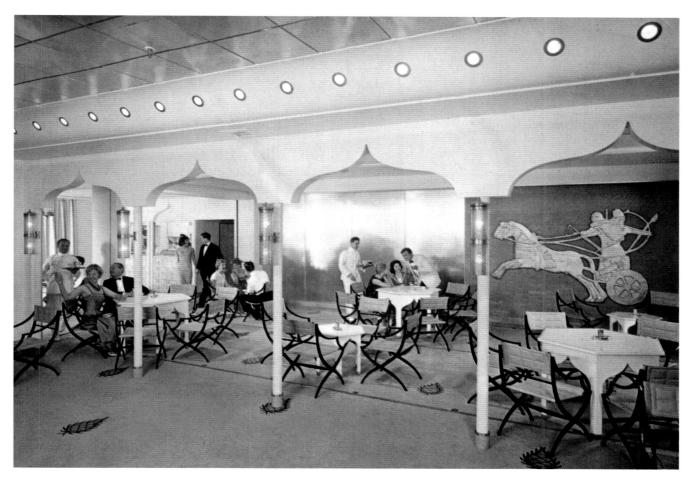

Above. The striking Golden Room café was decorated in what purported to be a Persian style. Below. Floral fabrics were a feature of many cabins. *(Clive Harvey collection)*

headed by Jean Munro who had been responsible for furnishing a number of British liners in a restrained but comfortable style. Another notable, and perhaps less conservative, member of the team was Jon Bannenberg. Overall, *Transvaal Castle* was furnished in lighter colours than her predecessors and in many areas laminated plastic materials were used rather than the wood veneers of old. And there was comment on the fact that the outside passenger decks were covered by a composition material rather than by the traditional teak.

The ship could carry up to 729 passengers. There was an ample number of public rooms and an air of spaciousness. Up on the Observation Deck, where the most expensive cabins were situated, there were two bars – the Cellar Bar and the Vineyard – and a quiet Drawing Room. Below that, the Promenade Deck was entirely taken up by public spaces, with the children's playroom (with its juke box) in a separate housing at the stern, well removed from the rest. Also on this deck was the Golden Room, described as a verandah café and decorated in what was claimed to be a Persian style with metal grilles over the widows, golden

lanterns and a gold ceiling. There were also a large lounge called the Assembly Room; a writing room; a small library which was, perhaps, the ship's most traditional room and was decorated in Regency style; the Orangery bar; and the smoke room. Lower down in the ship were the cinema and the 418-seater dining room, in one corner of which was a

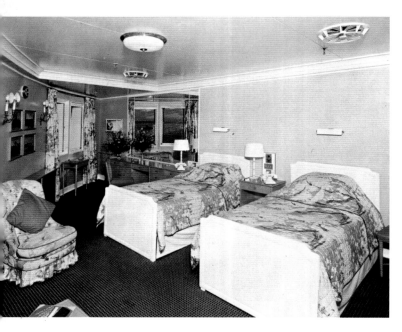

small private space called the Buttery. I suspect that the dining room must have been a difficult room to design, being a rectangular 'o' shape surrounding a closed-off central block (which contained the trunking of one of the cargo holds). From pictures, it would seem that the room fell between two stools - neither intimate nor imposing. Other facilities were a shop, the surgery and the hospital, two hairdressing salons, a passengers' laundry and a gymnasium. There was also a garage into which passengers' cars could be lowered by crane. Open deck space, with a single swimming pool, was very ample.

Transvaal Castle had a wide range of accommodation including a few very luxurious suites and cabins. *(Clive Harvey collection)*

Transvaal Castle was powered by four sets of steam turbines built by John Brown to a design from Pametrada. Developing 44,000 shp, they were double-reduction geared to twin screws. Like the other two mailships completed since the Cayzer take-over, she was fitted with Denny-Brown fin stabilisers which, although developed in the 1930s, were only now coming into general use. As we have seen, the Union-Castle mailships were big carriers of cargo. On the northward run, there would be large quantities of South African fruit during the season and accordingly the ship had 360,730 cubic feet of refrigerated cargo space. (Her total cargo capacity was no less than 643,000 cubic feet.) Another northbound cargo, much smaller in quantity but hugely valuable, was ingots of gold from the Rand mines – kept, of course, in a specially secure bullion room. *Transvaal Castle* had seven holds but mainly relied on quayside cranes to handle her cargo, having herself merely one crane forward and two kingposts aft.

The keel was laid on the 16th January, 1959 and the ship was launched by Lady Cayzer on the 17th January, 1961. Less than a year later, *Transvaal Castle* was completed. As was then the custom at the John Brown yard, members of the public were invited to come and inspect her In two days, over 20,000 people did so, more than for any ship built at Clydebank since the *Queen Mary* – an indication of just how important the new Union-Castle liner was considered to be. She ran trials in the Firth of Clyde on the 5th December and it was then necessary for her to sail all the way to Falmouth in the West of England to be dry-docked. After that, she returned to the Clyde to run speed trials over the Arran Mile and was then handed over to her owners on the 16th. John Brown & Co. (Clydebank), Ltd. proudly announced that she had been completed ahead of schedule and that work on her had been totally free from strikes or other labour disputes – in sad contrast to their experience with the next four liners they built, the losses on which brought about the demise of the yard as a builder of passenger ships. The new liner left the Clyde for a brief shakedown cruise to Southampton. There, she was prepared for her maiden voyage. The advent of this new ship led to the withdrawal of the 1926-built *Carnarvon Castle* some months later.

Transvaal Castle left Southampton on her maiden voyage on the 18th January, 1962 and put in at Las Palmas on the 22nd. Like Elder Dempster and several other lines which headed in a southerly direction, Union-Castle supplemented their passenger lists by offering holidays in the Canary Islands. Passengers would travel outwards to Las Palmas on one of the company's ships, stay there for a while – at one time, Union-Castle owned the Hotel Reina Isabel – and would either return on one of the northbound liners or by air. There was a similar arrangement for people wishing to holiday in Madeira, and on some voyages the ship would call there rather than at Las Palmas. On that first outward voyage, *Transvaal Castle* arrived in Cape Town on the 1st February. It was customary for the mailships then to proceed round the coast to Port Elizabeth, East London and Durban, where the new liner arrived on the 6th. On the return leg, she called at Madeira rather than Las Palmas.

She quickly settled down into a regular and mostly trouble-free routine, usually making 6½ round voyages in a year. Change was on the horizon, however. On the 1st January, 1966, she and her fellow mailship *Pretoria Castle* were sold to the South African Marine Corporation, Ltd. in what was described as 'the biggest shipping transaction in South Africa's history'. They were respectively renamed *S. A. Vaal* and *S. A. Oranje*. The deal was politically motivated. The South African Marine Corporation (known as Safmarine and partly-owned by the country's Industrial Development Corporation) was South Africa's national flag-carrier and had a fleet of cargo ships. The Afrikaner-led Nationalist government in Pretoria obviously felt that it was no longer appropriate that this lifeline service, which they were in effect subsidising by way of the mail contract, should be entirely in British hands. It was stated at the time that eventually a third Safmarine liner would enter what was now a joint Union-Castle/Safmarine service but, in fact, that never happened. For several years the two Safmarine ships continued to fly the Red Ensign and were operated by Union-Castle personnel.

The former *Transvaal Castle* was at sea when the change of ownership occurred and did not arrive at Cape Town until the 13th January. There she hosted a celebratory banquet attended by State President Swart (whose table manners apparently left something to be desired) and Sir Nicholas Cayzer. There had not been time to repaint her completely in Safmarine's livery and only one side of her hull wore their white colour. Her funnel was now grey, with its domed top in black and with, in descending order, black, white and red bands. The change of livery was completed when she reached Durban.

S. A. Vaal and *S. A. Oranje* were finally transferred from Safmarine's British flag subsidiary to the parent company in 1969. They now flew the South African flag and had South African crews. Before that, however, *S. A. Vaal* had, as a British-manned ship, been caught up in the 45 days-long seamens' strike of May, 1966 which had such disastrous consequences for the country's merchant marine. She had to be laid up in the Western Docks at Southampton amid a whole crowd of famous liners. *Queen Elizabeth* lay at her stern and *Arcadia* was at her bow. That regrettable episode apart, she led a relatively uneventful life, except for a couple of minor outbreaks of engine trouble.

A notable occasion in her South African career came on the 1st April, 1976 when, dressed overall, she represented her owners at the ceremonial opening of the new deep water port at Richard's Bay in Natal. However, the days of the old liner services were clearly numbered. The jet aeroplanes and the container ships were taking over and the rise in oil

MACHINERY INSTALLATION
Nº 720
MANUFACTURED BY
JOHN BROWN & Cº (CLYDEBANK) LTD
CLYDEBANK
1961

Now called *S.A. Vaal*, she is seen here in Safmarine colours. *(Clive Harvey collection)*

prices in the mid-1970s was an added woe. The *S.A.Vaal* was withdrawn in September, 1977 and later that month the flagship *Windsor Castle* made the final arrival at Southampton by a Union-Castle/Safmarine passenger-mailship. Then in October, the cargo-mailship *Southampton Castle* closed out the service for ever.

Safmarine had, in fact, already reached agreement for the sale of *S.A.Vaal* some months before her withdrawal. The buyers were to be Festivale Maritime Inc., registered in Panama. This unknown concern was, in fact, a subsidiary of the sometimes derided (but by now definitely up-and-coming) Carnival Corporation. Carnival Cruise Lines was the creation of the Israeli Ted Arison and had started operations as recently as 1972. It had survived its poverty-stricken beginnings to emerge as one of the most successful operators in the market for 'fun ship' cruises out of Florida. (If the brochures were to be believed, its smiling West Indian deck stewards were in the habit of balancing trays of drinks on their heads!) Already, it had two very sound vessels, both former Canadian Pacific 'Empresses', and the winding down of the Italian Line passenger fleet had given it the opportunity to employ numbers of experienced

Italian officers. This had undoubtedly added to the strength of the operation. Now another notable ex-liner was joining the fleet. Whereas the transformation of the two ex-'Empresses' (now bearing the suitably high-spirited names of *Mardi Gras* and *Carnivale*) into tropical 'fun ships' had taken place gradually as cash flow had allowed, Carnival was by now in a position to raise enough finance to spend an instant $20 million (in addition to the purchase price) on a far-reaching conversion of the *S.A.Vaal*. The winning tender for the work had come from an unusual source, Kawasaki Heavy Industries of Kobe. The Japanese had – to the detriment of established European, and particularly British, yards – become a potent force in the shipbuilding world, mass-producing huge numbers of freighters and, particularly, enormous tankers. But they had not so far made an impact on the international passenger ship market. By winning this important contract to convert the *S.A.Vaal*, they were seen to be putting down a marker. In the event, although Japanese yards have produced a few notable cruise ships in the succeeding years, they have never really established themselves in competition with the Italians, Finns, Germans and French. Nevertheless, Kawasaki obviously made a good job of transforming the *S.A.Vaal*.

She sailed from Southampton bound for Kobe on the 29th October, 1977 with the Safmarine stripes on her grey funnel already painted out and bearing her new name *Festivale* and Panamanian registry. The plan was that she should be turned into 'The Ship of the Eighties'. Her superstructure was extended both fore and aft, arguably improving her appearance; she was given two swimming pools and a paddling pool; and the public rooms were modernised in a style more in keeping with Carnival's tastes. Not everyone approved. For instance, Peter Knego comments: 'I thought the interior renovation was utterly tasteless, running the gamut of clashing colours, neon and glitz that would become Carnival's interior architect Joe Farcus' trademark. But what did I know? She was actually his first fully-fledged Carnival commission and, to his credit and the ship's, led to his becoming perhaps the most successful and well-known designer on the seven seas.'

Festivale now had a large casino, a night club, a cinema and a discotheque called Fanta Z (pronounced in the American manner, Fanta Zee); and her passenger capacity was hugely increased from 729 to about 1,300. Extra berths were squeezed into existing cabins and many new cabins were built into former cargo spaces. 180 of these would, it was said, have 'queen-size' beds. She was painted white with her funnel bearing the jazzy Carnival 'new moon' design in red, white and blue. The main technical change was that she was fitted with a bow thruster to reduce her dependence on

Cruise *the "Fun Ships"* to the Caribbean

Carnivale · Festivale · Mardi Gras

expensive tugs when docking. Another saving was that she would now be running at slower speeds and would therefore be less fuel-thirsty.

The original intention was that the *Festivale* should enter service in May, 1978 but this proved to be too ambitious a target and her debut was put back to October. She then began her new career in the Caribbean cruise market from Miami, usually running on 7-day circuits which at first called at St. Maarten, St. Thomas and Nassau (later Nassau, San Juan and St. Thomas). As a Union-Castle and Safmarine liner, she had always been rather overshadowed by her slightly bigger and perhaps more prestigious running-mate *Windsor Castle* but now she was undoubtedly the finest ship in Carnival's fleet and – until the advent of the *Norway* (ex-*France*) – in the whole Miami cruise market. She was a huge success.

The 'Eighties were a time of hectic expansion at Carnival which began to order new, purpose-designed cruise ships rather than relying on being able to pick up unwanted former liners. The conversion of the *Festivale* had been satisfactory enough to prompt the ordering of the first of these new ships from the Kawasaki yard but eventually price escalations caused Carnival to negotiate a better deal with a Danish builder. As the new and bigger ships gradually came into service, there was a 'trickle down' effect, with the older vessels being shifted to different schedules or to new and experimental routes. In 1986, *Festivale*, was moved to a new home port, San Juan in Puerto Rico, to which her American passengers were flown and from where she sailed on a weeklong circuit taking her to St. Thomas, St.Maarten, Dominica, Barbados and Martinique. The following year, she was given a major refit which involved a further increase in her passenger capacity from 1,300 to 1,750, changes to the public rooms, the addition of a new sports deck and the fitting of new diesel generators. At one stage, there had been thoughts of giving her a much more

With her passenger spaces vastly extended, Carnival's *Festivale* was tremendoulsy succesful in the Caribbean cruise market. (*Clive Harvey collection*)

With his brash, gaudy designs for *Festivale*'s interiors, Joe Farcus set the style which was to define Carnival Cruise Lines for three highly successful decades. *(Clive Harvey collection)*

far-reaching rebuild which would have extended the superstructure further out along the long cargo ship fore deck and would have seen the bridge rolled forward. In the event, more modest modifications were made which still increased her capacity very usefully.

In 1990, as one of the sanctions imposed by the U.S. government against the dictator General Noriega, Panamanian-registered ships were banned from American ports. This caused a stampede of cruise ships to other flags of convenience, with the Carnival fleet shifting its allegiance to the Bahamas. The following year, Peter Knego saw *Festivale* again at St. Thomas and, whatever his opinion of her interiors, remarks that outwardly she looked magnificent – 'her bow may have been the most perfect ever fitted to a passenger liner' - and that her 'full-throated Tyfon steam horn was blasting wonderfully'.

Festivale ran successfully for Carnival until 1996. In April of that year, they chartered her to the Dolphin Cruise Line, a relatively small Greek-owned concern which was well-established in the short and medium cruise markets out of Miami. There were cordial relations between the two companies and indeed at one time Dolphin was to have been a third party in a quickly abandoned partnership between Carnival and Epirotiki in the Mediterranean cruise market. Dolphin renamed the ship *IslandBreeze* (note the lack of a space between the two words) and she wore their stylised dolphin logo on her now white-painted funnel and had 'go faster' stripes painted along her hull. Starting in May, she was based in New York for a programme of five-night cruises to Halifax, Portland and Newport and two-night 'cruises to nowhere' during which she loitered about 60 miles outside American territorial waters with her bars and the casino doing a roaring trade. Ted Scull sailed on one of these cruises and remembers that 'while hardly stylish, she still had a most attractive profile and served her market well. Most of the original public rooms had been remodelled and hundreds of extra cabins had been squeezed in – six had even been built into the original swimming pool and consequently had curved bulkheads! However, all cabins now rated en suite facilities.'

This New York programme was briefly interrupted in August when *IslandBreeze* was chartered to take a large party of *Titanic* enthusiasts to witness a chunk of the bow of the sunken White Star liner being raised from the sea bed. Disappointingly for the Titanophiles, the salvaged section fell back to the bottom before it had reached the sur-

Now called *IslandBreeze* and at first running for Dolphin Cruise Lines and later for Thomson Cruises and Premier Cruises, the much-modified ship continued for a while to be successful. Here she is seen leaving Port Everglades in 1999 *(Andres Hernandez)*

face. Then, for winter employment *IslandBreeze* was shifted to Montego Bay for seven-day Caribbean cruises.

Within a few months, she had proved sufficiently successful to persuade Dolphin to enter into a form of maritime hire purchase intended eventually to give them full ownership. A clause in the contract limited the competition she would pose to Carnival by stipulating that she would not operate in the Caribbean for more than four months a year. In May, 1997, in order to bring her into compliance with new safety regulations, she was sent to Genoa for a refit which was stated to have cost $10 million. Dolphin had now chartered her to Thomson Cruises, a branch of the big Thomson travel group, for a programme of Western Mediterranean cruises out of Palma de Majorca to be marketed in Britain. For this she wore Thomson's white, blue, yellow and red funnel colours.

Meanwhile, a company called Cruise Holdings had bought out not only the Dolphin Cruise Line but also Seawind Cruises and Premier Cruises and eventually the three fleets were combined under the Premier name. Most of the ships were given an extremely smart new livery with both funnels and hulls painted dark blue and with a narrow gold strake along the length of the hull which also bore the words Premier Cruises towards the stern. However, *IslandBreeze* continued under charter to Thomson Cruises and for much of the time wore their colours. She remained with Thomsons until April, 2000, still running out of Palma de Majorca in the summer months but switching in the Autumn to cruises between the Canary Islands, Madeira and Casablanca; and then crossing the Atlantic for Caribbean cruises from Santo Domingo in the Dominican Republic in the Winter. Here she had two alternating schedules which took her to Curaçao, La Guaira, Grenada, Martinique and St. Croix and to Barbados, St. Lucia, Guadeloupe, St. Maarten and St. Thomas.

After the end of the Thomson charter, *IslandBreeze* ran for Premier out of the Texan port of Houston on 7-day cruises to Vera Cruz, Cozumel and Playa del Carmen. Much to the regret of many liner enthusiasts, there had been a change in Premier's marketing policy and the dignified dark blue livery had been abandoned. Hulls were now painted in Premier's original brash red colour and three members of the fleet were given *Big Red Boat* names with *IslandBreeze* becoming *Big Red Boat III* (officially with a definite article – *The Big Red Boat III*). By now, she was registered in the ownership of Premier Cruise Lines.

As *IslandBreeze*, the former *Festivale* retained much of her Farcus-designed interior décor including the Grand Dining Room seen here. *(Bruce Peter collection)*

But these were difficult times in the cruise industry and there were several notable bankruptcies among the smaller, less well-financed companies. Premier, which had amassed a fleet of ageing but classic liners including not only *The Big Red Boat III* but also the former *Rotterdam*, *Federico C.*, *Southern Cross* and *Oceanic*, was not immune and, with travel agents reluctant to book passengers onto ships belonging to a company which they perceived to be insecure, the problems were compounded. Despite several refinancings, Premier collapsed in September, 2000. As sometimes happens when companies are teetering on the edge of the abyss, a series of misfortunes hastened the end. *The Big Red Boat III* contributed when she suffered boiler problems after leaving Funchal on the 5th January and repairs delayed her for several days. Then, in June, one of her propellers was damaged in a collision with a tug at Houston and she missed two cruises.

When the bankruptcy occurred, in September, she was immediately impounded at Cozumel in Mexico. She was carrying a mere 394 passengers. Eventually, she made her way to Nassau where she was laid up, later being shifted to Freeport. It seems that she had been stripped of some of her fittings by crew members who were unpaid and desperate. Peter Knego says, 'She was the mother ship of the retired Premier fleet, tied up next to *Rembrandt* (ex-*Rotterdam*) and across from *The Big Red Boat II* (ex-*Eugenio C.*). Her generators were left on so that she could house the skeleton crew with a fully functioning galley and air-conditioning as they looked after the three ships. I shot some video footage for ISP (International Shipping Partners) to help them find a buyer for *The Big Red Boat II* and they "paid" me by giving me *The Big Red Boat III*'s John Brown builders' plate, which I now proudly display in a mahogany and glass cabinet from her captain's office. The cabinet itself is most interesting because it has phoney leather-bound books that hinge open to reveal what was once a "speakeasy" bar – a special feature that must have come in handy in dry ports when a little "liquid persuasion" was necessary to get round tough regulations and officials, perhaps?'

In December, she was sold by auction to anonymous buyers, fetching $16 million. At first, it seemed that she might still have a future. Thomsons toyed with the idea of chartering her for the 2002 summer season but backed away. An Australian company proposed to use her for cruises out of Fremantle but that, too, came to nothing. The New York authorities inspected her for possible use as a floating hostel for the homeless but decided against. All the time, she was gradually deteriorating as she lay idle. Finally, in February, 2003 she was sold to Indian breakers. Necessary repairs delayed her departure but, bearing the abbreviated name of *The Big Boat*, she left Freeport under her own power on the 4th June, heading east via Gibraltar and Suez and arriving at Alang on the 9th July. She was beached on the 13th and scrapping of this fine old former liner began.

In this highly doctored publicity picture, *IslandBreeze* has been given a dark blue funnel and hull with a golden strake. *(Author's collection)*

After the collapse of Premier Cruise Lines, *The Big Red Boat III* was laid up at Freeport in the Bahamas; her fleetmate *Rembrandt* was tied up next to her. Later, now simply called *The Big Boat*, she was beached like a stranded whale and scrapped at Alang. Note the precarious ladder leading into the bow. *(Peter Knego)*

Avalon

Completed 1963.

6,584 gross tons.

Overall length: 405 ft. 0ins.

Breadth: 57 ft. 6ins. Draught: 15ft. 9ins.

Geared steam turbines. Twin screw.

Service speed: 21½ knots.

Converted into a car ferry, 1975.

5,142 gross tons.

Scrapped, 1981.

A handsome miniature liner, *Avalon* was built for the British Railways Board service from Harwich to the Hook of Holland. *(Bruce Peter collection)*

Although a notable ship, good-looking and very popular, the *Avalon* had an unlucky start to her career and, overtaken by events, did not last as long as she deserved. Superstitious old salts no doubt attributed it all to the unfortunate circumstances which surrounded her launch and her naming ceremony. Labour troubles delayed the former and at the latter, which did not take place until the completed ship was handed over to her owners, the champagne bottle failed to shatter on impact (although an official's timely blow with a hammer is said to have saved the situation). The choice of name, at any rate, was a happy one as, in 1864, one of the first railway-owned paddle steamers to run between Harwich and a Dutch port (Rotterdam) had been called *Avalon*.**

In 1961, the government-owned British Railways Board ordered a new ferry for this historic service, which by now had the Hook of Holland as its Dutch terminal. She was to replace the 1935-built *Duke of York*. The British Rail ships ran the overnight crossings, while their Dutch counterparts of SMZ, the Stoomvaart Maatschappij Zeeland (Zeeland Steamship Company), handled the daytime sailings. The British Rail service was maintained by three vessels, although for much of the year only two were needed, the third being required during the peak Summer season and acting as a reserve for the rest of the year. But a British Rail official told *Lloyd's List* that the Board had 'little change out of £2 million for this ship – our intention is to make her work as hard as we can'. She was accordingly designed to be suitable for cruising in the Spring and Autumn. This was not a completely new idea: one of her predecessors, the *Vienna*, had run some weekend cruises out of Harwich before the War but it was now proposed that the *Avalon* should operate a much more ambitious programme.

The largest ship in the British Rail fleet, she was heralded as 'a miniature liner' and looked very handsome in her British Rail livery of black hull and buff funnel with a black top. (Soon, though, the fleet was given a trendier image: buff gave way to red, with a twin-arrowed logo superimposed, and the newly-invented fleet name Sealink appeared along the sides of the ships.) Partly, perhaps, because of her cruising rôle, the *Avalon* had a higher standard of passenger accommodation and facilities than was usually found on short sea ferries at that time. A few years earlier, Ward & Austin had become the regular interior design architects for the British Rail ships

and they had introduced a much smarter and more modish style. *Avalon* was a fine example of their work. The fleet's General Manager, though, wrote that the public rooms had been furnished 'without ostentation or over-elaboration' and added that 'the need to achieve economy in maintenance and cleaning was kept well to the fore'.

The order for the *Avalon*'s construction had gone to Alexander Stephen & Sons, Ltd. of Linthouse, Glasgow, where she was yard no. 680. By now, they were using modern prefabrication techniques and the ship was of all-welded construction. Her design was mainly the work of the Railways Board's own naval architects. It is arguable that the Board's management hobbled their designers and compromised the ship's future by not recognising 'the shape of things to come'. A few years later, the *Avalon* would undoubtedly have been given drive on / drive off facilities for cars, if not lorries, and would have been powered by the more economical diesel engines rather than by steam turbines. In mitigation, it can be said that perhaps it was thought that quiet and smooth-running turbines were more suitable for a 'night boat'. Ferry service, with its frequent dockings and undockings, dictated that the low cruiser stern and much of the hull were protected by the traditional rubbing strip.

There was no doubting the modernity of the *Avalon*'s exterior, however – she had a raked bow; a curved bridge front; two streamlined masts, the forward one placed above the wheelhouse; and a single tapered funnel with a raised top. And some other aspects of her design were definitely ultra-modern. It was claimed, for instance, that she was the first British sea-going passenger ship to be fitted with biological sewage disposal equipment. She was particularly manoeuvrable, having twin rudders at the stern and a bow rudder, too. In addition, a side-thrust unit was fitted near the bow. The radar installation was 'believed to be one of the most comprehensive afloat'. Air-conditioning was not only provided for all passenger spaces but also for the crew accommodation. And passenger comfort during the sometimes turbulent North Sea crossing was further enhanced by the fitting of Denny-Brown-AEG stabilisers.

Two sets of Pametrada-type turbines from the ship's builders developed an output of 14,500 shp and drove the twin propellers. At first, these turbines proved distinctly troublesome. Although primarily a passenger-carrier, the new ship had

** *I cannot resist reviving the familiar old joke about the famous slogan 'Harwich for the Continent' which used to appear on posters in railway stations throughout the country. Some wit is said to have scrawled underneath 'but Frinton for the incontinent' – Frinton-on-Sea being a nearby resort, very select and much loved by the elderly retired.*

The *Avalon* was intended for cruising as well as ferry service and her first class public rooms were quite stylish. Here we see the forward-facing lounge and the restaurant. *(Bruce Peter collection)*

three small cargo holds, two forward and one aft. A few cars could be carried in the 'tweendecks but she had no cranes of her own, the vehicles being lifted on and off by the quayside units. It was stressed that her aft hatch was big enough to take 'large American-type cars'.

As built, the *Avalon* could carry up to 750 passengers. Being a 'night boat', she had 280 cabins which could sleep 331 first class passengers and 287 second. The remainder snatched such rest as they could in aircraft-type seats. Included in the tally of first class accommodation were six de luxe and four special cabins, all very separately situated on the Promenade Deck and all with their own facilities. The de luxe cabins in particular were very stylishly furnished. As was common on overnight ferries at that time, the other cabins were small and had washbasins but no toilets of their own. Notably for the time, however, they did have sockets for electric razors.

All first class spaces were in the forward part of the ship and they included a smoking room and a handsome lounge, furnished very much in the modern manner and looking out over the bow. The first class restaurant was panelled in teak and could be entered from either end so that second class passengers who wished to eat in style could cross the barriers of caste and dine there. Comfortable though the first class rooms were, even there many of the floors were covered in old-fashioned linoleum out of deference to the need for hygiene and the declared requirement for easy and economical cleaning. Second class passengers had their own lounge and a cafeteria. Each class had its own shop.

The *Avalon* was due to be launched on the 10th April, 1963 but a four week strike of electricians meant that she could not take to the water until the 7th May. The customary launching ceremony had to be cancelled. When the ship was finally completed, the usual trials took place on the Clyde and she eventually arrived at her home port of Harwich in mid-July, a remarkably short time after the launch. The shipyard had remained at work for several days of the traditional Clyde holiday period in order to deliver her. It was at Harwich that the *Avalon* was finally named by Mrs. Ella Beeching, the wife of the much-reviled chairman of the British Railways Board, Dr. Richard Beeching. (At the time, he was embroiled in controversy due to his application of ruthless economics to the railway system by closing several hundred branch lines.)

This very period picture (note the lady's beehave hairstyle) shows one of the comfortable first class de luxe cabins.
(Bruce Peter collection)

Dressed overall, *Avalon* makes a brave sight. She was, though, one of the last of her type, soon outdated by the growth of motor traffic on the short sea routes. *(Bruce Peter collection)*

Mrs. Beeching presented the ship with a water colour of the original *Avalon*.

The new ship entered service on the 25th July, apparently assured of a successful future. Indeed, she carried 6,600 passengers on her first ten crossings. However, the ill omen of her naming ceremony seemed to be justified when, outbound on the night of the 9th August, she was forced to return to Parkeston Quay, Harwich with an overheating bearing. Her 695 passengers were transferred to the next sailing of the SMZ company's *Prinses Beatrix*; the faulty part was rushed back to Linthouse; and the *Avalon* limped up to Immingham for repairs to be made. She left there, apparently cured, on the 21st. But mechanical problems persisted: she missed her 9th December sailing and on the following 4th February had to put back to Harwich yet again. She encountered further ill-luck later in 1964 when, on the 12th December, she struck the quay while leaving the Hook of Holland in a gale and gashed her hull quite badly. She was sent to the Wilton-Fijenoord yard at Schiedam, Rotterdam.

(This yard had already become her customary resort for repairs and overhauls.) Thereafter, her luck changed and she led a less troubled existence.

Her cruises, although never numerous, proved to be very popular. The first was a short trip to Amsterdam and back starting on the 24th April, 1964 but later she made longer voyages, visiting such places as the North Cape, Copenhagen, the Baltic ports, St. Nazaire, Bordeaux, Santander, La Coruña, Vigo, Lisbon, Oporto, Seville, Cadiz, Gibraltar, Tangiers, Agadir and Casablanca. When used for cruising, she was restricted to about 320 passengers. Even so, she must have been rather short of open deck space. If she was sailing to sunny destinations, an awning would be erected over her after deck.

She also attracted a few charters. In August, 1966, for instance, she inaugurated the new England-Sweden Line's service from Gothenburg to Hull. (Ironically, in view of her own history, she took the place of Ellerman Wilson's *Spero* which was late in being delivered by the shipyard.)

Avalon was built as a 'night boat'. She was a member of the British Railways fleet and, appropriately, the officer collecting tickets at the foot of the gangway wears his peaked cap at a railwayman-like angle. *(Bruce Peter collection)*

This charter, in a way, was a portent of the future – the new service was a drive on-drive off operation and, since *Avalon* did not have the necessary facilities, another vessel had to be brought in to carry the cars. Then in October, 1968, the *Avalon* was chartered to take guests to the opening of the new Gulf Oil terminal in Bantry Bay and to act as a floating hotel. Laurence Dunn was on board for this trip and remembered the high standard of the *Avalon*'s public rooms, her food and her service.

By now, however, she was already outdated. When she was planned, most passengers on the route were expected to arrive by train. (Indeed, timetables warned those coming by other means to join their ship as early as possible as she would sail as soon as the rail passengers had embarked.) But by 1966, only three years after the *Avalon* entered service, British Rail and their Dutch partners found it necessary to order two car ferries for the Harwich – Hook route. The first of these, Sealink's (i.e. British Rail's) *St. George*, entered service in July, 1968. Her SMZ partner, *Koningin Juliana*, followed in the October. The new car ferries now operated the night service and two of the remaining 'classic' ships ran the daytime sailings. *Avalon* was mainly kept as a reserve vessel – very necessarily in view of the uncertain reliability of the *St. George*'s machinery – and continued her off-season cruise programmes. The arrival of a third car ferry, the solid-looking *St.Edmund****, at the end of December, 1974

*** see the first volume of the author's *Liners & Cruise Ships* series.

rendered the *Avalon* redundant after only eleven years of rather intermittent service.

Sealink had plans for her, however. On the 29th December, she sailed for the Tyne, where Swan, Hunter converted her into a car ferry for the service across the Irish Sea between Fishguard and Rosslare. The cost was said to be about £1 million. The cabins on Main and Upper decks were stripped out and gave way to two vehicle decks loaded through a vertically-opening stern door. There was now space for up to 210 cars. It seems to have been an ingenious conversion but limited headroom meant that no more than eight high-sided lorries could be carried. As with many of the passenger/vehicle ferry conversions and newbuilds of a few years earlier, failure to anticipate the growth of lorry traffic quickly curtailed the ship's usefulness.

During the conversion, the shelter deck superstructure was extended aft. This, and the necessarily chunkier stern, slightly spoiled the *Avalon*'s handsome appearance. The new superstructure did, however, accommodate a much bigger second class lounge – very necessary as the ship could now carry up to 1,200 passengers (as against the original 750). As a result, at one stage of her Irish Sea career she was fitted with two extra lifeboats. She was still a two class ship but there were now only 19 first and 13 second class cabins, accommodating just 72 berthed passengers. Among the casualties of the conversion were the de luxe and special cabins on the

Above. *Avalon* in her original livery and (opposite page, top) with the new Sealink logo on her funnel. *(Bruce Peter collection)*

Promenade Deck. With much less demand for cabins on night sailings on the Irish routes than on the North Sea service, *Avalon*'s character underwent something of a change.

She took over the single-ship Fishguard – Rosslare service in July, 1975. However, her lack of adequate space for lorries became an increasing problem and in March, 1979 she was replaced by a chartered Swedish ferry, the *Stena Normandica* (1974 / 5,443 gross tons). This rather ugly vessel had much less style than the *Avalon* but, crucially, she had a capacious vehicle deck, with both bow and stern doors. *Avalon* was now transferred to the service between Holyhead and the pleasant port of Dun Laoghaire, conveniently close to Dublin. (She was not a complete stranger to this route, having deputised on it for at least one stint during her time at Fishguard.)

It is a measure of the lack of progress in the British ferry scene that in 1910 advertisements for the service between Holyhead and Dun Laoghaire (then known as Kingstown) were proclaiming that it was maintained by 24 knot ships – somewhat faster than the *Avalon* and her running mate 69 years later. *Avalon* was the secondary vessel on the route. During the peak season, she was scheduled to make either one or two crossings in each direction every 24 hours. For most of the rest of the year, she stood by as a reserve ship. Again, her lack of adequate space for vehicles limited her usefulness and it was often necessary to complement her sailings with a ro-ro vessel departing half an hour later. Her 1979 season was, in fact, interrupted by a bout of boiler trouble and by an unexpected recall to the Fishguard – Rosslare service for several weeks when the *Stena Normandica* also broke down.

Sealink's Irish Sea services were, in fact, bedevilled by the unreliability of their ships. In 1980, not only did the *Avalon*

miss sailings in January and May-June, but her running mate *St. Columba* was also suffering breakdowns. In the end, enough was enough – it was decided that the *Avalon* must go. Considered unreliable, inadequate and fuel-thirsty, she made her last two-way crossing from Holyhead on the 8th September, 1980 and on the 24th sailed for Barrow-in-Furness and lay-up. In November, she was sold to a Cypriot concern called Seafaith Navigation Co. who, with a single economical stroke of the paintbrush, renamed her *Valon* – taken to be an indication that they had no intention of returning her to service. Sure enough, when the *Valon* sailed on the 20th December, with her funnel now painted plain black, she was bound for Gadani Beach and the scrappers' torches. The career of this once-notable ship had lasted for not much more than 17 years.

The conversion of the ship into a car ferry necessitated considerable changes at the stern, where she now had a ramp. *(Ambrose Greenway collection)*

Queen Elizabeth 2

Completed 1969.   65,863 gross tons.

Length overall: 963 ft. 0ins. Breadth: 105 ft. 3ins.

Draught: 32 ft. 7½ins.

Geared steam turbines. Twin screw.

Service speed: 28½ knots.

Became 66,852 gross tons (1972) and 67,140 gross tons (1977). Converted to diesel-electric propulsion, 1987; gross tonnage now 66,450.

1995 gross tonnage: 70,327.

Laid up 2008.

The *Queen Elizabeth 2* represented an abrupt break with Cunard tradition. *(Bruce Peter collection)*

I find it hard to write dispassionately about *QE2*. She has been one of my favourite ships – along with *Black Prince*, *Maxim Gorkiy*, *Oceanic* and a few others. And she has always had star quality. I remember so well the spectacular send-off she was given by the port of Trieste after one of her rare calls there. And people coming down to the harbour at Funchal to see her depart even after her umpteenth visit (and dozens of German passengers on the *AidaBlu* flashing their cameras as we sailed past). Then there was the lovely exhibition of *QE2* memorabilia mounted in the Hamburg Chamber of Commerce by Stefan and Petra Behn. And not least, I remember watching from a crowded harbour boat in April, 2004 as the old *QE2* and the brand new *Queen Mary 2* made their double departure from New York with the skyscrapers of Manhattan silhouetted against the evening sky and a magnificent fireworks display adding to the excitement of the occasion. The event was really intended to celebrate the new ship but, hugely impressive though the *Queen Mary 2* was, I thought that the *QE2* stole the show. When seen almost from water level, the veteran liner's hull looked so very graceful and everything about her had such presence.

Then, sadly, there was that final departure from Southampton which I watched from the deck of the

Shieldhall along with a hundred or more other fans. When, having accompanied the great ship down Southampton Water, we turned and left her as she sailed off into the night, it was a hugely emotional moment. There have been so many memories.

Of course, *QE2* had her bad times as well as good and was often surrounded by controversy. When she was good she was very, very good; but when she was bad she was horrid. In truth, she could sometimes be disappointing. But somehow one always forgave her. Over the years, she changed character and not everyone approved. She had started as the epitome of sleek 'Sixties trendiness but, as refit followed refit, she regressed – at least, from the point of view of the modernists who had hailed her 'cutting edge' design – into a 'retro' evocation of what purported to be traditional ocean liner style. But many of her passengers preferred her that way and she was commercially successful.

Controversy had even started during her gestation period. By the end of the 1950s, the Cunard Steam Ship Company's weekly transatlantic express service between Southampton and New York was meeting formidable competition from the American speed champion *United States* and the other new liners which had come onto the scene; and also, more ominously, from the piston-engined aircraft and then, after October, 1958, from the jet 'planes. *Queen Mary* was reaching the end of her active life and obviously, too, *Queen Elizabeth* had a limited future. Cunard, though, had plans for a new liner under way and in 1959 the decision was taken to go ahead with the project.

The original intention was that the new ship should be only slightly smaller than the 80,000-ton *Queen Mary* which she would replace. She would observe the tradition of carrying her passengers in three strictly segregated classes and, although suitable for out-of-season cruising, she would be mainly used for transatlantic crossings. However, the outlook for those regular liner voyages was becoming ever more obscure and the political situation, too, was changing. This was important because the new ship would have to be partly financed by a government loan which Cunard would gradually repay – an arrangement similar to those which had made possible the building of *Lusitania* and the first *Mauretania* and, later, *Queen Mary* and *Queen Elizabeth*. But the case for the new ship, code-named *Q3*, was much less clear and voices were raised in Parliament and in the Press, asserting that tax-payers' money should not be wasted on financing a liner which could well turn out to be a White Elephant. On the other hand, supporters of the

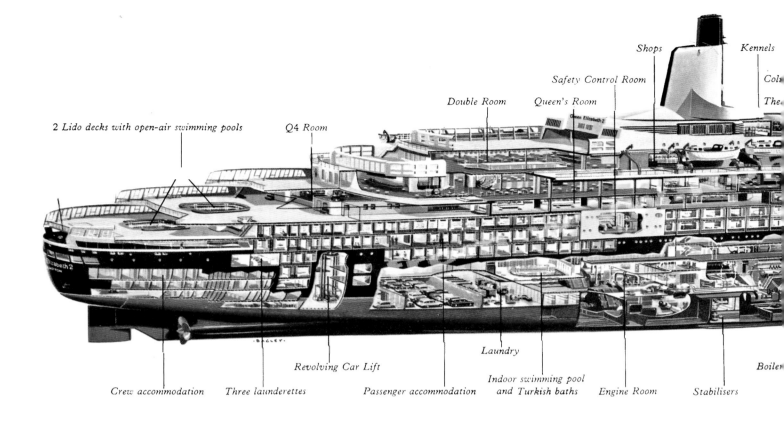

2 Lido decks with open-air swimming pools

Q4 Room

Double Room

Safety Control Room

Queen's Room

Shops

Kennels

Col

The

Crew accommodation

Three launderettes

Revolving Car Lift

Passenger accommodation

Laundry

Indoor swimming pool and Turkish baths

Engine Room

Stabilisers

Boiler

project argued that, for reasons of national prestige, Britain must still have a modern Atlantic liner and that the country's struggling shipbuilding industry needed the work.

In 1960, a government-appointed committee came down in favour of Cunard's plans more or less as they stood and the design and development work continued. Despite their long relationship with the John Brown yard at Clydebank, Cunard had to put the contract for the new ship out to competitive tender among the major British shipbuilders. When the tenders were opened in 1961 it was found – to the dismay of Browns and, no doubt, of many of their friends in Cunard – that the offer jointly submitted by Vickers-Armstrongs and Swan, Hunter & Wigham Richardson had eclipsed that from Browns both on price and on delivery date. More significantly – although that may not have been generally realised at the time – the two successful companies had also put forward an alternative specification for a somewhat smaller, much less traditional, less expensive ship which would be more economical to operate. There is still a certain amount of resentment among veterans of Vickers' Barrow-in-Furness yard that, although they were given a contract for preliminary development work on a ship of this more modest type, the one for her actual construction eventually went to John Brown. (This time, the tender submitted by Browns was the lowest.) However, in view of the disastrous consequences which ensued for Browns, it may be that Vickers had a lucky escape.

The Q4, as this new, smaller ship was then known, was in some respects as controversial as the previous project. Cunard were instinctively conservative but, in their fine if somewhat polemic book QE2, Britain's Greatest Liner, the modernist Bruce Peter and his co-authors Philip Dawson and Ian Johnston describe the way in which the company was pressured into weeding out most of the designers originally chosen to work on the ship's exterior and interiors, replacing them with others of a trendier bent. The two key figures in the new team were James Gardner, who was responsible for the overall external shape, and Dennis Lennon, who co-ordinated the design of the interiors. Other notable contributors included Jon Bannenberg, David Hicks, Michael Inchbald (one of the few survivors from the original team) and Sir Hugh Casson. Interestingly, two of Sir Hugh's student pupils were given the task of designing the facilities intended for children and teenagers. It is said that the relationship between the newly-recruited stylists and the down-to-earth naval architects and engineers responsible for technical matters was sometimes uneasy.

Nevertheless, the eventual result was a fine ship – and a very modern one. In particular, all cabins and suites were placed within the hull, while the public rooms occupied the superstructure. This was in sharp contrast to the traditional layout, as had been recently exemplified by Canberra and to a lesser extent Oriana. For many years, dining rooms had tended to be low down in the hull, in

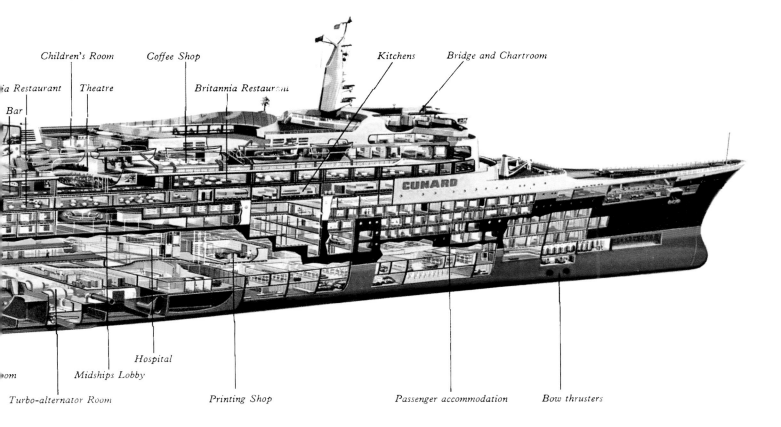

Children's Room   Coffee Shop   Kitchens   Bridge and Chartroom

a Restaurant   Theatre   Britannia Restaurant

Bar

Hospital

Midships Lobby

Turbo-alternator Room   Printing Shop   Passenger accommodation   Bow thrusters

the most stable part of the ship, while most of the first class cabins and suites occupied the superstructure where passengers could enjoy the best sea views and have ready access to the open air. It had mainly been the less expensive passengers who were accommodated within the hull. And most of the lounges were usually at main deck level or thereabouts.

Although Cunard had originally intended their new liner to be a three-class ship, in the event they followed the new orthodoxy and she carried her passengers in just two classes. These were designated first and cabin. However, in tune with the times, division between the classes was much less rigid than of yore, particularly when the vessel was in cruising mode. By now, it went without saying that she was air-conditioned throughout.

The décor in both classes was dramatic in the brightly-coloured, trendy style which the World had come to associate with the Swinging 'Sixties 'scene'. The calculation was that some of the International Jet Set could be attracted back to sea travel and that even staid, middle-aged, middle class passengers could be seduced into shedding their reserve while sailing in this startlingly modern ship. (Somehow the general public always thought of her as a haunt of the rich and famous, even towards the end of her long career. I remember chatting with a lady over afternoon tea on a routine Mediterranean cruise during QE2's final season. 'But where are the celebrities?' she wondered.)

The architect James Gardner was responsible for the revolutionary shape of the ship so dramatically displayed in the cut-away drawing (at the top of the page) which appeared in publicity material when she was introduced. (Paolo Piccione collection)

Perhaps the favourite space on the ship – and one of the most enduring – was the first class Queens Room, a ballroom which also served as the setting for those famously stylish afternoon teas, served by white-gloved stewards while a string trio played refined music in the background. Taking in the side passages, the room stretched over the full width of the ship and, although serving a very traditional purpose, was gracefully modern with its slender, trumpet-topped columns and back-lit, slatted ceiling. As was the case throughout the ship, the furniture was also ultra-modern – in this instance consisting of pedestal chairs obviously inspired by the famous tulip-shaped designs of Eero Saarinen. A bust of the young Queen Elizabeth II provided a touch of gravity.

Another notable first class room was the small and darkly sumptuous Midships Bar. Even the first class lobby was memorable, a circular space centred around another slim, trumpet-topped column which led up into a ceiling consisting of concentric plastic circles. (Modern, easily cleaned but decorative materials were widely used throughout the passenger quarters. At the time of the launch, it was stated that a million square feet of Formica would be consumed in fitting out the new ship. Later reports mentioned a figure of two million.) The first class dining room was known as the Columbia Restaurant and adjacent to it was a discreet Grill Room. There was a lounge and night-club known as the Q4 Room which led out to the first class swimming pool on an after deck. And first class passengers also had the exclusive use of a conference room, a card room and a library.

Another striking space, this time mainly intended for the cabin class passengers but in fact open to everyone, was the Double Room. For the most part, the Q4 did not aspire to the palatial scale of her predecessors but, as the name implied, the Double Room rose through two decks – a lounge, bandstand and dance floor on the lower level were overlooked by the balcony of an upper lounge. A whole wall was spectacularly covered with claret-coloured suede (which, unfortunately, was already peeling off when I first travelled on the ship some years later.). The two levels were

The Queens Room was one of the most famous lounges at sea. Although the trendy 'Sixties furniture was replaced during the ship's many refits, the room remained essentially unchanged throughout her career. *(Bruce Peter collection)*

Above. The spectacular Double Room and (below) the broad arcade which was in effect an extension to the starboard side of the Queens Room. *(Bruce Peter collection)*

connected by a sweeping, metallic double staircase and, indeed, dulled aluminium was a prominent element in the décor of many of the public spaces.

Also double height was the relatively plain but effective theatre (actually used mainly as a cinema and for lectures, recitals and the traditional Church service conducted every Sunday by the captain). Nearby was the busy and brightly coloured Theatre Bar, in which even the grand piano was painted red. The 736 Club was the cabin class's angular equivalent of first's Q4 Room nightclub. (736 had been the ship's yard number at John Brown's while, as we have seen, *Q4* was her pre-launch code name.) The huge Britannia Restaurant was only marginally less sophisticated than its first class equivalent and contained a colourful statue of the lady herself, poised to rule the waves. Forward of the Britannia Restaurant was the Lookout Lounge, from which one could gaze out over the bow. Cabin class also had its own library.

Each class had both an outside and an indoor swimming pool and there were saunas and Turkish baths. Young passengers were provided with a room suitably named The Juke Box and there was a 24-hour Coffee Shop. There were two long shopping arcades; and the other rooms included a small but very dignified synagogue designed by Mischa Black and panelled in lovely wood – quite a number of the transatlantic passengers were likely to be New York Jewish – and an art gallery. In the latter, works by estimable artists were offered for sale (in contrast to the largely inferior art sold to unsuspecting punters on some ships these days). Unlike the synagogue, the art gallery did not last long. Another regrettable casualty of early refits was the Lookout Lounge. Indeed, by the end, very few of the original rooms had survived – in addition to the synagogue, the Queens Room remained (albeit with less modish furnishings) as did the Midships Bar (by now somewhat altered and called the Chart Room), the theatre and the entrance lobby (although the latter had been 'traditionalised'). Times changed, the 'Sixties ceased to swing and the ship acquired a more comfortable, middle-brow ambience. Like many shocking young ladies she gradually became a dignified and highly respectable old lady. It is interesting to speculate how dated the original décor would have seemed if it had still been in place several decades after it first grabbed attention. And would some of the modern materials which were used have lasted as well as the traditional woods on the earlier ships?

In her original form, the ship accommodated up to 564 passengers in first class and 1,441 in cabin class, although when she was sent cruising the numbers were reduced. All cabins and suites in both classes had private facilities and as many as three-quarters of them had either windows or port-

The first class Columbia Restaurant (top) was representative of the ship's original style. Work proceeds (lower) on the sweeping staircase of the Double Room. *(Bruce Peter collection)*

Like the *Queen Mary* before her, *QE2* had a synagogue for her many Jewish passengers. It was simple but beautiful. *(Maurizio Eliseo)*

holes (in a few cases this was made possible by giving the rooms an interlocking configuration rather similar to that of the old-time Bibby cabins). There was a very wide range of accommodation, from small two-berth cabins low down on Deck Five to 46 luxurious suites, in addition to de luxe rooms which could be combined to form suites. In fact, quite a number of cabins had connecting doors to the neighbouring room, thus giving an unusual degree of flexibility in accommodating families or other passengers who required more spacious quarters. Also, for many years the ship had more single cabins than any other vessel in the cruise market.

But it was not just her interiors which were the height of modernity. Her outer shape was equally modish. Her design, though, did benefit from Cunard's and John Brown's long experience of building the hulls of generations of Atlantic liners and, as a consequence, she soon gained the reputation of being 'a good sea boat', well able to cope with the worst of conditions. Sleek and elegantly shaped and with a bulbous forefoot, the hull had a beautifully raked, fine-lined bow. Another graceful feature was the rounded stern topped by curved windshields which sheltered those passengers, wrapped in those famous Cunard rugs, who were enjoying their morning bouillon on the open after decks. The solitary mast, over the bridge, was so shaped that it became an architectural feature. And then there was the controversial funnel – a narrow pipe partly shrouded by a broader outer casing which was painted white and had curved wind deflectors at its base. No doubt it was admirably efficient at throwing the exhaust from the furnaces well clear of the decks but it was not only tradition-

alists like me who regretted that Cunard's 129-year old funnel colours had been discarded, although that distinctive orange-red did peep out from the insides of the wind deflectors. Nevertheless, the ship's very recognisable shape became so widely admired that when Royal Cruise Line converted the former *Doric* (ex-*Hanseatic*, ex-*Shalom*) into their *Royal Odyssey*, she emerged as a very close cousin of the great Cunarder.

The *Q4* was an all-welded ship and, as was becoming customary with big liners, her superstructure was constructed of aluminium alloy – 1,100 tons of it. This was said to have reduced top-weight by a half but, as the years progressed, worrying cracks began to appear round window apertures and elsewhere. Also, welding the steel and aluminium structures together where they joined just above the promenade deck had presented difficulties and required the use of special techniques.

While not intended to be a record-breaker, the *Q4* was an express liner designed to cross the Atlantic in five days, to do which she required a service speed of 28½ knots. As yet, there could be no question of using diesel engines on such a large, fast liner – but in any case Cunard were so wedded to steam turbines that they even specified them for their container ships while the other partners in the Atlantic Container Line all went for diesels. The *Q4* was given two sets of turbines designed by Pametrada and constructed by John Brown Engineering (Clydebank), Ltd., which together developed over 110,000 shp transmitted through double reduction gearing to twin propellers. Each set of turbines consisted of a high pressure and a low pressure unit, fed with steam from the biggest marine boilers ever built.

The first class suites and cabins combined a light modernity with an air of luxury. *(Bruce Peter collection)*

Cunard also made much of the fact that many of the *Q4*'s functions were controlled by the largest computer yet installed in a merchant ship. There were side-thrusters and two sets of fin-type stabilisers. Of the six small holds, only one was reached through a hatchway. It was served by two cranes. Access to the other holds, which were intended for carrying cars, baggage and stores, was through side ports. The keel was laid on the 5th July, 1965 and the Queen performed the launching ceremony on the 20th September, 1967. It is customary that a lady who has launched a ship should receive a gift and in this case, Her Majesty was given a speedboat for installation on the Royal Yacht *Britannia*. I have hitherto referred to this new flagship of the British merchant marine as the *Q4* – deliberately so since, as with the *Queen Mary* before her, her intended name was known only to those in the innermost circle and it had still not been painted on the hull when she was launched. Her Majesty proclaimed: "I name this ship *Queen Elizabeth, the Second*" but was that perhaps a Royal mistake? In fact, the ship was officially called *Queen Elizabeth 2* – although she very quickly became known to half the World simply as the *QE2*. Whether or not this was a deliberate abbreviation, it turned out to be a brilliant marketing ploy. (Rather less brilliant was the *QE2* logo, decipherable only with difficulty, which was used for the silver medal commemorating her maiden voyage - on this page - as well as in some of the early publicity material but was then discarded.)

The launch of a vessel as big as the *QE2* in a confined space presented huge difficulties and the Clyde Port Authority had dredged that stretch of the river in order to accommodate her. Seven tugs were needed to handle her and to shepherd her to the fitting out basin (also specially dredged). The launch was a joyous occasion, watched by thousands of people. Yet the omens were not good. These were difficult times for shipping and for shipbuilding. Three days previously the great old *Queen Mary* had begun her final crossing from New York. On the Clyde, the famous Barclay, Curle yard had ceased to build ships. In Copenhagen, workers were voting on a scheme to save the Burmeister & Wain yard from closure. Furthermore, the eventual cost of building the *QE2* had caused financial problems for the already troubled Cunard and it had become necessary for the government to make an extra loan to the company, bringing the amount it had lent to

£24 million (to be repaid over 12 years). In the end, the total cost of the ship was £29½ million.

John Brown's success in winning the contract to build the *Q4* had been greeted with relief in Clydebank. The future of the fitting out department – and possibly of the whole yard – depended on it. By the time the ship was launched, however, negotiations were going on for the John Brown yard (but not the company's wider engineering interests) to be taken over by a new government-sponsored concern called Upper Clyde Shipbuilders, Ltd. which would also absorb several other local shipyards.

The problems were not only financial. Management and labour were often at loggerheads and the construction of the *QE2* was bedevilled by overtime bans and strikes (and also by theft). It had become almost impossible to deliver ships on time and the famous yard lost money on each of the last four passenger ships it built – *Centaur*, *Kungsholm*, the *QE2* and *Blenheim*. In the end, Upper Clyde Shipbuilders decided that enough was enough. No more passenger vessels would go down the ways at Clydebank. Nevertheless, the *QE2* was a source of great pride and, in the days before she was due to leave, about 24,000 shipyard workers, family and friends were taken on conducted tours over her.

Completion of the *QE2* had inevitably taken longer than scheduled and when, on the 19th November, 1968, she finally left the fitting-out basin to go into the Scott-Lithgow drydock at Greenock she was still unfinished. She ran trials off Cumbrae and Arran from the 26th to the 29th November but an oil leak caused contamination of the boiler feedwater and, humiliatingly, tugs had to be called to stand by in case there was a complete breakdown as she returned to Greenock. It was announced that a charity cruise which was to have taken place at Christmas and would have raised £40,000 for the National Cancer Relief Fund would have to be cancelled. Trials were not resumed until the 17th December when the ship achieved a speed of 32.46 knots over the measured mile off Arran, with her turbines producing 117,000 shp. Despite everything, she had easily exceeded the targets set in the contract.

On the 23rd December she left on a trial voyage to the Canary Islands. Her 500 'passengers' were Cunard employees and their families. But it proved to be a shakedown cruise in more senses than one when serious vibration developed in one of her turbines. Cunard refused to accept delivery of the ship which, in any case, was still incomplete. On the 2nd January, 1969, the new national flagship limped into Southampton to what *Lloyd's List* described as 'a quiet welcome'. She lay at the Ocean Terminal for nearly three months while re-designed turbine rotors were manufactured in Scotland and flown down to Southampton to be installed. The episode led to an acrimonious public spat between Cunard and John Brown Engineering, which at one stage threatened to descend into legal action. Meanwhile, more than 1,400 workers were striving to finish the ship, some of them housed in a former Irish Sea ferry which was moored nearby. The *QE2*'s problems generated a great deal of unfavourable publicity for British engineering and one journal (published on Tyneside) described her as 'a 963-feet long advertisement for technical imprecision'. It may have been little consolation that the *Hamburg*, the new flagship of the German-Atlantic Line, was also said to be having turbine problems at the same time.

It was not until the 24th March, 1969 that the *QE2* started further technical trials which took three days and were followed by another shakedown cruise which lasted eight days and covered 5,000 nautical miles. This time things went well and, finally, on the 18th April Cunard accepted delivery. There was then what was described as a preview cruise, on which she took her first paying passengers to Las Palmas, Tenerife and Lisbon. *QE2*'s life began in earnest, however, on the 2nd May when she set off on her much-delayed maiden transatlantic crossing. Despite all the adverse publicity which she had attracted, her departure was a celebratory occasion marked by a fly-past by aircraft from the Fleet Air Arm in an anchor-shaped formation. After calling briefly at Le Havre she headed for New York, where she arrived on the 7th May. The normally blasé newspapers and radio and television stations in that hard-bitten city gave her a welcome which was perhaps not equalled until the maiden arrival of the *Queen Mary 2* in April, 2004. There's something about a Cunarder.

Revealingly, when the *QE2* made her New York début, Sir Basil Smallpiece, the company's reforming chairman, was reported as saying, 'With this ship we are out of the transportation business and into the leisure business'. Indeed,

Doubts about the uncertain future of the shipyard are temporarily forgotten as the great ship enters the water (above) and (opposite page) the upper portion of the mast is lowered into place. All subsequent Cunard passenger ship newbuilds have been given masts of this distinctive shape. *(Bruce Peter collection)*

her introduction and the withdrawal of the old *Queen Elizabeth* marked the final acknowledgement by Cunard that a regular year-round transatlantic service was no longer a viable proposition.

The sleek and trendy new liner now settled down to what was to become her regular routine. Between May and October each year she made 5-day transatlantic crossings, with occasional calls at Cobh en route and sometimes at Boston. (After May 1972, Cherbourg replaced Le Havre as the regular French port of call on these voyages.) They were interspersed by cruises from Southampton which took her variously to Norway, Iberia, the Atlantic islands and the Mediterranean. Then she would embark on a winter-long season of Caribbean cruises out of New York, sometimes picking up additional passengers at Boston or Hampton Roads. A typical Caribbean itinerary would be New York –

St. Thomas – Fort de France – Bridgetown in Barbados – Grenada – Caracas – Port au Prince – New York.

Already, the *QE2* was shewing that knack of attracting headlines which she continued to exhibit throughout her career with Cunard. On the 9th January, 1971, while on a Caribbean cruise, she raced towards the French liner *Antilles*, which was aground and on fire off the island of Mustique, and took on board 501 passengers and crew members, some of whom she landed at Bridgetown, the rest at La Guaira.

Later in 1971, there was a significant development which probably changed the *QE2*'s career. The Cunard company was taken over by Trafalgar House Investments, Ltd., a building and construction concern which had diversified to become a broad conglomerate whose speciality was the acquisition of problematic but undervalued assets (such as

the *Daily Express* group of newspapers). Over the years, Trafalgar House had the *QE2* refitted several times, aiming to improve her commercial potential. This gradually altered her character – I was going to say radically, but there was nothing at all radical about what was done to her.

The first of these refits took place at Southampton in October and November, 1972. The most obvious alteration was the insertion on the top deck between the mast and the funnel of a two-deck high structure containing twenty new first class suites, each with a balcony. At the same time, the upper level of the Double Room became a shopping arcade and the Lookout Lounge was replaced by an additional galley, thus regrettably depriving the ship of a forward facing observation room. Other spaces to disappear were the Art Gallery, the Coffee Shop and the 736 Club. On the other hand, the occupants of more of the first class cabins could now enjoy discreet dining, either in a new Queen's Grill or in the original grillroom, now known as the Princess Grill. A new casino was also constructed. Not unusually, the refit took longer than expected and when the *QE2* departed for Boston she was several days late. In order to make it possible to complete the work during the crossing, she sailed without passengers.

She was such a high-profile ship that, inevitably, there were times when security became a concern. There were consistent rumours that I.R.A, sympathisers among the crew were smuggling arms into Ireland and in October, 1971 some sub-machineguns and hand grenades were found in luggage being landed at Cobh. Then in May, 1972, Cunard's New York office received a 'phone call alleging that primed explosives had been secreted on board and demanding a ransom of $350,000. The threat was taken sufficiently seri-

Opposite page. The *QE2*'s beautifully shaped stern. Above. Moran tugs handle the *QE2* on her maiden arrival in New York. Strangely, she was not dressed overall. Note the sports deck just aft of the mast. It was later replaced by luxury suites.
(Bruce Peter collection and Maurizio Eliseo collection)

The original Grill Room, here seen in its later form as the Princess Grill, was eventually supplemented by the exclusive Queen's Grill and the Britannia Grill. *(Maurizio Eliseo)*

ously for four bomb disposal experts to be flown out by the R.A.F. and parachuted into the sea in mid-Atlantic. They were picked up by one of the ship's launches but they found no trace of explosives. Eventually the perpetrator of the hoax was traced and arrested. He pleaded guilty and a New York court sent him to prison.

Security was again to the fore when, in April, 1973, the *QE2* sailed from Southampton under charter to a Jewish organisation, taking a party of passengers to Ashdod and Haifa to attend the celebrations of the 25th anniversary of the foundation of the state of Israel. (Questions were asked in the British parliament about who was paying for the frogmen and security guards who attended the ship before she left Southampton – apparently, the bill was sent to Cunard. There was also controversy in Israel since her presence in Haifa harbour for several days seriously disrupted the import of grain.) But it seems that there may have been a very real risk – it was alleged that the Libyans had planned to attack the liner as she sailed through the Mediterranean

and were only prevented from doing so by the intervention of the Egyptian government. The I.R.A. also saw her as a potential target but a plot to blow her up while she lay in Southampton was discovered and foiled by MI5 and in November, 1976 a court sentenced two men to 20 years in gaol and a third conspirator to 16 years.

For some years, the *QE2* was spectacularly breakdown-prone. Most notably, on the 1st April, 1974 all her boilers had to be closed down during a Caribbean cruise from New York. Once again, oil had contaminated the feedwater. Cunard was forced to charter Flagship Cruises' *Sea Venture* which hastily landed her own passengers in Bermuda and rushed to take on board the *QE2*'s passengers whom she also landed in Bermuda (they were then flown back to New York). Two tugs towed the *QE2*, again to Bermuda where repairs were made. The total cost (including the cancellation of the following cruise) was said to be £750,000. Then on the 23rd July, 1976, a serious fire broke out in the engine room while the ship was about 80 miles west of the

Scilly Isles, outbound from Southampton. It caused considerable damage to one engine and raged upwards, reaching as far as the funnel casing. One man was seriously injured but the blaze was extinguished after about six hours. The *QE2* was forced to return to Southampton on one engine and repairs cost about £1 million.

When she was in cruising mode, she would usually carry no more than 1,400 passengers and class divisions would be somewhat relaxed. In her early years, most of her cruises were relatively short, 7 or 14 days. But on the 10th January, 1975 she left New York on a much more ambitious voyage – her first round-the-World cruise. After a call at Port Everglades, this took her eastwards to such exotic places as Colombo and Hong Kong and it was from the latter port that 500 passengers were able to make a 3-day overland excursion to Canton. In those very authoritarian days in China it was regarded as remarkable that so large a party of westerners, particularly Americans, was allowed to enter the country. Thereafter, the ship would make at least one long-distance cruise every year, often a complete circumnavigation but sometimes a Pacific Circle cruise or a lengthy voyage round South America. Her first call at Sydney, in February, 1978, was a particularly notable event.

Marketing of her regular transatlantic service now included some very attractive packages, such as ones coupling a sea voyage one way with a flight in the other direction, usually with B.O.A.C. (the predecessors of British Airways). Particularly notable in later years was a very classy combination of a *QE2* crossing with a transatlantic flight by *Concorde* and a stay at either the Waldorf-Astoria in New York or the Ritz in London. Cunard, in fact, became *Concorde*'s biggest customers; and for some years they were also said to be the biggest buyers of Beluga caviar. Although *QE2*'s startlingly trendy décor may have been somewhat diluted by now, her reputation as a favourite of the wealthy classes was being maintained.

It has to be said, however, that in the 'Seventies and 'Eighties, passengers lower down the social scale were not always treated well. I think that it was only in 1987, when her sometimes grumpy and unwilling British stewards were replaced by a multi-national crew, that standards improved. Earlier, the Tables of the World Restaurant had become almost infamous. This room – divided into five areas intended to be suggestive of different culinary cultures – was the result of a remodelling in less modish style of the Britannia Restaurant during a far-reaching refit in 1977, this time at the Bethlehem Steel yard in Bayonne, New York. More successful was the insertion at the same time of two huge split-level first class penthouses between the mast and those top deck suites which had appeared during the 1972 refit.

In 1982, the *QE2* went to war. On the 4th May, while she was at Southampton preparing for her next cruise, she was requisitioned by the British government to join the diverse fleet of nearly fifty merchant ships which was taking troops and equipment to counter the Argentine invasion of South Georgia and the Falklands. Many ships, including the liners *Canberra* and *Uganda*, were already well on their way but more troops were needed. I was told by a senior naval officer that doubts were expressed whether such an important and prestigious vessel as the *QE2* should be risked in so hazardous an exercise but that, on being told that there was no alternative, the redoubtable Mrs. Thatcher immediately squashed the faint-hearted 'wets' by saying, 'Right, we'll have her.' There could be no further discussion. Of course, if the *QE2* had been sunk, quite apart from the dreadful loss of life which might have resulted, the triumph for the Argentines would have been immense. The requisition did not come as a complete surprise, however – Cunard had already taken out insurance cover against the possibility.

Some amazing feats of ship conversion were carried out in a very short time in those anxious days, not least the modifications made to the *QE2* by the Southampton firm of Vosper Thornycroft. Two enormous helicopter pads were installed, one of them some way forward and the other over the after decks where the ship's structure was already well reinforced to carry the weight of the swimming pools. This involved the demolition of the Q4 Room and the removal of those stylishly slanted windshields which gave the stern its characteristic look. Refuelling At Sea gear was also installed. Within only eight days, the *QE2* was ready to sail, having embarked 3,150 troops together with large quantities of stores, aviation fuel, ammunition and equipment. She left Southampton for the South Atlantic on the 12th May, manned by volunteers from her peacetime crew. Indeed, far more than were needed had offered to go and about 300 had to be left at home. For most of the long voyage, she sailed without escort but, unlike *Canberra*, *Uganda*, *Norland* and some other brave merchant ships, she was not sent into the battle zone. Nevertheless she was at considerable risk – not only from attack but also while feeling her way through a vast field of over a hundred icebergs in fog while approaching South Georgia. Once there, she transferred her troops and military cargo to *Canberra* and *Norland* which took them onwards to the Falklands. She then returned home with 700 casualties, including many injured men from the lost H.M.S. *Antelope*, H.M.S. *Ardent* and H.M.S. *Coventry*, arriving back in Southampton on the 11th June. Among those giving the *QE2* and the troops an extremely heartfelt welcome was the Queen Mother on board the Royal Yacht *Britannia*.

While the *QE2* was being refitted to restore her to peacetime condition, certain changes were made. Most obviously, the hull was repainted in light grey and, happily, the anonymous white of the funnel casing gave way to the traditional Cunard colours. More fundamentally, the Q4 Room was not re-instated but was replaced by a new buffet and lounge called the Club Lido which led out to one of the open air pools. The whole area was later given a retractable Magradome glass-panelled roof (which tended to leak and was eventually done away with).

The liner's return to civilian service on the 14th August was a great occasion, her departure from Southampton being watched by thousands of spectators. Unhappily, her old propensity for breakdown which, very fortunately, had not been evident during her time at war, soon re-asserted itself. In September, she was immobilised for over three days by a broken pump off Falmouth. Boiler trouble followed in December and in June, 1983 there was a serious

turbine problem. It proved necessary to replace one of the rotors. While a new one was being made, the ship went temporarily back into service at reduced speed. By the time repairs were completed, she had missed a cruise and two Atlantic crossings and the total cost of the breakdown had amounted to £2½ million. While she lay at Southampton, the opportunity was taken to repaint her hull black (or, to be more precise, dark charcoal grey). That November, her annual refit was, for the first time, entrusted to a German yard – the Lloyd Werft in Bremerhaven – which caused anguish in the British press and disappointment in Southampton.

The technical problems continued when a generator failed off the Virgin Islands in May, 1984; and then an electrical fire put one of the turbines out of action in October, 1984, causing the ship to be two days late in arriving at Southampton. This was her sixth breakdown in less than three years and it had been known for some time that

During her long career with Cunard, *QE2* entered her homeport of Southampton nearly 700 times. Here she is returning at the end of the Falklands campaign. *(R. Bruce Grice)*

Cunard were seeking tenders to re-engine her with diesels, which would, it was hoped, not only obviate the problems but would make her more economical to operate. It was variously estimated that fuel consumption would be reduced by either 40% or 50% and it was expected that the cost of the conversion would be recouped within five years. An added bonus was that the ship's life would be extended by twenty years. Again, the contract went to the Lloyd Werft, where she arrived on the 27th October, 1986. In a massive operation, the boilers, turbines and generators were stripped out and no less than nine new MAN B&W 9-cylinder diesel engines with a total output of 130,000 bhp were inserted, each coupled to a new generator. These not only provided the power for the two electric propulsion motors which now drove the ship but also for all the other equipment on board. The whole system was fully automated. The original turbines had, by the way, been offered for sale but there were no takers.

At the same time, other changes were made. Apart from a general upgrading and refurbishment, a further eight penthouses were erected on the top deck; overall passenger capacity was increased to 1,870; the Tables of the World was refurnished as the Mauretania Restaurant; the lower level of the Double Down Room was further changed and now became the Grand Lounge; the shopping arcades were extended; a new Yacht Club was constructed; controllable-pitch propellers were fitted, behind which were patent devices called Grim wheels which were said to increase efficiency but which started to disintegrate during trials and were later removed; and a new and much stouter funnel had to replace the previous slim structure in order to accommodate the large number of uptakes which were now necessary. The whole transformation of the ship was an enormous, complicated job costing well over $160 million and the contract stipulated that the work must be completed in no more than 179 days. This was a busy time for the Lloyd Werft as, while the yard was altering the QE2 so fundamentally, it also refitted Canberra.

Sea trials during mid-April, 1987 were several times interrupted by technical mishaps but the QE2 eventually achieved 33.1 knots over the measured mile. (Later, on her delivery voyage to Southampton, she easily reached 35 knots, which prompted an optimist in Cunard to tell Lloyd's List that an attempt on the United States' Blue Riband record of 35.39 knots for an entire westbound crossing might be made. That was almost certainly wishful thinking.) The QE2 finally left the yard on the 25th April, on schedule but with a great deal of outfitting unfinished and with a team of eighty workmen still on board. As a result, the 'maiden voyage' departing Southampton for New York on the 29th April was a very public disaster. Ted Scull who

was a passenger on that unfortunate trip speaks of 'a litany of problems. There was an appalling level of vibration in the after section due to the trouble with the Grim wheels; Five Deck was closed off; there were cabins without furniture, bathrooms without water and doors without keys or even locks; the laundry was not working; and 'Niagara, Niagara' was repeated over the Tannoy as water cascaded from ruptured pipes.' When the ship arrived in New York on the 4th May, the British and American press seized upon these shortcomings and disappointed passengers were in a particularly complaining and, indeed, litigious mood.

And yet... Once the initial problems had been sorted out, the QE2 embarked upon the most successful phase of her long career. In fact, without the conversion she could probably not have survived for more than a few more years.

QUEEN ELIZABETH 2
TRANSATLANTIC TIMETABLE 1983

INCLUDING QE2, CONCORDE AND NEW YORK HOLIDAYS FROM £950

● QE2 ROUND-TRIP EXCURSIONS WITH ONE-WAY FREE: FROM £755
● SAIL ONE-WAY, FLY THE OTHER FREE: FROM £595
● TAKE YOUR WIFE FREE: FROM £765 FOR TWO
● QE2 AND HOLIDAYS IN AMERICA: FROM £495

British airways

For a brief period, QE2's hull was painted light grey. More permanently, her funnel was at last given the historic Cunard colours. (Author's collection)

Now, despite the high cost of fuel, she was much more viable. She was popular with passengers. She was still a true transatlantic liner – after the withdrawal of the *Stefan Batory* in 1988, the only one. And with that imposing new funnel she looked the part. More than ever, she was something very special. Furthermore, she was economically important, described by one newspaper as 'one of the U.K.'s single biggest currency earners'.

It was at this time that the *QE2* started a love affair between Cunard and the north German public which has persisted ever since – ironically, since the British company had historically been the great rival of the big German lines on the Atlantic. The Japanese also became besotted with her. Between the 30th March and the 9th June, 1989 she lay at Yokohama, providing additional hotel accommodation during the celebration of the city's 130th anniversary. Prices were high - it was reported that the cost of a suite for a single night was the equivalent of £1,690. Later, she spent the first half of 1990 under another charter, this time acting as a floating hotel during the World Exposition at Osaka and then making several cruises from Japanese ports. In July of that year, Cunard celebrated the 150th anniversary of the first voyage by the wooden paddle-steamer *Britannia* of just 1,135 gross tons, inaugurating their pioneering transatlantic mail and passenger service. By 1990, the Cunard Line may have been sadly shrunken from the mighty concern which once bestrode the Atlantic but it was still regarded as a great British institution and the *QE2* had become one of the most recognisable and famous ships anywhere. She made several celebratory voyages including a short cruise to ports with which Cunard had been particularly associated – Cobh, Liverpool (once the company's headquarters), Greenock on the Clyde (the river from which so many Cunarders, including the *QE2* herself, had come) and Cherbourg. She received a great welcome, particularly in Liverpool where, it was reckoned, a quarter of a million people turned out to see her arrival.

Then, on the 27th July, she was the centre of attention in a special Royal Review at Spithead in which, from the deck of the Royal Yacht *Britannia*, the Queen inspected three Cunarders (the *QE2*, *Vistafjord* and the container ship *Atlantic Conveyor*, the replacement for a vessel of the same name which had been sunk during the Falklands War) and a number of naval vessels. It was all an amazing Royal compliment to the company. To complete the occasion, *Concorde* flew overhead. That, though, was not the end of the ship's excitements in 1990 – during a cruise across the North Sea, she acted as a control centre during the rescue by helicopters of 49 oil rig workers from an accommodation platform which had broken loose from its tow in 80 mph winds. Also in 1990, in her annual refit, the *QE2* was

given a third grill room for first class passengers, the Britannia Grill.

Twice during the following months, the benefits of her new propulsion system were demonstrated. The latter stages of the 1991 world cruise had to be re-routed via the Cape as the Iraqi invasion of Kuwait made it advisable for her to avoid the Middle East. Although this involved a much greater distance, the *QE2* had sufficient extra speed in reserve to be able to catch up on her planned schedule. Then in June, 1992, one of her nine engines suffered a breakdown but she was able to continue in service without losing speed.

However, on the 7th August, while she was returning from a cruise from New York to Newfoundland, she scraped a hitherto uncharted rock near Martha's Vineyard and sustained serious wounds stretching over 400 feet of her hull and breaching three ballast tanks and a fuel tank. There was also damage to the keel. She was temporarily patched up in drydock at Boston before sailing to the Blohm+Voss yard at Hamburg for permanent repair. It was not until early October that she was able to return to service. Some experts were of the opinion that she was saved by her heavy scantlings and that a more modern, flimsier ship would have become a constructive total loss.

The parent Trafalgar House company was by now running out of momentum and into financial difficulties but it seemed that rescue was at hand when, in late 1992, Hong Kong Land, a subsidiary of the influential Jardine Matheson group, took a large stake. Jardine Matheson are one of the great Hongs (famous old British trading houses operating out of Hong Kong). Like Cunard, they are an extremely historic firm. Their origins go back to the 1830s and over the years they acquired long experience of the shipping industry through their Indo-China Steam Navigation Co. subsidiary. For a time, they seemed to bring new energy to Trafalgar House and to Cunard, particularly through the purchase of the name and goodwill of the prestigious Royal Viking Line and its remaining ship, *Royal Viking Sun*. Also, at one stage, it was proposed that the *QE2*'s transatlantic crossings should in future be co-ordinated with similar voyages to be run by Cunard's old rival, the *United States*, which had been bought by new owners who had ambitious plans for her restoration. In fact, as we all know, those plans never came to fruition and the greatest American liner of all time lies in an almost moribund state at Philadelphia to this day.

In June, 1994, the *QE2* was involved in yet another notable event when she was one of the fleet of well-known passenger ships which took veterans to the French coast to celebrate the 50th anniversary of the D Day landings.

In November, 1994, she returned to the Blohm+Voss yard for yet another major refit, this time costing about $60 mil-

The control panel and one of the two engine rooms, containing a total of nine diesel-generators, following the transformational refit of 1986-87. *(Maurizio Eliseo)*

lion. One of the main alterations was the relocation of the main first class dining room, now called the Caronia Restaurant, and the transfer of the Mauretania Restaurant to the space formerly occupied by the Columbia Restaurant. In addition, the Theatre Bar was replaced by the Golden Lion Pub. (This was regarded by some as a symptom of an increasing polarisation of the QE2's passenger lists. Certainly, karaoke night in the Golden Lion was hardly calculated to attract her more sophisticated passengers. I have to admit, though, that I have spent some very enjoyable lunchtimes there eating fish and chips and listening to good jazz.) With Cunard now keen to emphasise their history, an interesting display of models and memorabilia known as the Heritage Trail was laid out round the ship. Again, there was a change of livery, with the hull being re-painted navy blue but, as before, the old charcoal grey soon returned.

It was becoming almost a tradition that the QE2's immediate post-refit voyages would end in tears but, even by past standards, this one was an utter débacle. Blohm+Voss subsequently claimed that their own part of the contract had been completed on time but that sub-contractors separately employed by Cunard had failed to meet the tight time schedule. By the time the ship sailed from Southampton on the 17th December, structural modification to the Club Lido area at the after end of the superstructure still remained to be done and outfitting was far from complete. To add to the misery of the crossing, the QE2 encountered a very nasty Force 8 gale. The arrival at New York on the 22nd December was a nightmare for Cunard with some angry passengers anxious to brief the press about the emotional trauma they had suffered and demanding very substantial compensation (which was eventually conceded, to the dismay of others in the cruise industry). The company's woes increased when the mandatory inspection by the U.S. Coast Guard proved to be particularly contentious and as a result the ship was a day and a half late in leaving on her next Caribbean cruise. Nevertheless, once again the QE2 seemed quite quickly to brush off the damage which had been done to her reputation.

Inevitably, a ship which for much of the year was making long trans-ocean voyages would encounter dangerous weather from time to time. On the 11th September, 1995, while on a cruise from New York to the

The spectacular circular Midships Lobby was refurnished and given murals depicting the Cunard Line's history. The illuminated silver model is now to be found on board the new *Queen Elizabeth*. (*Maurizio Eliseo*)

Caribbean, she ran into Hurricane Luis and was battered by winds gusting up to 130 knots and by a rogue wave said to be 95 feet high. Almost exactly ten years earlier, during a brush with Hurricane Gloria, she had suffered damage which reached even to her funnel. However, the *QE2* had been built to withstand such onslaughts. Over the years, her transatlantic programme had been extended, with one crossing even taking place every December. In fact, this late voyage, with its high risk of Atlantic gales, proved popular with liner enthusiasts, some of whom – including a hardy group of New York regulars – probably went down on their knees every night and prayed for bad weather. To them, rough seas were part of the Atlantic experience

The situation of the Trafalgar House group did not improve and in April, 1996 it was taken over by Kvaerner, a Norwegian company with interests in the construction and engineering industries, including shipbuilding.

Kvaerner made no secret of the fact that they did not see Cunard as a long-term holding but that they intended to retain the company until they had placed it on a firmer footing, making it a more attractive proposition for possible buyers.

The 1997 season saw a change in the transatlantic voyages, with the ship crossing on a more southerly course and now taking six days instead of five. Greater fuel economy was probably the motive behind this move but it marked the abandonment of any pretence that a liner voyage could be taken seriously as pure transport – the transatlantic crossings may still have had a very different atmosphere, and often attracted a different type of passenger, from the cruises but most people now took them more for pleasure than as a purposeful means of travel.

In April, 1998, the future of Cunard was settled at last. For years, the grand old line had been losing ground to more aggressive, more expansionist companies.

The 'retro' styling of the Caronia Restaurant of 1999 epitomises the way in which the character of the ship was changed in successive refits. *(Maurizio Eliseo)*

This is how one likes to remember the *QE2*: a true express liner at speed in mid-Atlantic.
(Maurizio Eliseo)

The Cunard fleet, although it contained several very fine passenger ships which had been bought second-hand, often seemed to lack focus. Latterly, only the *QE2* was a true Cunarder – and, despite all the money which had been spent on her, she was beginning to shew her age. Now, Kvaerner sold the line to the Carnival Corporation, at first with a minority stake being held by Norwegian interests who, however, soon withdrew. From uncertain beginnings in 1971, Carnival had become the biggest cruise group in the World, consisting not only of the mass-market Carnival Cruise Line but also Holland America, Costa and Seabourn, each operating in its distinct sector of the market. Now, with the acquisition of Cunard, Carnival had another arrow in its quiver, a historic and very British line of huge prestige – even if that prestige had become a little tarnished of late.

And the cash-rich Carnival group had the means to restore Cunard to something approaching its former glory. Within months, Micky Arison – the son of Carnival's Israeli-American founder and now the group's president – was announcing that a new Atlantic liner would be built.

It had been assumed that the *QE2* would be the last of the breed but now she was to have a successor. This prospect did nothing to diminish the old ship's appeal or success, however.

1998 also produced excitement of a different kind when a 66 to 1 outsider named Taufan's Melody won the classic Caulfield Cup horserace in Melbourne, Australia. It belonged to a syndicate of *QE2* crew members, led by one of the bartenders, who had bought it cheaply sometime previously.

Then, in 1999 *QE2* returned to the Lloyd Werft for yet another refit. Again, the Mauretania and Caronia restaurants swapped places, with the Caronia being given a faux-Edwardian décor. Then on the 11th September, 2001 (9/11) she was once more affected by world politics when the infamous terrorist attack on New York brought about the temporary closure of the port. The *QE2* was heading in that direction at the time

and had to be diverted to Boston. For some months, the Manhattan piers remained out of action but by the time she called on her World Cruise in January, 2002 the *QE2* was able to dock there as usual.

2002 also saw an important milestone in her career: on the 29th August she clocked up her 5 millionth nautical mile. She had travelled the equivalent of nine trips to the moon and back, calling at New York 680 times and at Southampton 598. This demonstrated very vividly how hard-worked modern passenger ships are in comparison with most of their predecessors who would spend several days in port at the end of each voyage. Later, in 2006, the *QE2* became the longest serving Cunarder ever, surpassing the *Scythia* (1921 – 1958).

With the arrival of the massive new *Queen Mary 2* in 2003, the *QE2*'s life changed. She would still make her World Cruise every year but otherwise she would be largely devoted to shorter cruises from Southampton for

The takeover of Cunard by the Carnival group made it possibile for the previously unthinkable to happen - the construction of another transatlantic liner. Here the *QE2* is seen in New York harbour with her successor, the *Queen Mary 2* at the start of a tandem crossing to Southampton. *(Cunard Line)*

The *QE2* was built to cross the North Atlantic at speed in almost any weather. Here we see how confidently she pitches into a heavy swell during a tandem crossing with the *Queen Victoria*. *(Steve Swanson)*

Above. In recent years Cunard has made much of its heritage. Here we see a vitrine on the *QE2* displaying memorabilia from previous Cunarders. Below. Two of the most popular features of the *QE2* were the bookshop (left) and the library (right). *(Maurizio Eliseo)*

the British market. The transatlantic crossings and the cruises out of New York would now become the preserve of the new flagship. The handing over of the baton, as it were, was staged spectacularly in New York in April, 2004. One of Cunard's most historic possessions, the silver cup which had been presented to the original *Britannia* by the city of Boston in 1840 and which had been displayed on board the *QE2,* was transferred to the new ship. Then, as already mentioned, the two liners, *Queen Mary 2* and the *QE2*, set off together on a tandem crossing during which they were within sight of each other throughout the entire voyage to Southampton. The change rather altered the atmosphere on the *QE2* as her passengers would now be largely British, but still with a few Americans, Japanese and Continentals who were attracted by the prospect of sailing on this famous ship. It shewed in a number of ways – the shops, for instance, found that their turnover fell sharply as Brits tend to be much more parsimonious than the free-spending Americans.

The *QE2* encountered various technical problems during 2005 but nevertheless Cunard announced confidently that, despite the fact that they had by now ordered another new ship, to be called *Queen Victoria*, the old liner would continue in service and that a series of 'rolling refits' would make it possible for her to comply with the new SOLAS (Safety of Life at Sea) regulations which would come into effect in 2010. Suddenly, however, in July, 2007 there came the hugely surprising announce-

ment that late the following year she would be sold for $100 million to Istithmar, a company owned by the Royal Family of Dubai. She would be converted into a floating hotel and museum and would become a special feature of the spectacular new development being constructed on an artificial island off the city of Dubai by Nakheel, an associated company. The price being offered for so old a ship was presumably just too tempting and, in any case, the sale solved the problem of how to dispose of a high profile, asbestos-ridden ocean liner at a time when scrapping on a beach in India was becoming increasingly controversial, as the owners of *Norway* (ex-*France*) discovered.

The *QE2* went out on a high. Throughout 2008, she attracted both repeat passengers wanting to make one last trip on the old girl and newcomers who wished to do so before it was too late. In January, she and *Queen Victoria*, which had been delivered in 2007, made a tandem westbound crossing during which they encountered extremely rough weather and some spectacular pictures were taken of the *QE2* pitching her way through the waves while *Queen Victoria* laboured to keep up (see page 201). A few weeks later the *QE2* met up with *Queen Mary 2* in Sydney harbour and together they attracted enormous crowds. Then, in April, there was a threesome meeting of the *QE2*, *Queen Mary 2* and *Queen Victoria* in Southampton. The *QE2* was honoured by Royalty when, on the 2nd June, Her Majesty the Queen paid a farewell visit. On the 30th September, the old liner left Southampton on a special cruise round the British Isles, this time taking in Cobh, Dublin, Douglas (her

The *QE2* generated excitement wherever she went. Here we see the great liner in 2008 making her final visits to Trieste (above) and the Clyde. *(Maurizio Eliseo and Bruce Peter)*

first visit to the Isle of Man), Liverpool, Belfast, Greenock, South Queensferry (for Edinburgh) and Newcastle. On the 10th October, she departed on her final westbound transatlantic crossing for New York and on the 16th, at the beginning of the return trip, she and *Queen Mary 2* sailed down the Hudson together, the *QE2* in the lead.

Arriving back from her final Mediterranean cruise on the 11th November, she ran briefly aground when approaching Southampton but fortunately got off undamaged and in time to leave as scheduled late that afternoon on her delivery voyage to Dubai, on which she carried a full load of passengers. Before she sailed, she was visited by the Duke of Edinburgh and she was then given a fine send-off with a fireworks display and an accompanying flotilla of small boats, a Red Funnel ferry and, of course, *Shieldhall*.

She arrived in Dubai on the 26th November and was handed over to her new owners on the same day. There was great speculation among liner enthusiasts. What would be done to her? Would the kind of people likely to visit her in Dubai be aware of – or even interested in – the heritage of a great ocean liner? How could she be made to meet the expectations of visitors used to the most luxurious five star hotels? Speculative drawings were circulated purporting to shew the new owners' intentions and it was said, for instance, that her funnel would be replaced by a replica containing luxurious suites. But although she was drydocked, little seemed to be happening to her. Then plans were announced to send her to Cape Town to act as a floating hotel during the 2010 World Cup football tournament but these were scuppered by the local authorities. By the end of 2009, Nakheel was in financial difficulties and was struggling with some of the loans it had taken out in order to help pay for its immensely ambitious projects in the real estate market. Indeed, the state of Dubai itself was in financial trouble. As this is written, the *QE2* remains at Port Rashid, Dubai awaiting the outcome of it all.

Whatever happens in the end, the *QE2* will long be remembered as one of the best-known and best-loved ships there have ever been. Indeed, she has been a *Favourite British Liner.*

In 2011 the new *Queen Elizabeth* visited Dubai where she encountered her celebrated predecessor, the *QE2*, now laid up but still looking magnificent. *(Cunard Line)*

The second Oriana

Completed 1995.

69,153 gross tons.

Length overall: 853 ft. 0ins.

Breadth: 105 ft. 9½ins.

Draught: 26 ft. 10ins.

Twin screw. Diesel engines.

Service speed: 24 knots.

Designed specifically for the British market, the second *Oriana* has built up a strong following. *(William Mayes)*

When she entered service, the second *Oriana* was an important ship, an affirmation by P&O of their continuing commitment to the British cruise market in which, at one time in the late 1980s, they had been represented solely by the ageing *Canberra*. Although still very popular, particularly since her heroics in the Falkland War, *Canberra* was struggling to meet the requirements of the modern cruise market and, by the 1990s, was clearly nearing the end of her career. Preliminary discussions regarding a replacement began in 1988.

When they finally introduced the new *Oriana* with much fanfare in 1995, P&O hinted that they hoped that she would supersede the *QE2* as the national flagship. In fact, she has never achieved that level of recognition but she has always been very well-liked, a favourite with many passengers. William Mayes, the much-travelled shipping author, has written that she 'set the standard that many others have yet to achieve'.

In their introductory brochure, P&O asserted that the new *Oriana* 'has been conceived from the beginning as a specif-

The second *Oriana* is about to leave the massive enclosed building hall at the shipyard at Papenburg in Germany. (Meyer Werft)

Above. More views of the 'float out' of the *Oriana* in 1994. Note her distinctive tiered after decks. Below. The beautiful Curzon Room, since converted into a restaurant. *(Meyer Werft and William Mayes)*

ically British ship [...], she possesses the sea-keeping qualities and the speed necessary for sailing swiftly from Britain to the sun [...], she is the fastest liner (*sic*) built for over a quarter of a century.' They had a point – she is not as quick as *Canberra* or the original *Oriana* (both designed partly for the express service to Australia) but she was built to be able to hurry through the Bay of Biscay or the North Sea so that her passengers have less exposure to the discomforts often experienced in those turbulent areas.

Apart from ferries, she was the first major passenger vessel to be built for British owners since the *Cunard Countess* and *Cunard Princess* of 1976-7; and she was the biggest British passenger ship since the *QE2* of 1969.

Regrettably, there was no longer any possibility of having her built in a British yard. Instead, in 1992, the order went to the well-regarded Jos. L. Meyer company of Papenburg on the River Ems in Germany. The keel was laid on the 11th March, 1993 and she was floated out on the 30th June, 1994. A formidable team had been assembled to design her, including Robert Tillberg (co-ordinating architect), John McNeece (responsible for the main public rooms) and Petter Yran (for the cabins). The result was one of the better-looking modern cruise ships, with some

echoes of *Canberra*, notably the twin side-by-side funnels, although in *Oriana*'s case they are actually Siamese twins. Comparisons with *Canberra* are instructive, indicating the changes which have taken place in passenger ship design since 1961. The *Oriana* is only slightly longer and broader than the older ship but she is so much more built-up that her gross tonnage (i.e.: internal space) is over 50% larger. Her breadth is the maximum possible if she is to pass through the Panama Canal.

The ten passenger decks are arranged in a layered manner: extensive open sun decks and the less formal rooms are at the top of the ship; and then, in descending order, the better cabin accommodation (including, notably for a ship built in the early 'Nineties, an entire deck with balconies); two decks containing the main public rooms; and, finally, more cabin decks which also house the two main restaurants. Penetrating this arrangement is a four-deck high atrium, complete with waterfall and a Tiffany ceiling.

Ships no longer segregate their passengers into completely separate classes but *Oriana* carries a very wide variety of people and so she has been given a range of public rooms calculated to appeal to different tastes. You gravitate towards those areas where you think you will find compatible company and the ambience you prefer. For instance, the lively beer-drinking crowd are comfortable in Lord's Tavern which, like its equivalent on *Canberra*, is decorated with cricketing memorabilia while, at the other end of the spectrum, Anderson's is a quiet lounge which, in cruise-speak, has a club-like atmosphere. For many years, habitués of Anderson's were also likely to enjoy the rather grand Curzon Room with its slight hints of the P&O of the Imperial age but in 2006 it was replaced by a Gordon Ramsay extra-tarriff restaurant. (More recently, another celebrity chef, Marco Pierre White, has taken over this restaurant.) Apart from that, the two main formal dining rooms are the Peninsular Restaurant and the Oriental Restaurant and there is also a buffet, called The Conservatory, which compensates for its rather bland décor (and food) by giving its occupants fine sea views. It opens out at the stern to overlook the gracefully tiered after decks. It was perhaps a commentary on changing British tastes (and waistlines) that after only a couple of years the Aerobics Disco was replaced by an al fresco pizzeria.

Very much in the modern cruise ship manner, the Crow's Nest is a smart, spectacular two-tiered observation lounge situated over the bridge. Other public spaces include a dedicated ballroom named Harlequins; the well-equipped Theatre Royal with its revolving stage and steeply raked auditorium (and air-conditioning in the backs of the seats!); the Pacific Lounge which is a venue for cabaret and lectures; the Chaplin cinema, which has two statues of the eponymous Charlie by the door; Crichton's, a card room; Thackeray's, a small writing room; a library; and, of course, a casino.

1 The Terrace Pool
and jacuzzi

2 Children's Play Area and Paddling Pool
outside the playroom, Peter Pan's (not shown)

3 Pacific Lounge
cabaret show lounge with dance floor

4 The Oriental Restaurant

5 The Terrace Bar

6 The Conservatory
informal restaurant with additional open-air seating

7 Decibels and Outer Space
teenagers room and video games

8 The Lord's Tavern

9 Chaplin Cinema

10 The Crystal Pool

11 Crichton's
card room adjacent to The Library and writing
room, The Thackeray Room

12 Harlequins
Oriana's night-spot for all tempos

13 The Peninsular Restaurant

14 Deck Tennis
also available but not shown are deck quoits,
shuffleboard, golf nets and trap shooting

Other facilities include The Oasis complex of sauna, beauty salon and a gymnasium whose devotees enjoy a fine sea view. (Less energetic but still agile passengers can enjoy the views while walking round the mainly open promenade which encircles the superstructure.) There are three swimming pools and, until *Oriana* became an adults-only ship in 2011, there was also a children's outdoor play area with a paddling pool.

When *Oriana* entered service, Robert Tillberg told *Lloyd's List* about his approach to designing a ship for the British market. He had taken a cruise on *Canberra* and had studied her passengers – 'I really liked them and saw how individualistic they are.' He tried to reproduce something of *Canberra*'s atmosphere although, in fact, the result – criticised by some as too conservative – lacks the 1960s radicalism of *Canberra* or, indeed, of the previous *Oriana*. In marked contrast to the many cruise ships which have been designed with an eye to the American market, Tillberg gave

the new *Oriana* 'smaller, more intimate public rooms with muted colours and traditional fabrics and as much use of wood as possible.' The ship was decorated with a number of pictures and sculptures by contemporary British artists. Some interesting old paintings of P&O ships hang in Anderson's lounge but otherwise P&O does not emulate its rival (and now stable-mate) Cunard in paying tribute to its history with lavish displays of memorabilia. On *Oriana*, though, there is a nod in that direction with the naming of some of the public rooms after men who have played a part in the line's long story and in calling the two main restaurants Peninsular and Oriental. There, the curries for which P&O ships have been famous for a century and a half are still on the menu and throughout the ship the line still employs mainly Indian and Goanese stewards rather than the Filippinos and Eastern Europeans now favoured by many other companies.

As built, *Oriana* had accommodation for a maximum of

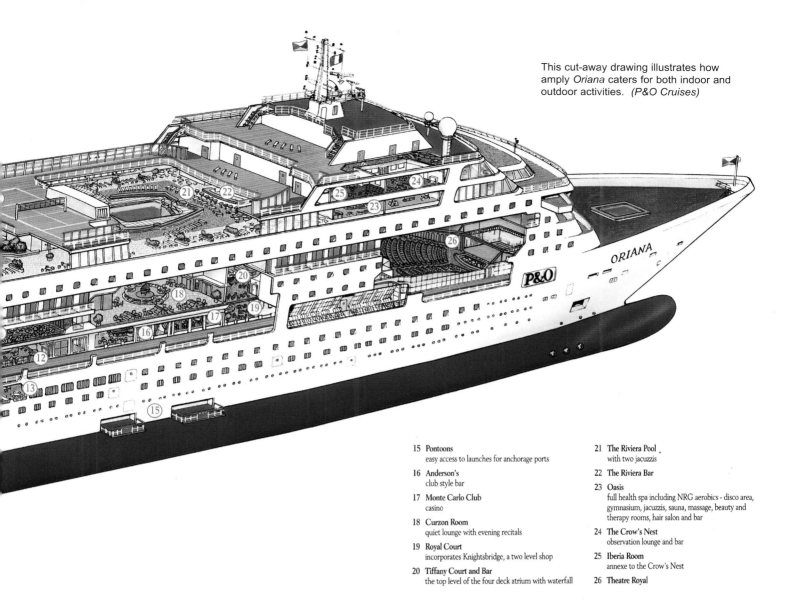

This cut-away drawing illustrates how amply *Oriana* caters for both indoor and outdoor activities. *(P&O Cruises)*

15	**Pontoons** easy access to launches for anchorage ports	21	**The Riviera Pool** with two jacuzzis
16	**Anderson's** club style bar	22	**The Riviera Bar**
17	**Monte Carlo Club** casino	23	**Oasis** full health spa including NRG aerobics - disco area, gymnasium, jacuzzis, sauna, massage, beauty and therapy rooms, hair salon and bar
18	**Curzon Room** quiet lounge with evening recitals	24	**The Crow's Nest** observation lounge and bar
19	**Royal Court** incorporates Knightsbridge, a two level shop	25	**Iberia Room** annexe to the Crow's Nest
20	**Tiffany Court and Bar** the top level of the four deck atrium with waterfall	26	**Theatre Royal**

1,975 passengers (standard occupancy 1,760) in 913 two-, three- and four-berth cabins, all fully equipped. Some of the two-berth cabins were offered for single occupancy. At the top end of the price range, there were twenty-four Premier suites and De Luxe staterooms. At the time of the ship's introduction, the comfort of the accommodation she provided for her passengers evoked much favourable comment.

The hull has, of course, all the usual appurtenances of a large modern cruise ship – a bulbous bow; three side-thrusters forward and one aft; fin stabilisers (of an innovative design by Brown Bros. and claimed at the time to be the largest in the World).; twin rudders. Although, as on most modern ships, the hull lacks sheer, it is not inelegant. The sharply raked bow carries the traditional P&O sunrise badge. As is now customary, the lifeboats are stowed inboard over the open side promenades.

Oriana's much-vaunted speed comes from two 9-cylinder and two 6-cylinder MAN diesel engines, rated at 64,040 bhp and coupled to twin controllable-pitch propellers by a system of clutches, flexible couplings and single reduction gearing. P&O had gone against conventional thinking at the time in opting for a diesel-mechanical drive rather than a diesel-electric one.

The days before the ship was delivered were fraught with anxiety. The initial sea trials in the Skagerak in March, 1995 were disrupted by Force 10 winds and stormy seas and there were further problems when, near Papenburg, *Oriana* touched bottom, damaging her propellers. (She was the biggest ship built in Germany since the *Bismarck*, later the *Majestic*, which was completed in 1922; and the waters in the River Ems are notoriously constricted.) Repairs were made at Hamburg. Then, during another series of trials in which she achieved 26.2 knots, serious vibration became evident when she was driven at speed. Relations between the shipyard and the shipowners are known to have become very tense and, in the end, P&O did not take delivery of the ship until the 2nd April. She arrived at Southampton on the 3rd, only three days before she was due to be named by the Queen. The ceremony, a great honour for the ship and for P&O, took place at the Ocean Dock.

Oriana left Southampton on her maiden voyage on the 9th April. It took her to Madeira and ports in the Canaries, then to Casablanca, Praia da Rocha and Lisbon. For the rest of that first year, she was occupied with mainly 14- or 15-night cruises to the Mediterranean, but with one to Norway and Iceland and one to the Baltic plus two longer cruises to the Caribbean and back. It was on one of these, in October, that she encountered two hurricanes which forced her to miss three ports. Presumably because she then had to sail at full speed in order to catch up on her schedule, the vibration problem was particularly apparent, adding to the very vocal discontent of some of her passengers. (I have been told that, ever since she had entered service, it had been necessary to slow her down to little more than 15 knots during meal times so that passengers could enjoy their food in comfort.) Various possible cures had been considered and now the intention was that new blades should be fitted to the propellers during hurried maintenance work at Southampton in early January, 1996. Unfortunately, high winds made this impossible and on the 6th January she sailed on her first World cruise still with the original blades. The new ones were finally installed in April, on her return to Southampton.

Nevertheless, that first World cruise was a success with *Oriana* receiving a particularly warm welcome at Sydney. It was a measure of the extent to which, for generations, the ships of the P&O and Orient lines had been a feature of the harbour scene there that the arrival of this successor to the first *Oriana* and eventually, everyone realised, to the *Canberra*, was a cause for spectacular celebration. She was greeted by a fleet of small boats and ferries, not to mention a large manned model of the first *Oriana*, and, among all the other festivities during her stay, there were two fireworks displays, one partly mounted on Sydney Harbour Bridge.

For some years, *Oriana*'s schedule did not vary greatly, although sometimes her annual World cruise took her in a westward direction and sometimes eastward. On a few of these circumnavigations, she sailed via the Cape rather than through the Suez Canal. In 1997, for instance, she visited Madeira, the Caribbean, the Panama Canal, San Francisco, Hawaii, New Zealand, Australia (including, of course, Sydney), Bali, Hong Kong, Mauritius, South Africa and the Atlantic islands, taking 91 days and calling at 23 ports. On her 1998 World cruise, on the other hand, she returned via Japan, Singapore, India and Suez.

Oriana in her element: moored offshore at Castries, St. Lucia, during a Caribbean cruise, the kind of assignment for which she was built. *(William Mayes)*

When she came out, *Oriana* was considered to be a large ship. Today she is described as been 'mid-sized'. She is now one of three P&O ships which are 'exclusively for adults' rather than 'family friendly'. *(P&O Cruises)*

Oriana proved to be a popular ship and, in her early years, may to some extent have helped to stimulate the notable growth in the number of Britons taking a cruise. In 1997, *Lloyd's List* expressed the view that 'The arrival of the *Oriana* has been one of the factors providing a major boost to the strength of the U.K. market.' It was clearly not coincidental that P&O placed an order with Jos. L. Meyer for a modified and slightly larger version of the *Oriana* which they also intended for the British trade. They called her *Aurora*. Inevitably, *Oriana* has encountered problems from time to time. In May, 1999, for instance, a stern tube failure led to the cancellation of a 3-day charter cruise from Southampton and an 11-day cruise to northern Europe so that repairs could be made in the King George V Dock.

The early years of the new century were a momentous time for P&O. In 2000, the group's cruise interests were split off to form a separately quoted company, P&O Princess Cruises PLC. But that new concern had only a brief independence as in 2002 it was taken over by Carnival Corporation after they had waged a fierce battle with Royal Caribbean. Throughout these changes *Oriana* continued to sail successfully.

In 2004, for the first time, she did not make a World cruise. Instead, the former *Sea Princess* – newly transferred within the Carnival group from Princess Cruises' American-based

operation to P&O's British fleet and now called *Adonia* – ran a half-World cruise while *Oriana* cruised to the Caribbean. But the *Adonia* was suffering from serious engine problems and was perhaps a little too American in style to appeal to some British passengers and in 2005 she was returned to Princess Cruises. However, with the British cruise market growing at a heady rate, P&O's British fleet was being expanded. This has made it possible for *Oriana*'s schedule, which originally contained a very heavy preponderance of cruises to warm weather destinations, to contain slightly more summer voyages to such places as Norway and the Baltic. Also, after missing out in 2004, she has resumed her annual World cruises. By now, P&O ships are making four World cruises per year.

In 2011, the fleet consists of seven ships. *Oriana* is the oldest and the second smallest of them but she continues to hold her own. In December, 2006, she was sent to Bremerhaven for a refit which included some re-arrangement of her public spaces. In addition to the replacement of the Curzon Room by a restaurant, the Lords Tavern was expanded. At the same time, she was taken off the British register and transferred to the Bermudan one. *Oriana* continues to be a very popular cruise ship and, all being well, will remain a successful member of the P&O fleet for some years to come. That certainly seemed likely when I took a Caribbean cruise on her in Spring, 2010.

Two favourite British liners. Above, the first *Oriana* turning at full helm to starboard while steaming at full speed on her sea trials in November, 1960. Below, the second *Oriana* passing the venerable *Passat* at Mariehamn. *(Bruce Peter collection and Stefan and Petra Behn)*

Primary sources and bibliography

Primary Sources (often made available by the helpful staff at Guildhall Library, London):

Lloyd's Confidential Index.
Lloyd's Register.
Lloyd's Shipping Index.
Lloyd's Voyage Records.
Lloyd's Weekly Casualty Reports.
Various brochures and timetables.

Periodicals:

Daily Telegraph, The.
Lloyd's List.
Marine News (journal of The World Ship Society).
Motor Ship, The.
Sea Breezes.
Seascape.
Shipbuilder, The.
Shipbuilding and Shipping Record.
Shipping Today & Yesterday.
Shipping World, The.
Ships in Focus Record.
Ships Monthly.
Steamboat Bill (the journal of The Steamship Historical Society of America).
Times, The.

Books:

Stephen J. Card, *Cunarder*, Carmania Press, London, 2005.

Alan L. Cary, *Liners of the Ocean Highway*, Sampson Low Marston & Co., Ltd., London, 1936.

Anthony Cooke, *Emigrant Ships*, Carmania Press, London, 1992.

James E. Cowden & John O. C. Duffy, *Elder Dempster Fleet History, 1852–1985*, Mallett & Bell Publications, Coultishall, Norfolk, 1986.

Ambrose Greenway, *A Century of North Sea Passenger Steamers*, Ian Allan, Ltd., Shepperton, 1986.

R. Bruce Grice and David F. Hutchings, *Southampton Shipping*, Carmania Press, London, 2006.

C. J. Harris & Brian D. Ingpen, *Mailships of the Union-Castle Line*, Fernwood Press, Vlaeberg, 1999.

Clive Harvey, *The Last White Empresses*, Carmania Press, London, 2004.

Ann Haynes, *Union-Castle Line Purserette*, Mallett & Bell Publications, Coultishall, Norfolk, 1999.

David F. Hutchings, *QE2 - A Ship for All Seasons*, Waterfront Publications, Poole, 1991.

F. E. Hyde, *Cunard and the North Atlantic, 1840-1973*, The Macmillan Press, Ltd., London, 1975.

W. A. Laxon and F. W. Perry, *The British India Steam Navigation Co., Ltd.*, World Ship Society, Kendal, 1994.

Charles F. Morris, *Origins, Orient and Oriana*, Teredo Books, Ltd., Brighton, 1980.

Peter Plowman, *Emigrant Ships to Luxury Liners: Passenger Ships to Australia and New Zealand, 1945-1990*, New South Wales University Press, Kensington, N.S.W., 1992.

Don Ripley & Tony Rogan, *Designing Ships for Sealink*, Ferry Publications, Kilgetty, Pembrokeshire, 1995.

C. M. Squarey, *The Patient Speaks*, Thos Cook & Son, Ltd., London, 1955.

Roger Villar, *Merchant Ships at War: the Falklands Experience*, Conway Maritime Press and Lloyd's of London Press, London, 1984.

Ocean Liners of the Past: The Cunard Quadruple-Screw Liner Aquitania, Patrick Stephens Ltd., London, 1971 (reprint from "The Shipbuilder").

The Bank Line, (pamphlet): *The Syren & Shipping*, London, 1934.

The Cunard White Star North Atlantic Twin-Screw Geared Turbine Passenger Steamship Mauretania, "Shipbuilder & Marine Engine Builder", London and Newcastle-on-Tyne, 1939.

Web-site:

SSCanberra.com

Printed in Rijeka, Croatia
September 2011

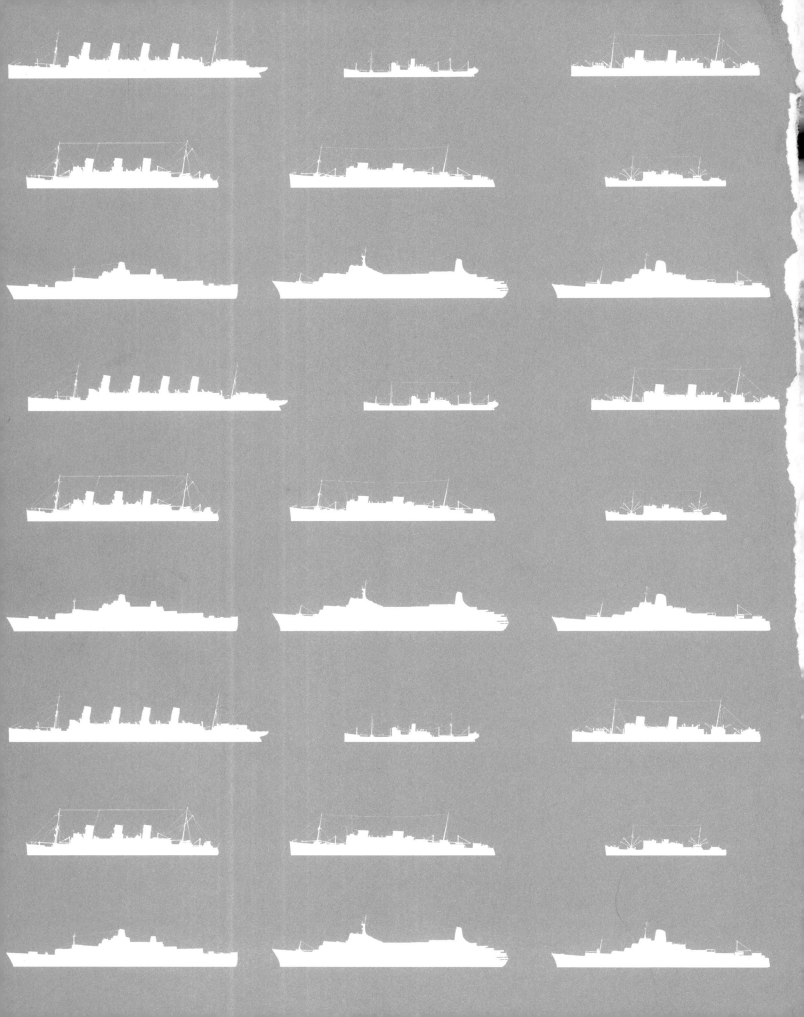